D1500136

THE LADIES OF ZAMORA

To

ROBBIE

– Professor R. E. Robinson, CBE, DFC –

Historian of Empire,

Old chum

and

Tutor

The Ladies of Zamora

PETER LINEHAN

THE PENNSYLVANIA STATE
UNIVERSITY PRESS

UNIVERSITY PARK, PENNSYLVANIA

Copyright © Peter Linehan 1997

Published in 1997 in the United States of America and Canada by
The Pennsylvania State University Press, University Park, PA 16802

ISBN 0-271-01682-5

Library of Congress Cataloging in Publication Data
A CIP catalog record for this book is available from the Library of Congress.

Printed in Great Britain by Bookcraft (Bath) Ltd.

This book is printed on acid-free paper.

It is the policy of The Pennsylvania State University Press to use acid-free
paper for the first printing of all clothbound books. Publications on uncoated
stock satisfy minimum requirements of American National Standard for
Information Sciences–Permanence of Paper for Printed Library Materials,
ANSI Z39.48–1992.

Errata

The Ladies of Zamora
by Peter Linehan

page xii. For Santa Sabrina, read Santa Sabina

page xv. For Embalse de Almendra (above), read
Embalse del Elsa

page xvi. Scale of Map 2: for 500 m. read 1000 m.

page 47. The reference to "the late J. H. Mundy" is
mistaken. The author profusely apologizes
to Professor Mundy for his blunder.

CONTENTS

PREFACE

My reasons for revisiting the Ladies of Zamora and writing about them again are stated at the beginning of Chapter Two. But for the incitement of Alain Boureau, however, and his friendship and encouragement, I would probably have left the Ladies where I abandoned them in 1971 and have allowed them to rest in peace. Part of the blame for what follows is due to Alain Boureau, therefore.

It has long been a commonplace amongst historians that the arrival of the friars on the scene at the beginning of the thirteenth century destroyed Western society's delicate ecological balance. With the material resources of that society already hard pressed by the demands of an ever-growing population, the laity's enthusiastic response to the mendicants' pastoral commitment dealt the economic interests of the ecclesiastical establishment a mortal blow. All over Europe, bishops and chapters, monks and parish priests, at best viewed the newcomers with deep suspicion and as often as not attempted to run them out of town.

Yet in the land of Saint Dominic himself the process has been studied hardly at all.

The present investigation of the affairs of the Ladies of Zamora in these early years, and of the history of their convent on the left bank of the Duero, is intended as a small contribution both to the filling of this particular gap and, more generally, to an understanding of the social realities of a frontier society largely unaffected by the principles of reform (or 'reform') beloved of students of the two centuries which followed the death of Pope Gregory VII: a society at whose every level the rule of law, and of canon law in particular, remained subject to the whim of wilful men – and of course women.

In the course of writing it up I have incurred numerous debts. I am especially grateful to the Mother Superior of the Convento de las Dominicas Dueñas de Zamora for allowing me to consult the records of her community. I have been helped in various different ways by numerous friends. I have particularly in mind Maria João Violante Branco, Christopher and Rosalind Brooke, Jim Brundage, Francisco Cantelar, John Crook (for help with the Latin and much else besides), Ruth Daniel (for help with the proofs, not to mention the delight of her friendship), Heath Dillard, Tom Gallanis, Antonio García y García, Julian Gardner, Francisco Hernández, Jacques Le Goff, Miguel Angel González García (canon archivist of Orense cathedral), José Carlos de Lera (archivist of Zamora cathedral), the Revd Robert Ombres OP, Juan Ramón Romero and Cristina Usón at the Servicio de Reproducción de Documentos (Archivo Histórico Nacional, Madrid), Teo Ruiz, Patrick Zutshi, the Cambridge bagpiper (whose renderings of Cambridge laments beneath my window of summer afternoons put me in the right frame of mind to sympathise with D. Suero), and the incomparable Vanessa Graham and her colleagues at Manchester University Press, who have been absolute bricks. Though to some of them more than others, for a variety of reasons I am obliged to them all.

P.A.L.

A NOTE ON MONEY VALUES

In the second half of the thirteenth century the kingdom of Castile experienced a series of debasements and reissues of its currency which as well as provoking political mutiny at the time continue to this day to exercise and perplex its historians. Since, moreover, the base value of the maravedí in the kingdom of León (within which Zamora lay) was different from that of the kingdom of Castile in this period, it is extremely difficult to be altogether sure of the real value of money. Nevertheless, on the strength of F. J. Hernández's recent study (*Las rentas del rey*, i, especially pp. clxxi–clxxii, clxxxi, ccxiv), it can be stated with some confidence that one effect of Alfonso X's issue of the so-called 'moneda de la guerra' in and after 1265 was something like a sixfold devaluation of the maravedí in relation to the *livre tournois*, and that by the mid-1290s it had declined even further. Thus, in the bequests he made in 1285 Bishop Suero of Zamora was careful to distinguish between maravedís of what he called 'good money' (i.e. the pre-1265 gold coin) and those of the post-1265 'new money' of debased silver. However, it was not only the king who stood to profit from the volatile state of the currency, and it is not only historians of kings and money who need to keep a close eye on the exchanges. For in claiming to have spent sums of the order of 5,000 and 6,000 maravedís on his church in the early 1260s (pp. 22, 84), Bishop Suero was surely expressing his expenditure in post-1265 values, and was thereby inflating its significance accordingly. That said, the 3,300 maravedís which the Ladies paid for their site in 1264 and the 200,000 maravedís 'de la guerra' with which Queen Violante endowed the convent of Allariz in 1292 were both substantial sums (see pp. 13, 138). The former would have purchased 825 head of cattle at official 1258 prices and is to be compared with the 60 maravedís which it had cost Bishop Pedro I to build a palace and two houses at Maalde (*Cortes de los antiguos reinos de León y de Castilla*, ed. Real Academia de la Historia, i, Madrid 1861, 60; *Doc. zamoranos*, no. 147), while, as the queen's will indicates, the present that her son Sancho IV sent Cardinal Ordoño Alvarez in 1285 (p. 100) would have been sufficient for the purchase of 1,000 new Franciscan habits.

ABBREVIATIONS

Litt. encyc.	*Litterae encyclicae Magistrorum Generalium Ordinis Praedicatorum ab anno 1233 usque ad annum 1376*, ed. A. Frühwirth, MOPH 5, Rome 1900
MHE	*Memorial histórico español*, ed. Real Academia de la Historia, ii, Madrid 1851
MIöG	*Mitteilungen des Instituts für österreichische Geschichtsforschung*
MGH	Monumenta Germaniae Historica
MOPH	Monumenta Ordinis Fratrum Praedicatorum Historica
Po.	A. Potthast, ed., *Regesta Pontificum Romanorum inde ab anno 1198 ad annum 1304*, Berlin 1874–5
Reg. Bon. VIII	*Les Registres de Boniface VIII (1294–1303)*, ed. G. Digard, M. Faucon, A. Thomas and R. Fawtier, Paris 1907–39.
Reg. Clem. IV	*Les Registres de Clément IV (1265–68)*, ed. E. Jordan, Paris 1893–1945.
Reg. Clem. V	[Benedictines of Monte Cassino], *Regestum Clementis Papae V ex Vaticanis archetypis S. D. N. Leonis XIII P. M. iussu et munificentia, cura et studio monachorum ordinis S. Benedicti editum*, Rome 1885–92.
Reg. Hon. IV	*Les Registres d'Honorius IV (1285–87)*, ed. M. Prou, Paris 1888.
Reg. Inn. IV	*Les Registres d'Innocent IV (1243–54)*, ed. E. Berger, Paris 1881–1921.
Reg. Nich. IV	*Les Registres de Nicholas IV (1288–91)*, ed. E. Langlois, Paris 1886–1905.
'Rule'	'Liber constitutionum sororum Ordinis Praedicatorum' (The Rule of Humbert of Romans, 1259): *Analecta Sacri Ordinis Fratrum Praedicatorum*, iii (1897), 337–48
TB	*Tumbo Blanco* (AC Zamora)
VI	Liber Sextus
X	Liber Extra

PLATE I   Tomb of Munio of Zamora,
Church of Santa Sabrina, Rome. Photo: Alinari

PLATE 2   Tomb of Munio (detail).
Photo: Julian Gardner

PLATE 3   Seal of Munio.
Archives du Nord, Lille

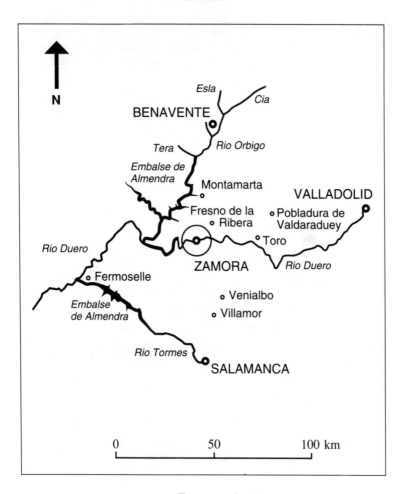

MAP I   Zamora and region

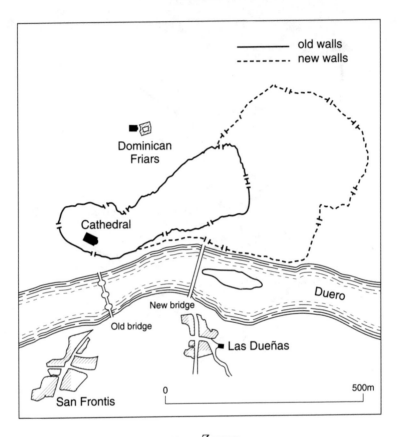

MAP 2 Zamora
in the thirteenth century

CHAPTER ONE

❀❀❀❀❀❀❀❀❀❀❀❀❀❀❀❀❀❀❀❀❀❀❀❀❀❀❀❀

'Nichilominus tamen . . .'

ONE evening some seven centuries ago there was a disturbance at the great gate of the convent of Dominican nuns in the cathedral city of Zamora in western Spain. Cervantes mentions Zamora for the sound of its bagpipes. But it was not the skirl of the pipes, it was not even the sound of music that disturbed the peace on that thirteenth-century evening. It was the rustle of rustic intimacy. And there was worse to come. As one of the nuns who claimed to have been there was later to recall:

> In defiance of the bishop's instructions Doña Xemena, Doña Stefanía, Doña Perona and various other nuns opened the great gate to the friars and spoke with them there. Brother Juan Yuáñez surveyed the convent and said: 'This would make a fine love-nest for brother Nicolás.' And then and there he and Ines Domínguez made love. Meanwhile brother Pedro Gutiérrez was on the loose. For fear of him the girls hid themselves in the oven. Also, brother Juan de Aviancos was roaming the convent looking for nuns. All this was the cause of the scandal.

It was 'all this' that Sol Martínez remembered in July 1279 when together with thirty-three other nuns she appeared before the bishop of Zamora's tribunal. In the next chapter we shall return to the convent gate and accompany brother Pedro Gutiérrez and brother Juan de Aviancos within. But before that there are certain pre-liminaries to be attended to.

Pope Honorius IV was very old when he died in April 1287 and so con-sumed with gout that in the last months of his life it was only with the assistance of a contraption which as contemporary accounts describe it sounds like a Zimmer frame that he was able to celebrate

I

mass. Yet according to the chronicler Salimbene, it was not the pontiff's general state of dilapidation that eventually finished him off. According to Salimbene, what finished him off was prayer. Honorius IV died – the Franciscan gossip-monger reported – because he was prayed to death. He had been bought by the bishops (the 'ultramontane bishops') for a hundred thousand pounds and was on the point of depriving the mendicant orders of their licence to preach and hear confessions when the combined force of Franciscan and Dominican intercession had its desired effect and doubled him up for ever.[1]

How different, how very different, it had all been as recently as a year and a half earlier when the pope, who was at Tivoli at the time, had had his attention directed to the affairs of the Dominican Order in the land of the Order's founder. Then, in the autumn of 1285, he had reacted very much as all his predecessors since the early years of the century had reacted whenever threats to mendicant interests had been brought to their attention. In September 1285, just five months into his pontificate, and sixty-four years after Saint Dominic's death, Honorius IV had received complaints from the Friars Preacher of the Spanish province about those who 'did not blush to receive the name of the Lord in vain'. The words were his, the pope's, in the letter he issued on the subject, but the sentiment was the friars', and the friars meant the bishops. Spanish bishops – though not all Spanish bishops, and for that matter not only Spanish bishops – had long been notorious at the curia for their persecution of friars.

In the previous May, within a month of his own election and just a matter of days before that of the Spaniard Munio of Zamora as Master General of the Dominican Order, the pontiff had had to intervene yet again in the increasingly violent and apparently interminable dispute of the cathedral chapter and the Dominicans of the city of Burgos.[2] Now, in mid-September, he appointed the archbishop of Toledo, Gonzalo Pérez, as protector of the interests of the entire Spanish province of the Order,[3] and four days later followed this by directing the same prelate to investigate reports of what on the face of it was a particularly flagrant case of friar-baiting.

The Dominicans of the city of Zamora had informed the pontiff of the sufferings they were experiencing at the hands of their local bishop. D. Suero Pérez had declared open war on them. He had banned them from the churches of his city and diocese. He had forbidden the laity to make their confessions to them, attend their sermons, have them present when they made their wills, or be buried by them. He had excommunicated them and had even had one of their number unceremoniously ejected from the pulpit. Worse still, he had denied them all access to the convent of Santa María, a community which 'by grant of the Apostolic See had assumed the rule of Saint Augustine and the institutions and habit of the Order of Preachers'.[4] And when the prioress and the sisters had protested, he had 'infamously and publicly loosed his tongue' both against them and against the friars. He had invaded the convent 'as an enemy', deposed the prioress, and replaced her with a creature of his own. He had confiscated the convent's seal, imprisoned various of the sisters, excommunicated others, starved them out and driven some forty of them away, vowing that until they abandoned their rule, their institutions and their habit, he would never let them return. 'For many years', therefore, the good sisters had been miserably eking out a rootless existence, to the danger of their souls, the shame of the friars and the friars' order, and the scandal of the faithful.

If true, it was a shocking story, so shocking indeed that, if the archbishop found it to be true, rather than dealing with the matter himself he was to cause the bishop to appear at the papal curia within four months in order to answer for himself to the pope.[5]

The friars had done well to secure the appointment of the archbishop of Toledo to investigate their grievance. For there was no Castilian prelate more sympathetic to their cause, and *prima facie* none better placed to bring their tormentor to book, than Archbishop Gonzalo Pérez. In 1282 the Dominican General Chapter meeting at Vienna had acknowledged the magnitude of its debt to him as one of the Order's staunchest friends. Conversely, the archbishop was heavily indebted to the Order. At the time of his translation from Burgos to Toledo in 1280 he had owed the local convent the sum of twelve thousand maravedís.[6] Also, he knew the lie of the land in the diocese of Zamora. Almost twenty years before, while dean of Toledo, he had intervened in the long-running dispute between Bishop Suero and the *concejo* of Toro. Even so, the archbishop failed to produce the alleged miscreant at the papal court, for the sufficient reason that by the following summer the bishop of Zamora was dead.[7]

As will be seen, had Bishop Suero been spared long enough to provide his own version of the events that had occurred just across the river from his cathedral and of his dealings with the local Dominican friars and the ladies of the local convent of Santa María over the previous fifteen years or so; or had he been represented by a proctor at the papal curia sufficiently competent to challenge the friars' allegations in the autumn of 1285; or, rather than leaving the archbishop simply to report back if he found those allegations to be well founded, had the pope instructed him to do so with an account of what he had discovered; or had Cardinal Ordoño Alvarez had words with the pope before he, too, died later that year, then history might well have followed a significantly different course. Not the history of the world perhaps, but certainly the history of the Dominican Order towards the end of the Order's first century – as well, of course, as the history with which we are here concerned.

No apologies are offered for all these 'or hads'. The story that follows is from beginning to end a story of contingencies.

It begins on reasonably firm ground, however, on the banks of the river Duero in the year 1258.

In the city of Zamora some time in that year, the knight Ruy Peláez, son of Pelayo Rodríguez of Toro, and his wife Elvira Rodríguez decided to go their separate ways. In order better to serve the lord Jesus they agreed to end their marriage. In the man's world which they inhabited it was Ruy Peláez who defined the terms of their separation. Renouncing all the rights he enjoyed over Elvira's person, he declared his intention of joining the military Order of Santiago. Elvira was free to join the Order of Santiago too, he stated – or indeed any religious order of her choice.[8]

The eventual consequences of this singular resolution of a mid-thirteenth-century mid-life crisis were to be both considerable and far-reaching. For Ruy Peláez they were both considerable and immediate. For almost at once he changed his mind, only to find that there was no going back, and in particular that there was no going back to Elvira. In May 1259 he petitioned in the court of the archdeacon, Master Esteban, to have his wife restored to him. His petition was heard by the archdeacon's vicar, Pedro Benítez, *magisterscolarum* of Zamora, and was refused.[9] We hear nothing further of the unhappy Ruy Peláez.

Divorce Zamora-style – or, strictly speaking, separation by mutual consent on religious grounds – was not provided for in the local law-

＊＊＊＊＊

code, the *Fuero de Zamora*. But there was ample allowance for it in canon law. Had they consulted the Gregorian Decretals, the witnesses at the hearing of Ruy Peláez's failed appeal in May 1259 would have found no fewer than twenty-one entries on the subject.[10] And in the Order of Santiago, had she opted for it, Elvira Rodríguez would have encountered a comfortable enough lifestyle, and within a community of married men and women whose connubial arrangements rendered it unique in the West would have had all the time in the world to pray, service the warriors, and educate their pre-nubile daughters. What was more, there were two houses of the order nearby – San Mateo de Avila and Santa Eufemia de Cozuelos in the diocese of Burgos – which doubtless would have welcomed her in.[11] Perhaps it was to one of these that her husband had expected her to go. But Doña Elvira had ideas of her own. A woman of resource as well as of not inconsiderable resources, she preferred something both nearer home and spiritually more up to date.

The identity of the witnesses to her former husband's unsuccessful plea indicates the direction in which her spiritual fancy was turning by the spring of 1259. Apart from two members of the cathedral chapter (Master Gil, the *cantor*, and the bishop's vicar, canon García Móniz), all those present were Dominicans, the prior and community of the local convent *en masse*. It was plain enough which way the wind was blowing, the wind that was soon to carry Master Gil himself, together with all his worldly wealth, into the Order of Preachers.[12] Moreover, those present would also have been aware not only that in the previous January Pope Alexander IV had granted the petition of the noblewoman Jimena Rodríguez of Zamora to establish a convent of women 'under the order of Saint Augustine and according to the Dominican rule'[13] but also that Jimena Rodríguez and Doña Elvira were sisters. In short, the 'other order' which Doña Elvira had been allowed the option of favouring was the 'Order of Saint Augustine . . . according to the Dominican rule'.

But what precisely was it that the sisters were committing themselves to in 1259? What did membership of the 'Order of St Augustine . . . according to the Dominican rule' imply?

For Alexander IV the question was readily answerable. For him, membership of the 'Order of Saint Augustine . . . according to the Dominican rule' implied whatever membership of the Order's Madrid convent entailed – the Madrid convent which Saint Dominic

5

himself had established in 1218 as his very first Spanish foundation. Originally a male community, well before 1259 it had been taken over by women.[14] In 1259 there was just one female community associated with the Order: Madrid practice was normative therefore. Accordingly, the prior provincial was instructed to arrange for the transfer of two sisters from Madrid to instruct the members of the new community in their duties.[15]

Yet the question remained. What precisely *were* the rules in 1259? Madrid rules, said the pope, the rules which Dominic had prescribed in about May 1220. But the rules prescribed in 1220 had been a simple set of rules for relatively simple times. They had required the nuns to observe the rule of silence in refectory, dormitory and oratory. They had forbidden them to leave the convent or to permit anyone else to enter it, other than the diocesan (the archbishop of Toledo) or another prelate coming there to preach or visit the place. In 1220 the duty of obedience to the prioress had been paramount. Also there was to be no chattering.[16]

By 1259, however, the days of piecemeal regulations of this kind were numbered. At the Valenciennes General Chapter in the June of that year, five months after the pope's letter to Jimena Rodríguez, the Master General of the Order, Humbert de Romans, promulgated a uniform rule addressed to 'all the sisters committed to the care of the friars of the Order of Preachers'.[17]

In issuing the first rule of its sort in the Order's history, Humbert stated, his purpose was to 'remove confusion'. Even so, the scope of his new rule was strictly limited. It extended only to the *de facto* situation. It did not address the *de jure* issue which had remained unresolved ever since the founder's death in 1221, the issue whether the Order should accept responsibility for women, *cura monialium*, at all. In 1235 the Bologna General Chapter had divested the Order of that responsibility, and four years later Pope Gregory IX had confirmed this decision and instructed bishops to desist forthwith from clothing women in the habit of the Order. Yet despite the pronounced reluctance of the friars regarding female communities, female foundations nevertheless continued to proliferate and the queues of women to join existing foundations continued to lengthen.[18] Hence in 1257 and 1259, just as the Zamora convent was being established, the instructions of the General Chapters of Florence and Valenciennes to priors provincial to report on the number of female houses within their provinces, the number of 'our sisters' inhabiting them, their material resources, and the authority by which they had been established.[19]

The demands which these communities were making on the Order's limited resources were matched by the Order's own ever-increasing demands on the limited resources of Western society at large. Since the early years of the century, while Europe's capacity to feed itself was ever more heavily strained by its mounting population, the mendicant orders had been making great and greatly resented inroads into the ordinary income and future expectations of the eccle-siastical establishment. At the Fourth Lateran Council in 1215 that establishment had opposed the foundation of new orders, and had had its opposition to them enshrined in the conciliar legislation.[20] However, as was reported at the Second Council of Lyons in 1274, that 'considered prohibition' proved a dead letter: 'Not only [had] the troublesome desire of petitioners extorted their multiplication, but also the presumptuous rashness of some [had] produced an almost unlimited crowd of diverse orders, especially mendicant, which [had] not yet merited the beginnings of approval.'[21]

For most of the bishops whose voice was again heard in 1274, it was not the orders which Rome had not authorised that were the problem, however, but those which 'to the evident advantage of the universal Church' (as the same decree asserted) it had, and in particular the Dominicans and the Franciscans. And it was less on account of the 'grave confusion in God's Church' which the prospect of the latter had portended in 1215 than of the threat that they represented to the material interests of cathedral, collegiate and parish churches from one end of Europe to the other that many of those bishops continued to resent their existence.

As mendicants, the friars ought, of course, not to have affected the ecclesiastical establishment's material interests at all. Such indeed had been the assurance that Bishop Martín II of Zamora had received from the prior provincial of the Dominicans, Sueiro Gomes, regard-ing the convent of the order which was established in his episcopal city some time after 1219 – when (according to tradition) Dominic visited the city and his aunt María de Guzmán provided him with a house for the purpose at Puebla de la Vega outside the walls.[22] As well as promising obedience to the bishop (a promise underwritten by the local *concejo*), the friars vowed not to come between the bishop and his flock. They would neither take tithes nor, except with episcopal licence, receive oblations. They would neither accept bequests, bury the dead (other than their own) nor, unless the bishop invited them to, preach. They would do none of these things because according to their own constitutions they could not, and any friar coming from afar and attempting otherwise would be denied houseroom.[23]

Yet despite those constitutions and despite those assurances, in the years that followed the friars of Zamora proceeded to do all the things that they had promised not to do. And they did so because the flock itself found the friars irresistible. At Zamora as elsewhere, because they were able to offer what the bishop in the cathedral had proved incapable of providing, the friars were converged upon in droves. In their search for spiritual solace, at Zamora as elsewhere laymen and laywomen – and members of the cathedral chapter, too, at Zamora the *cantor* Master Gil, for example – packed out the little lean-to churches on the wrong side of the river, and found there what they had sought in vain in the cathedral. And, having found that consolation, they then set about bringing those who provided it nearer home so that in life they could have easier access to the most accomplished confessors of the age and in death be buried within their walls with them for ever.

To this pattern of events – the succession of penitents, the corpses making tracks for the scruffy suburbs, the move towards the city centre, the building of a great stone church within sight of the cathedral – of stone, for fear of fire, according to Franciscan tradition, though in the case of the Castilian Dominicans flood was a hazard as well[24] – in the late 1240s Catalonia provided a rare exception. As is so often the case, Catalonia was running ahead both of Castile and of the rest of the West, too. In Catalonia the Dominicans were not circling the cathedral. Due largely to the influence of Raymond of Peñafort, Master General of the Order and the king of Aragon's confidant as well as the pope's, by the late 1240s they were already installed there. Before the Franciscan Order had made any such impression anywhere in the West, by then the province of Tarragona had as many as five Dominican bishops in office.[25] And though further west, in the kingdoms of Castile, León and Portugal, the thirteenth-century friars never captured the cathedrals as they had in Catalonia, across the whole peninsula that impact was considerable. In 1250 the provincial chapter held at Toledo assigned members of the Order to a total of twenty convents. By 1275 there were at least half as many convents again.[26]

The rate of Dominican growth in the third quarter of the thirteenth century is a phenomenon awaiting systematic investigation region by region. Why these years should have witnessed so rapid an expansion of mendicant activity, and why that expansion should have occurred where it did, in Spain and Germany, whereas in France and England the age of expansion had almost ended by mid-century, are questions the answers to which remain as uncertain today as they were in 1968 when Jacques Le Goff posited some sort of relationship between the distribution of mendicant foundations in thirteenth-century France and the incidence of urban expansion there.[27] What Le Goff identified as a feature of all the mendicant orders, namely the concentration of their offensive in the larger cities, the Franciscan Salimbene had recorded at the time as a characteristic peculiar to the Dominicans.[28] After 1968 it remained therefore to test the hypothesis in other areas of the old Christian West. Hungary and Germany apart, however,[29] the hypothesis remains untested. In common with their colleagues elsewhere, students of thirteenth-century Spain have resisted the temptation to hurry towards premature conclusions.[30]

Of course, the counting of heads and of houses is not everything. 'Le quantitatif n'est pas l'histoire.' But equally, 'il ne peut plus y avoir désormais de l'histoire sans base quantitative'.[31] In the case of the Spanish Dominicans, however, it has been claimed that no such enquiry is feasible because Napoleon's troops and the liberal governments that followed in their wake destroyed the means of attempting an assessment – that 'in relation to the past the loss is irreparable', as one of modern Spain's most distinguished historians of the Order has maintained.[32]

Such claims appear unduly pessimistic. True, the records of many convents are irrevocably lost. But not all of them are. Some are in the National Archive in Madrid, which is a different thing. Moreover, the *acta* of at least some of the chapters of the Spanish province are available. Since in the case of only four of the eleven chapters (those of 1250, 1275, 1281 and 1299) do the *acta* mention place-names,[33] as to precisely what they denote judgement may, of course, differ. However, if the Dominicans did indeed gravitate towards the cities and the larger towns – because, as Humbert de Romans remarked, in the towns there were more souls to be saved[34] – then the evidence of the provincial chapters should be capable of shedding at least some light on the urban history of thirteenth-century Spain and Portugal too. On the face of it the revelations it provides are startling. If the data are reliable then by 1299 no fewer than twenty-one of the peninsula's fifty-one episcopal cities – those in which the Dominicans had chosen not to settle – were in decline,[35] in contrast to the fifteen non-episcopal centres, all but one of them in the north or centre of the peninsula, in which convents had been established.[36] The list of Dominican foundations by the year 1299 implies significant changes in the distribution of human settlement since the peninsula's ecclesiastical map had been redrawn in accordance with Visigothic precedent.

But *are* they reliable? If by that question is meant, are they statistically exhaustive?, then the answer is surely no. For the records of the provincial chapters contain only the names of those of the Order's houses between which individual members of the Order were transferred.[37] But they are none the less valuable for that. Between 1250 and 1299 the proportion of Dominican houses in episcopal cities declined, and declined sharply, from nineteen houses in twenty cities to thirty in fifty-one.[38] In the second half of the thirteenth century – the half-century with which the present enquiry is concerned – the Spanish province of the Order was diversifying and expanding on all fronts.

The mendicant boom of the late thirteenth century was fuelled and fed by those who were themselves well-nourished – in Spain by Alfonso X's bastard daughter the Infanta Beatriz, for example, who even after her marriage to King Afonso III of Portugal continued to shower favours upon the Poor Clares of Alcocer.[39] As to the hungry, historians are more in the dark – though Humbert de Romans cannot only have had the upper reaches of European society in mind when in 1255 he instructed his friars to exercise discretion by not preaching at the same hour as the bishop was preaching in the cathedral.[40] Precisely what calibre of corpse it was that the Dominicans of Palencia had buried, on account of which the local bishop had excommunicated them, Alexander IV's letter two years later failed to reveal.[41] All that is clear is that, as was usually the case in disagreements between the friars and the local bishop, on this particular occasion the pope sided with the friars, and also, as was also usually the case, that the bishop of Palencia paid scant attention to the pope's admonitions.[42]

Conditions were tight in mid-thirteenth-century Europe, with men standing shoulder to shoulder and only venturing from their place in the line in order to gather up the crust discarded by another. Up to a point Castile was no exception. In Castile the effect was the same. It was the causes that were different. Whereas elsewhere in the West in 1250 there were too many people and not enough land, in Castile there was too much land and not enough people. In a single generation the extent of the kingdom of Castile had increased by some 80,000 square kilometres, it has been calculated.[43] By creating a vacuum for human endeavour, the Great Leap Forward into Andalucia after the crushing of the Almohad army at Las Navas de Tolosa in 1212 had disrupted the north and centre of the kingdom. Economic historians continue to debate the demographic consequences of the Reconquest of Seville in 1248. In the opinion of some it shifted the peninsula's centre of demographic gravity southwards, pouring its human resources towards the frontier and thereby aggravating problems already endemic north of the Duero.[44] For others it had no such universal effect: there were areas of the north where the problem was not the lack of manpower but an excess of it.[45] Doubtless both views are correct, as the conflicting views of economic historians are so often found to be. Possibly the archbishop of Toledo who reported the spectacle of the mass of humanity attracted to reconquered Córdoba 'as to a king's wedding', so that there were not enough houses to accommodate them, and the king of Castile who presided over the crisis of his kingdom between 1252 and 1284 – and for once the jaded concept of crisis is not altogether out of place – were both ill-informed.[46]

Certainly that king's own vainglory played a part. In March 1256 Alfonso X embarked on the imperial adventure which was to end in humiliation and failure nineteen years later. And meanwhile the weather turned. In the seven years after 1255 the Spanish peninsula experienced famine of biblical proportions, the result of a combination of unseasonal drought and widespread flooding. And in 1257–8, with their churches and dioceses impoverished by forced contributions to the cost of the previous half century's military adventures, the Castilian bishops as well as the Castilian weather turned against the king.[47]

Castile in the late 1250s was in a state of post-reconquest *tristesse*, dejected, exhausted and subversive. Small wonder that the regular clergy of Palencia were scrabbling over corpses. If as many as 11,000 had starved to death there in a single year, as Alexander IV and the cardinals were later said to have been informed,[48] in the kingdom's increasingly straitened circumstances corpses were big business. With inundated mendicants seeking higher and drier ground towards the historic centres of the kingdom's cathedral cities, small wonder either that just six months after approving the foundation of the Zamora convent it was reported to Alexander IV that various monks and secular clergy had been touring León and Castile obliterating the stigmata from statues of Saint Francis.[49]

The onset of widespread hostility directed specifically at Saint Dominic's order seems to have been somewhat delayed. Part of the explanation for this may have been a sense that, although God had proved not to be Castilian after all, as he had appeared to be when Fernando III had been sweeping through Andalucia in the 1240s, at least there was no question about Dominic's nationality. Also there was the fact of the Dominicans' preference for non-episcopal cities. Further investigation of Le Goff's hypothesis will need to allow for the case of Pamplona, for example, where while Franciscan migration towards the city centre resulted in the cathedral chapter's denunciation of the Friars Minor as heretics and 'worse than Jews or Saracens', for the time being the Preachers, who had directed their attention to Estella instead, remained on the best of terms with the canons.[50] At Burgos too, furiously though the battle would rage once it had been joined, with hooded men sent to steal the friars' privileges and building materials as well as papal emissaries tipped into the Arlanzón, until the mid-1260s relations between the Dominicans and the cathedral chapter appear to have remained on the whole cordial.[51] Likewise, when in March 1264 the sisters Jimena and Elvira Rodríguez approached the bishop and chapter of Zamora with a request to purchase the site 'iuxta Sanctum Frontonem' recently abandoned by the Franciscans[52] and establish themselves there together with a number of other ladies of similar religious disposition, the bishop and chapter were altogether willing to oblige.

True, three years earlier the dean and chapter of Zamora had obtained from Alexander IV a privilege preventing (after a fashion) the establishment of further monastic foundations within the city and diocese.[53] As well as being flawed, however, that prohibition had come too late to stand in the ladies' way. For by then their plans were already in train. In 1264, moreover, the bishop who was later to be denounced as the hammer of the mendicants was wholly sympathetic to the Preachers – so much so indeed that in the following year he provided the Salamanca convent of the order with an indulgence to assist them to rehouse themselves after they too had been flooded out.[54] At Zamora, therefore, the ladies' desire to 'assume the habit and order of the friars preacher' presented no problem. On their payment of a 1,000 maravedís deposit towards the sale price of 3,300, the deal was done: 'And we the said bishop promise to give the said ladies Doña Jimena and Doña Elvira the said habit and order', the agreement stated, understandably enough.[55] For in 1264 3,300 maravedís was a large sum. And for the bishop of Zamora in 1264 it was a windfall. It was one and a half times the sum that his immediate predecessor, D. Pedro I, had spent on diocesan improvements over a period of sixteen years.

Coming just three years after the promulgation of *Virtute conspicuos* − Alexander IV's privilege to the Dominicans whereby 'independence of everyone save the pope was finally and completely attained'[56] − with hindsight the arrangement envisaged by Bishop Suero might seem exceptionally naive. On 26 March 1264, however, the agreement was one into which both parties entered freely and to which the ladies would readily have set their seals, if they had possessed seals − as it was, the abbots of Moreruela, Valparaíso and S. Miguel del Monte performed this service for them. In a further agreement on the same day, the ladies pledged 'obedience, subjection and reverence' to the bishop and his successors, entrusted him with the stewardship (*procuratio*) of their house as its worldly fortunes improved, and acknowledged his right to exercise discipline there and their obligation to pay him tithes on their possessions, promising neither to acquire parishes or parishioners nor to accept bodies for burial except with the licence of bishop and chapter. Nor would they seek any indulgence or privilege in derogation of these arrangements. On the contrary, they would seek papal confirmation of all that been agreed.[57] These questions of jurisdiction duly settled, two days later Elvira Rodríguez swore obedience on the altar as first prioress of Las Dueñas.[58]

Ostensibly, therefore, the issue of episcopal jurisdiction over the new foundation was not an issue at all in 1264. The establishment of the convent of Las Dueñas was conducted in strict conformity with those business principles in accordance with which Bishop Suero liked all transactions to be conducted. The church of Zamora had no present use for the site, but it did have the heavy debts to clear with which his predecessor, Bishop Pedro I, had saddled it.[59] Hence the prominence of financial provisions during those spring days. As soon as there were twelve sisters installed – the number needed to make the community viable, presumably – the bishop was to receive half the goods of all subsequent recruits (other than their clothes, furniture, beds and bedding), or the money equivalent, as surety for payment of the balance of the purchase price of the site;[60] all of which sounds as unremarkable as it was businesslike.

In reality, however, Zamora's circumstances on 26 March 1264 were anything but unremarkable, as yet another agreement concluded between the parties of that day amply demonstrates. Here the conditions of near-anarchy in which these negotiations were being conducted are revealed. Bishop and chapter commit themselves to defend the ladies in their possession of their new property across the river ('ultra flumen'). Of course. But now it is acknowledged that the ladies might not be allowed to enjoy their new retreat undisturbed. Now it was admitted that at any time the exercise of superior force just a few hundred yards from the cathedral might require them to abandon the site altogether. Whence the need for both parties to address the issues of reparation and indemnity.[61] The possibility of the need for a decent alternative 'in suburbio Zamorensi' had to be allowed for. Contingency plans had to be envisaged regarding the twelve-sisters provision, whereby any sister opting for a quiet life (rather than a cloistered existence on the front line) would have the proportion of her goods restored to her which under the initial arrangement would have been acquired by the bishop[62] – all of which is reminiscent of the small print of a contract drafted on the slopes of Etna.

In these circumstances the Ladies of Zamora were able to drive a hard bargain too. And they were shrewd businesswomen, these ladies. As has been indicated, the establishment of their convent quite closely resembled the foundation of a limited liability company. Indeed, that was what from the outset Las Dueñas was, a limited liability company, the founders of which were its shareholders. Though their bishop may not fully have appreciated the implications of this, the pope did. In the year after their foundation the ladies received Clement IV's assurance that although they had withdrawn from 'the world' individually, they remained fully in control of the worldly possessions which were theirs by just title.[63] The Ladies of Zamora in 1264 may have been inclined to religion. But they remained women of the world.

On the other hand, Bishop Suero was a prelate of the hard-headed school and nobody's fool. Like so many members of the hard-headed school, however, he was also gullible to a fault. Proceeding on the blithe assumption that 'the said ladies Doña Jimena and Doña Elvira' and their successors would meekly accept 'the said habit and order' from his hands, the bishop of Zamora in 1264 appears to have been acting in total disregard of the implications of the rule which the Master General of the Dominican Order had promulgated five years before for 'the sisters committed to the care of the friars of the Order of Preachers'. The possibility that the status of such female communities was about to be transformed seems not to have occurred to him.

True, he cannot be blamed for having failed to anticipate the saga of copulation, cross-dressing and general mayhem which was soon to be enacted across the river from his episcopal residence. Many bishops lack imagination. What is extraordinary is that a bishop of Suero Pérez's training and experience should have failed to appreciate the extent to which his various agreements with the ladies were clouded in obscurity and riddled with inconsistencies. Regarding visitation of the convent and the appointment and removal of the prioress, in particular, there was a fundamental contradiction. 'Saving the *instituta* of the Order of Preachers,' the ladies promised, these tasks were to be carried out in accordance with those (same) *instituta*, 'as other ladies of the said Order of Preachers were visited and their prioresses appointed and removed'.[64] But what was this to mean in practice? What did the '*instituta* of the Dominican Order' actually amount to? If they were in conformity with the undertaking that immediately followed, the concession of these same functions to the bishops of Zamora in perpetuity, what purpose did the repetition serve?[65] And if they were not, or at some future date were construed not to be, what value attached, or would then attach, to the promise of perpetual submission to the bishop? The disjunctive 'nichilominus tamen' meant then what it means still: 'nevertheless however'. It was a device for squaring a circle.

'Nichilominus tamen . . .'. Here was a legal loophole wide enough to admit any number of ladies in line abreast, and this danger the old chancery hand ought to have recognised. But in this regard the Ladies of Zamora evidently had the advantage of the wordly-wise bishop. It was an advantage which some of them at least were to prove adept at exploiting.

And according to Humbert de Romans, in this the Ladies of

Zamora were not alone. According to the Master General there were many such ladies on the loose in mid-thirteenth-century Europe, ladies both eager to take advantage and fully capable of doing so. In the sermons he addressed to 'religious women of the Order of Saint Augustine' and to 'the sisters of the Preachers', Humbert gave expression to that current of profound scepticism which had run through the Order since its very foundation. Female enclosure was a sham, he warned. Far from providing a secure stronghold against carnality, female enclosure afforded a safe haven for its enjoyment. The women Humbert described may have assumed a new habit, but they had not renounced the old habits of their abandoned lifestyle.[66] In a critique as scathing as any penned by the Order's secular opponents, Humbert impressed upon the Dominican sisters the need for threefold protection ('triplex custodia'). As well as such feeble protection as enclosure itself afforded, they must be guarded against all manner of social intercourse, even conversations at the window. Also – and in the case of the Ladies of Zamora this was a prophetic warning – they must be guarded against the friars charged with their spiritual care.[67]

Within four years of the establishment of the convent of Las Dueñas, news was received from Rome well calculated to disrupt the agreement into which the ladies had entered for the reception of the Dominican habit and order from their bishop. Since 1264 the antifeminist tide within the Order had turned and begun to run strongly the other way – a development for which the first Dominican cardinal, Hugues de Saint-Cher (1244–63), was largely responsible – and on 6 February 1267 Clement IV, who had been a married man with children before becoming pope, finally entrusted the Master General and the priors provincial with entire responsibility for the 'diverse monasteries of nuns or sisters of the Order of Saint Augustine'.

Clement IV's privilege, *Affectu sincero*, delivered the nuns to the *magisterium* and *doctrina* of the friars. It did so, moreover, without so much as a mention of the existing rights of bishops to exercise jurisdiction over their communities or to visit and discipline them.[68] Later that same month the pope again overrode the interests of the ordinaries, this time in favour of the Franciscans,[69] and thereby refuelled the controversy regarding the mendicants' role in the Church which had first surfaced in the University of Paris in 1256. On that earlier occasion one of their opponents, William of Saint-Amour, had characterised the friars as hypocrites, men who pretended to have

16

abandoned the world, yet continued to aspire to its 'riches, pleasures and rewards', haunting the courts of kings and prevailing upon popes to provide them with ever more exorbitant privileges. The champion of the seculars quoted Saint Paul: 'Truly the signs of an apostle were wrought among you in all patience' (2 Corinthians 12.12). The cupidity of these self-styled apostles revealed them for the false preachers they were.[70]

His protests raised a storm, the storm moved the earth, and by the time the dust settled there were hairline cracks on the monumental façade of the Western Church itself. William of Saint-Amour was charged with having asked for a general council to consider the issue. He did not deny the charge.[71] In invoking 'ancient constitutional law against an abuse of papal sovereignty' he had appealed to a fundamental sense of the Church as a 'pluralistic institution'.[72] William's voice was that of the old Europe, of a once settled and confident Europe now betrayed from above, the voice of a Europe that had never spoken yet, a voice whose strident tones resembled those of agitated post-imperialists of more recent times. Combining (in Robert Bartlett's arresting phrase) 'the reproductive rate of the rabbit with the self-containment of the crustacean',[73] the mendicants were thirteenth-century Europe's immigration problem. With the blessing of distant authority they bred and spread across the continent. But their growth did not go unchallenged. For while Clement IV, having condemned William's *Tractatus de periculis*, was providing the friars with further aid and comfort, William himself returned to the charge with his monumental work of fundamentalist theology, the *Collectiones catholicae et canonicae Scripturae*.[74] This was in 1266–7.

As well as producing visceral reactions in certain recesses of the Church itself, the debates of these years – in which, as well as William of Saint-Amour and Gerard of Abbeville, both Saint Bonaventure and Saint Thomas Aquinas were actively involved – left a deep impression on the University of Paris. The University of Salamanca, however, appears to have remained unperturbed: testimony perhaps to the wisdom for once of Alfonso *el Sabio* in making no provision for theologians when he gave the place its charter in 1254.[75] Nor, it may be surmised, was theological speculation on the subject any livelier 60 kilometres to the north, in the immediate vicinity of the bishop of Zamora. The years 1266 and 1267 appear to have come and gone without particular incident along that particular stretch of the Duero.

Theological speculation may not have been the bishop of Zamora's forte, and though what he lacked in intellectual subtlety he more than made up for in episcopal robustness, it appears that in 1266–7 the time had not yet come for him to revise his views on the subject of the friars. When in due course it did come, that change of mind would owe more to the experience of having the convent gate slammed shut in his face than to exegesis of the text of 2 Corinthians or the promulgation of *Affectu sincero*.

This is not to suggest that *Affectu sincero* was not a thoroughly bad piece of law. It was. Partisan in conception and inept in execution, by neither safeguarding existing episcopal rights nor specifically abrogating them, it created battle-zones where none previously existed. But it was only the latest of a series of such papal violations of local rights and susceptibilities. Just two years earlier Clement IV had laid claim to the benefices of ecclesiastics dying at the papal curia, reserving them to the disposal of his successors for ever. True, that decree, *Licet ecclesiarum*, could be circumvented. However, for a bishop whose dean, archdeacons and canons were constantly setting off for Rome, as the bishop of Zamora's were, in order to denounce him there,[76] it was an irritation; yet another irritation, yet another sign of the times.

The signs of the times were clear enough to the likes of D. Suero. Red-blooded Spanish bishops were perfectly capable of interpreting them without the assistance of French logic-choppers. They were staring them in the face. And the pope was not the only offender. The tendencies of which Clement IV's two decrees were the most recent ecclesiastical manifestation were paralleled during those same years by changes within the kingdom's secular sphere. Times were hard. In November 1266 the dean and chapter of Zamora appealed against yet another imposition. On what they were left with they could hardly survive. But it was to the pope that they were reduced to appealing, the pope who had authorised the latest charge of a tenth of their resources. And the previous three such tenths had been exacted by the king.[77] Between the upper millstone and the lower there was no escape. The pressure created must seek release elsewhere.

The dean and chapter suspected that even if they were successful in resisting the demands of the papal executor (the archbishop of Seville, who was very much the king's man, anyway) the king would have his way with them none the less, and have it by main force.[78] By 1266 the

18

effectiveness of that force was making itself ever more insistently felt. In the previous year, it would appear, the royal law-code which would eventually come to be known as the *Siete Partidas* had been completed, a code which expressed Alfonso X's imperialist impatience with the peculiar foral institutions so dear to the local communities of the kingdoms of Castile and León.[79] In common with his episcopal colleagues elsewhere, the bishop of Zamora was therefore bound by a complex of loyalties as well as buffeted by the competing and complementary demands of increasing centralisation, both secular and ecclesiastical. The millstones were the same for him as for his dean and chapter. So were the pressures.

In the case of D. Suero himself this double pressure was never relaxed. For although in the summer of 1274 (while, as it happened, he was at Zamora) political reality impinged upon Alfonso X for once, sufficiently to persuade him to issue an *ordenamiento* modifying his master-plan for overall legal reform, otherwise, wherever he was able to do so, the king remained committed to the cause of restructuring the political society of his kingdom. The dynamics of that process are still less than perfectly understood. However, to judge by the course of events at Burgos, Alfonso's strategy was to seek a new basis for his rule by promoting the interests of the non-noble *caballeros villanos*, lavishing fiscal privileges upon them, to the considerable benefit of these urban oligarchs.[80]

Another beneficiary of the process was the king.[81] But there were casualties too. At Burgos those members of the cathedral chapter who had previously enjoyed the lion's share of the market in land and real estate apparently now found themselves increasingly excluded from its operations. And they in turn looked for scapegoats. Although Burgos had not yet seen the last of its ecclesiastical plutocrats (if only for the reason that there as in every other cathedral city of the kingdom, Zamora included, churchmen and laymen were all part of a single complex society),[82] there as elsewhere the ecclesiastical establishment vented its spleen on the representatives of that other privileged group for whom the third quarter of the thirteenth century was a period of uninterrupted prosperity, expansion and royal patronage, namely the Order of Preachers.[83] Similar alignments of forces are found elsewhere in these years. At Túy in the remote north-west, for example, while the municipality treated the friars to a warm welcome the canons of the cathedral greeted them with a fusillade of excommunications – and, there as at Burgos, the intervention of Gregory X had little effect.[84]

The exact sequences of events at Zamora during the 1270s, the degree to which they corresponded to this pattern, and the stages by which D. Suero's initial benevolence gradually curdled into bitterness remain uninvestigated and are destined so to remain for as long as the capitular records of these years are kept inaccessible – not unpublished, as they have been for seven centuries, but published and bizarrely not distributed.[85] Even so, it is already sufficiently clear that, for all D. Suero's privileged access to the king and the king's temporising *ordenamiento*, both before and after 1274 the corporate interests of the church of Zamora were under threat.

In September 1272 the bishop and chapter had raised with Alfonso the issue of their right to nominate a judge to the municipal *concejo*. Time out of mind such had been the custom (they claimed) until Alfonso had recently disenfranchised them.[86] Under pressure the king conceded the point.[87] But it was not until July 1278 that his concession was given effect. And then, just two months later, the king's son, the Infante Sancho, heard the case again, as one of six issues which the contending parties submitted to his arbitration at San Esteban de Gormaz.[88]

The infante's reconsideration of a dispute which his father had so recently determined is remarkable. But for the fact that the king's eldest son, as he described himself in September 1278, was also, as also he described himself, his father's heir, it would be inexplicable. By then, perhaps, the father's heir was already angling for his father's throne, the throne which – according to the infante's tutor, the Franciscan polymath Gil de Zamora, who assisted the infante in his arbitration on that occasion – Alfonso began to share with him in that year.[89] Be that as it may, in the summer of 1278 it may well have seemed to the bishop of Zamora that there were fault lines in the system which, if they were to be exploited, needed to be exploited while the opportunity presented itself. Perhaps also the same thought occurred to the Ladies of Zamora. Certainly there is a chronological coincidence to be observed between the deterioration in the relationship of D. Suero and the local convent on the one hand and the onset of political confusion at the centre on the other. As will be seen, although the battle lines had already been drawn by 1272, as late as September 1274 the bishop and the ladies were still on terms. It was not until the second half of the decade, as Alfonso X's control of affairs faltered, that the situation at Zamora reached flashpoint.

Bishop Suero of Zamora was an experienced judge of fault lines and a seasoned connoisseur of the main chance. A king's man *par excellence*, and one who owed Alfonso X his all, he remained loyal to the king for as long as the king remained effective. He had been elected to his see in 1254, just two years into Alfonso's reign, having risen through the chancery way to be notary for the kingdom of León. Up to a point, he was a model civil servant, a seasoned exponent of those arts of high-level collusion upon which the government of thirteenth-century Europe depended, one of a type indispensable to both Church and State. It had been in order to suit the king's convenience that in 1255 the pope had allowed his episcopal consecration to be postponed until he could be spared from his royal duties.[90]

Those had been his glory days. In September 1256 he had been the only bishop present in the royal chapel at Segovia when Alfonso had entered into his imperial commitments with the representatives of the commune of Marseilles.[91] He had been close to the king, and the warmth of that relationship had been shared by the chapter of Zamora. The chapter had much to be grateful to him for, and in the lengthy apologia he compiled towards the end of his life (the 'aduentarium quod confeci ... de melioracionibus in episcopatu factis' to which he referred in his final testament in May 1285)[92] he was at pains to record the enormity of the debt it owed him. In one of the snatches of autobiography which intersperse that record the ailing bishop recalled the occasion of his entry into his new see in 1255. Arriving in style, accompanied by almost forty horses, he had found there a lone lame mule.[93] A lone lame mule: fitting symbol of the dilapidated state in which his predecessor had left the church and from which over the next thirty years D. Suero set about rescuing it. As his end approached in the mid-1280s, it was in terms of the contrast with that squalid past that he desired his episcopate to be remembered.[94]

The earliest of his achievements, in the order in which he recorded them, was his securing from Alfonso X of the *villa* of Fermoselle to the east of the confluence of the Duero and the Tormes, at the Portuguese frontier of his diocese, the houses he built there to the very best of specifications ('domos perobtimas et nimis sumptuosas'), the vines he planted and the green-belt sites he acquired ('emi ortos ibi').[95]

The emphasis on material improvement pervades all that followed. Here restocking with cattle and fish and, by luring from elsewhere the *populatores* (those shady rustlers of thirteenth-century Spain's most valuable commodity), there with men, Bishop Suero was one of the great improvers of his age, a prelate for whom a diocese was a complex of estates and a bishop's principal function the business of estate management. To that end all other tasks were secondary. In the service of territorial rationalisation tithes could be treated as negotiable currency, canon law or no canon law.[96] Sumptuous was as sumptuous did.[97]

What enabled D. Suero to afford princely gestures on this scale were the contacts with the royal court that he continued to enjoy after moving to his one-mule cathedral city. As a fast-stream civil servant he had come to Zamora loaded with the richest pickings of the wealthiest churches of the kingdom, archdeaconries at Seville and Toledo and benefices at Compostela, León, Salamanca, Silves and elsewhere. The profits of these he had invested in 'good books' for the perusal of the canons.[98] And the benefits which his connexions at court conferred upon his church endured. He had prevailed upon the king to replace Zamora's old wax-sealed privileges with privileges sealed with seals of lead. The church of Zamora was the only church in the kingdom so favoured, Suero claimed.[99] He certainly kept his old chancery colleagues fully occupied. His cartulary, the *Tumbo Blanco*, contains copies of more than seventy royal mandates, most of them issued between 1252 and 1274 and all of them testifying to the strength of the career bureaucrat's faith in the system to which he owed his own ascent.[100]

In his church's cause he had selflessly followed the king all over the kingdom, trailing after him from Burgos to Segovia and from Segovia to Toledo, all at great wear and tear to himself, as well as considerable expense. Two and a half years he had spent shadowing Alfonso around Seville, Cádiz and Niebla (this must have been *c.* 1262). While doing so he had lost three of his men to enemy action and spent 6,000 maravedís of his own money (which was almost twice what the ladies were to promise to pay him just two years later). In 1270, and again in 1274, he had journeyed as far afield as Vitoria and Valencia, pursuing a ruler whose sights at the time were set on Milan and Rome with complaints about Toro and Fresno de Ribera.[101] And what contribution had the chapter made? What gratitude had they shown him? Precious little.[102]

The evidence of his remarkable memoir suggests that D. Suero died a bitter man.

And the will he made in May 1285 confirms the fact. The former civil servant who by the end of his life was not only out of favour at the king's court, but also apparently in exile from his own cathedral city, was determined that the chapter of his church should not benefit from the fruits of his worldly wisdom. All the property he possessed at Badajoz[103] and elsewhere was to be sold in order to fund the anniversaries he was establishing for himself and for others and the bequests he was making to members of his family, his servants, other ecclesiastical institutions, the lepers of Zamora and Toro, and the rest. For 'the moveables I now have are mine', he insisted and, expanding on the 'one lame mule' theme, recalled that when he had first come to Zamora the place was barely fit for human habitation, not even boasting a bed in which a simple cleric could spend the night.[104] In the service of the church of Zamora he had parted with almost 5,000 maravedis of his own money, not to mention additional expenditure on the purchase and recovery of church property. Perhaps his successor would think it right to recompense his family for all this, he reflected.[105]

Even so, even in May 1285 he had not despaired of the future entirely. The theological desert into which he had ventured thirty years before might yet prove capable of irrigation, he seems to have supposed.[106] Again, perhaps he was right. Himself more of a doer than a thinker – he was certainly not a member of Alfonso X's intellectual inner circle – in terms of the categorisation of human activity adopted by the Master of the Dominican Order in 1281, D. Suero was above all a man committed to the 'useful' rather than the 'curious'.[107] His own restless preoccupation with the affairs of his church can scarcely have allowed him much leisure to peruse the books he bequeathed it. Anyway, like the incoming bursar of a recently mismanaged modern college whose principal endowment is a rump of mutinous fellows, he appears to have regarded the leisure to read as a luxury reserved for future generations.

The books in the treasury at the end of the 1280s, five years after D. Suero's death, would have represented a more or less up-to-date collection at the end of the twelfth century, it has recently been observed, 'but not at the end of the thirteenth'.[108] The verdict does D. Suero less than justice. True, in the late 1280s there were only six law-books in the Zamora treasury, all of them canonist texts, and just one 'profane' work (the pseudo-Hippocratic *Epistola ad Maecenatem*). The comparison to be made is not with the late twelfth century, however, it is with the situation ten years into Suero's pontificate. For then, as emerges from the survey made in April 1265, the cathedral treasury contained no proper books at all. In April 1265 all its books were choir-books and two-thirds of its contents were vestments, materials suitable enough to serve as bedding therefore but hardly the stuff of scholarship.[109] Its silverware apart, in 1265 the most exotic item in the Zamora treasury was its missal 'de Tors'. Twenty years later that missal was still there,[110] together with the various reliquaries and silver vinegar-dispensers. By then, however, it was not with its missals, it was with the money of Tours that the canons of Zamora were pre-occupied. The likes of Fernando Martínez – archdeacon of Zamora, Bolognese regular, Alfonso X's envoy as well as collaborator, and legal author in his own right – did not depend for their references on the half-dozen law-books in the cathedral treasury. In common with 'the cardinal' (Cardinal Gil Torres, presumably) whose green chasuble was listed in the later list together with the archdeacon's brocaded bequest,[111] Fernando Martínez had accumulated a library of his own because he operated on a wider stage.[112] And part of the reason why he operated on a wider stage was that that was the stage on which don Suero operated and that don Suero was the bishop with whom, when he returned to base, the archdeacon of Zamora had to cope and to whom he had to answer.

A member of that band of pragmatic prelates whose commitment to the useful enabled the curious to realise their potential, Bishop Suero of Zamora left his church in better shape than he had found it. In marked contrast to the church of Jaén, that other refuge for super-annuated civil servants – where the local clergy, on having yet another Latinless ignoramus thrust upon them at the end of the reign of the wisest king in Christendom, reflected that it was the lack of literate and virtuous prelates that had brought the land to the state it was in[113] – the church over whose affairs the bishop of Zamora presided throughout the reign of Alfonso X was no place for sluggards.

No saint, no Spartan, and certainly no reformer, in the course of his thirty-year pontificate D. Suero is credited with just one diocesan synod of unknown date – and indeed even this may be an over-estimate, since the scope of the constitutions issued on that occasion appears to have been limited to the archdeaconry of Toro.[114] Though very much a law unto himself, and capable of regarding himself as exempt from the constitutions of his church enacted in the time of his predecessors,[115] Suero required the strictest compliance with the law from others. The glimpse of him that his old adversaries, the clergy of Toro, provided in 1265, crumpling Martín Fernández's charters and breaking their seals,[116] reveals him for what he was, a man of choleric temper and not one to be trifled with.

And trifling with him was what some time in the early 1270s the Ladies of Las Dueñas, or some of them, began to do. In 1267 presumably – and news of it cannot have been long delayed, for the priors provincial had been instructed to pass it on[117] – the ladies would have learned of Pope Clement's recent ruling entrusting them to the care of the friars. When some time after that the bishop came to pay them a visit, the ladies refused him entry – as indeed they appear to have been entitled to do: since the promulgation of *Affectu sincero* the visitation of communities such as theirs had been entrusted to the friars. And of this the bishop ought to have been aware. Perhaps he was. But whether he was or not, on being denied entry he responded with characteristic vigour, imposing sentences of excommunication and interdict, and when these were ignored, taking the matter further, to the papal curia itself. In October 1272 Gregory X – or rather the vice-chancellor of the Roman Church – instructed three dignitaries of the church of León to enforce the episcopal sentences. Accordingly, three months later, 'the prioress or subprioress' and the convent of Las Dueñas were directed to settle their differences with the bishop 'ami-cabiliter', failing which they were to present themselves before the judges at León in mid-March, on the day after Quasimodo Sunday.[118]

The effect of this communication was almost instantaneous. Within the month the ladies had come to heel and the sub-prioress Doña Jimena was providing the bishop with assurances of 'obedien-cia, subiection e reuerencia'.[119] This was followed in the following October by both the bishop and the prioress, Doña Stefanía, sub-mitting their 9-year-old agreement to Rome for papal approval, as Stefanía's predecessor had undertaken to do in 1264.[120] The texts of the agreement which bishop and prioress submitted for papal ratifica-tion were true to the original in all essentials and identical in detail.[121] On the face of it, the ladies had capitulated and confirmed their accep-tance of the terms on which their foundation had been authorised.

In reality, however, the events of October 1273 changed nothing. The papal mandate to the churchmen of León remained unimplemented. This was because the actual meaning of the 1264 agreement – and in particular its provisions regarding the issues of visitation and the institution and removal of the prioress – remained as capable as it had always been of more than one interpretation. And by 1273 the full implications of this ambiguity had become more evident. Since 1264 the ladies' perception of themselves had changed. Casting off their Augustinian disguise, they had come out into the open. Like Doña Elvira before her, Doña Stefanía now referred to her nuns as Dominicans *tout court*.[122] So also did the unidentified sub-prioress who in March 1274 supplicated Gregory X independently for confirmation of the 1264 agreement.[123]

What the sub-prioress's purpose was in replicating the prioress's recent approach to the pontiff we have no means of knowing. Perhaps the divisions within the convent, the full extent of which was to be brought to light in 1279, were already developing five years earlier. (As we have seen, the papal delegates in January 1273 were uncertain whether it was with the prioress of the convent or with its sub-prioress that they needed to communicate.) Possibly it was for that reason, incipient schism, that later in March 1274 D. Suero had Doña Stefanía's *supplicat* confirmed by a group of churchmen assembled at Burgos – a city not without mendicant problems of its own – a group in which he had the good sense to include Archbishop Gonzalo of Compostela and a brace of mendicant prelates.[124] The occasion of the gathering was the meeting of the last Cortes of his reign at which Alfonso X appeared more or less in control of events.[125] Evidently, questions remained which the ladies' simulated submission of February 1273 had left unanswered. Yet for almost seven years, the years during which the king of Castile sacrificed his domestic credibility on the altar of imperial ambition, no answers to those questions were received and the papal mandate of October 1272 was allowed to gather dust. For almost seven years the Ladies of Zamora turned a resolutely deaf ear to the dreadful authority of the Vicar of Christ and, perhaps with the concurrence of a temporarily more sanguine bishop, the papal judges delegate let the matter lie.

Hard-nosed bishops and canons turning a deaf ear to the supreme pontiff were a common enough feature of thirteenth-century Castile, where, as D. Suero's own career demonstrates, a capacity for dodging and weaving while papal sentences of excommunication rained down was a necessary qualification for episcopal office.[126] Such behaviour on the part of the otherwise apparently scrupulous Ladies of Zamora does deserve comment, however. And they *were* otherwise apparently scrupulous, those ladies, as was shown by their conduct regarding a certain church which they had purchased from the bishop. Having completed the transaction, an awful possibility occurred to them. Might this have been simony? So much did their consciences trouble them that in 1273 they consulted Gregory X. And so impressed was the pope that he took a personal interest in the matter. It was 'on his Holiness's own instructions' (as was explained by fr. Petrus de Regio, the papal chaplain and 'familiaris' to whom the matter was referred) that the conscientious ladies were to have their minds set at rest and enabled to sleep peacefully again[127] – which (barring other nocturnal disturbances) they could now settle down to do, secure in the knowledge that it had been they and not the bishop who had made a clean breast of it, and perhaps even confident in the expectation that that fact would have registered with the pope. And, although that impression would certainly have been unfair on a bishop who had been waging his own campaign against simony on an eleventh-century scale (Easter auctions of churches by laymen no less),[128] perhaps it had.

On the other hand, the pontiff who had concerned himself with their affairs did have so much else on his mind – the Holy Land, the Empire, Sicily *inter alia*. Not that that circumstance was to the ladies' disadvantage, either. If, for example, they had been assured that since the pontiff had no means of recalling the investigation into their affairs that he himself had so recently set in train, no risk attached to their drawing attention to themselves, then they had not been badly advised. And if they had also been assured that there was no need for them to refer to him the matter of their recent sale of the water-mill at Matarranas, they had not been badly advised either.

Even so, the particulars of the sale of that mill reveal both the bishop and the Ladies of Zamora for what they were worth. The date of the sale was August 1274, just a month after the conclusion of the Second Council of Lyons. Its purchaser was the *cantor* of Zamora, Pedro Johan, and with the 800 maravedís that it realised the Ladies of Zamora purchased a property at Montamarta. The vendors were two sisters, both of them members of the recently founded convent at Caleruega.[129]

❀❀❀❀❀

Notwithstanding the papal licence that they had received in 1265 permitting them to retain control of their worldly goods, it is surprising to discover the Ladies of Zamora engaged in entrepreneurial dealings with members of the convent of nuns situated in Saint Dominic's birthplace. Their activities would have come as no surprise to D. Suero, however, not least because he himself had given the conveyance his blessing – a conveyance which for good measure was signed and sealed in the Franciscan house at Zamora.[130] And even if he had been hitherto unaware of the extent of the ladies' capitalist ventures, which seems unlikely, then he certainly had his eyes opened just a fortnight later when he witnessed the will of Doña Elvira González. Doña Elvira was the owner of very extensive estates throughout the diocese of Zamora and beyond. Quite how extensive they were, the badly damaged state of her will conceals. But everything she had she left to the convent of Las Dueñas, either immediately or by reversion on the demise of sundry cousins and nephews. With her own children already dead, Doña Elvira bequeathed her all to the nuns into whose convent she hoped that her granddaughter would enter in due course.[131]

Nor will it have escaped D. Suero's attention that the exculpatory all-clear from Orvieto in the previous year had been addressed to the prior of the Zamora Dominicans, or that in witnessing Doña Elvira's will he had been accompanied by two members of the Order, fr. Fernán Domínguez and fr. Pedro de Roma.[132] Buying and selling, getting and spending, the Ladies of Zamora in the mid-1270s were indeed wiser in their generation than those world-spurning friars to whom Bishop Martín II had extended his wary welcome hardly half a century before.

On that occasion the friars had undertaken not to disturb the established order of parish and diocese – as in 1264 had the ladies themselves. By 1274, however, Bishop Martín's successor had sufficient reason for wondering not only at the spectacle of conspicuous formal piety combined with that spectacular contempt for the rules of engagement which the Ladies of Zamora so blatantly displayed in their dealings with their father in God, but also at the ease with which in the space of just ten years they had succeeded in adjusting to the transformation that the mendicant ideal had suffered in the course of the previous half-century.

In the memorandum listing some of the scandalous features of that transformation which he prepared in the very same year for the Second Council of Lyons, Humbert de Romans noted the need to restrict women mendicants from wandering unsupervised 'per villas et castra' in search of means of support.[133] True, in the case of the would-be mendicant Ladies of Zamora it was not penury that drove them from the cloister and out onto the streets and into the countryside. Far from it. As was soon to be reported, however, they were out there nevertheless. And, as the *acta* of the provincial chapter of the Order held at León in 1275 recorded, in the region around which they roamed there were many other evidences visible of the tarnishing of the mendicant ideal. These *acta* refer to both past and present. They commemorate Raymond of Peñafort, the representative *par excellence* of that ideal in its pristine state, who had died earlier that year. By the dispatch of friars to study at Paris, Montpellier and Cologne, they also confirm the international character that had distinguished the Order from its earliest days.[134] But at the same time they give notice of a series of less edifying developments nearer home: to a whole range of perennial problems at the provincial level; rifts and tensions; the scandalising of kings, princes and barons 'by words and sermons'; schism with the seculars; suspicion of conspiracy within the Portuguese houses; and the retention by individual friars of private property and bequests.[135] The evidence from 1275 strongly suggests that in the year after the General Council (at which the bishop of Zamora had not been present) there was no shortage of combustible material in the land of the founder's birth.

Notes

1 Salimbene de Adam, *Cronica*, ed O. Holder-Egger (*MGH*, SS. XXXII, Hanover and Leipzig 1905–13, 629–30). (Salimbene's hostility to Honorius presumably stemmed from the pontiff's indulgence to the minor mendicant orders and his relaxation of the campaign against them instituted at the general council of 1274: R. W. Emery, 'The Second Council of Lyons and the mendicant orders', *Catholic Historical Review* 39 (1953) 267–8.) For Honorius's condition and contraption, see Ptolemy of Lucca, *Die Annalen des Tholomeus von Lucca in doppelter Fassung nebst Teilen der Gesta Florentinorum und Gesta Lucanorum*, ed. B. Schmeidler, *MGH*, SS. rer. Germ. N.S., VIII, Berlin 1930, 204; *Willielmi Rishanger, quondam monachi S. Albani, et quorundam anonymorum, Chronica et annales*, ed. H. T. Riley, Rolls Ser., London 1865, 109.
2 Peter Linehan, 'A tale of two cities: capitular Burgos and mendicant Burgos

in the thirteenth century': *Church and City 1000–1500. Essays in honour of Christopher Brooke*, ed. D. Abulafia *et al.*, Cambridge 1992, 98.

3 AHN, Clero 3022/8 (13 September 1285).

4 'que ex concessione Sedis Apostolice regulam beati Augustini et institutiones ordinis fratrum Predicatorum et habitum susceperunt' (*Reg. Hon. IV*, 147 (17 September 1285)).

5 *Ibid.* The convent (or, as will be seen, one of the factions within it) acquired an exemplar of the papal mandate (Zamora, Archivo de las Dueñas (unnumbered)).

6 AHN, Clero 3021/17; AC Toledo, A.7.G.1.4; Linehan, 'A tale', 95.

7 See below, p. 83.

8 'que tome la sobredicha Orden ou outra qual le plougier': *Documentos zamoranos*, I. *Documentos del Archivo Catedralicio de Zamora. Primera parte (1128–1261)*, ed. J.-L. Martín, Salamanca 1982, no. 164.

9 *Ibid.*, no. 156.

10 X 3.32 *De conversione coniugatorum* (E. Friedberg, ed., *Corpus iuris canonici*, i, Leipzig 1881, 579–87). Cf. *Fueros leoneses de Zamora, Salamanca, Ledesma y Alba de Tormes*, ed. A. Castro and F. de Onis, i, Madrid 1916; J. Rodríguez Fernández, *Los fueros locales de la provincia de Zamora*, Salamanca 1990; J. A. Brundage, *Law, Sex and Christian Society in Medieval Europe*, Chicago and London 1987, 375–6.

11 M. Ferrer-Vidal, 'Los monasterios femeninos de la Orden de Santiago durante la Edad Media' (*Las Ordenes Militares en el Mediterráneo occidental (s. XII–XVIII)*). Coloquio celebrado los días 4, 5 y 6 de mayo de 1983, Madrid 1989, 41–50; M. Echániz Sans, *Las mujeres de la Orden Militar de Santiago en la Edad Media*, Salamanca 1992, 58.

12 *Doc. zamoranos*, no. 164. C. Fernández Duro prints the inscription in the cloister of the Zamora convent ('Istam domum fecit cum caelis frater Egidius magister in iure, quondam cantor Ecclesiae Zamorensis, cuius anima requiescat in pace') (*Memorias históricas de la ciudad de Zamora, su provincia y obispado*, i, Madrid 1882, 395–6).

13 'quoddam monasterium sororum ordinis Sancti Augustini secundum instituta ordinis fratrum predicatorum' (ACZ, 1/3).

14 *Libellus de principiis Ordinis Praedicatorum Iordani de Saxonia*, ed. H. C. Scheeben, MOPH 16, Rome 1935, c. 59 ('que nunc est monialium').

15 'ut ipsarum magisterio sorores instituende ibidem institutis regularibus informate dignum reddere valeant Domino famulatum': (ACZ, 1/3).

16 *Monumenta diplomatica S. Dominici*, ed. V. J. Koudelka, MOPH 25, Rome 1966, no. 125.

17 *Litterae encyclicae Magistrorum Generalium Ordinis Praedicatorum ab anno 1233 usque ad annum 1376*, ed. A. Frühwirth, MOPH 5, Rome 1900, 50–1; *Analecta Sacri Ordinis Fratrum Praedicatorum*, iii (1897) 337–48; R. Creytens, 'Les Constitutions primitives des soeurs dominicaines de Montargis (1250)', *AFP* 17 (1947) 57–64; E. T. Brett, *Humbert of Romans. His life and views of thirteenth-century society*, Toronto 1984, 57–73.

18 H. Grundmann, *Religiöse Bewegungen im Mittelalter*, Hildesheim 1961,

208–53, 284–303. Cf. Dominic's directive to the Madrid community only to admit women recommended by friars and approved of by the prioress and community (*Mon. dipl. S. Dominici*, no. 125).

19 *Acta Capitulorum Generalium Ordinis Praedicatorum*, I. *Ab anno 1220 usque ad annum 1303*, ed. A. Frühwirth, MOPH 3, Rome 1898, 88, 98.

20 IV Lat. c. 13, *De novis religionibus prohibitis: Decrees of the Ecumenical Councils*, trans. N. P. Tanner, London and Washington, DC 1990, 242.

21 II Lugd. c. 23, *De religiosis domibus, ut episcopo sint subiectae* (*ibid.*, 326).

22 Fernández Duro, *Memorias históricas*, i. 393.

23 'non recipiatur Zamore in consortio fratrum, immo per episcopum et concilium repellatur' (ACZ 13/24 (undated)).

24 J. Le Goff, 'Ordres mendiants et urbanisation dans la France médiévale', *AÉSC* 25 (1970) 929.

25 Peter Linehan, *The Spanish Church and the Papacy in the Thirteenth Century*, Cambridge 1971, 78–82. Cf. W. R. Thomson, *Friars in the Cathedral. The first Franciscan bishops 1226–1261*, Toronto 1975, 27–40.

26 In Douais, 611–12, 618–19, thirty are mentioned (cf. R. Hernández, 'Las primeras actas de los capítulos provinciales de la Provincia de España', *Archivo Domenicano* 5 (1984) 27–32; 'Pergaminos de actas de los capítulos provinciales del siglo XIII de la Provincia Dominicana de España', *Archivo Domenicano* 4 (1983) 14–17). The Bordeaux General Chapter of 1277 recorded thirty-five 'in provincia Hispaniae' (J. Quétif and J. Échard, *Scriptores Ordinis Praedicatorum recensiti*, i, Paris 1719, p. i).

27 J. Le Goff, 'Apostolat mendiant et fait urbain dans la France médiévale: l'implantation des ordres mendiants. Programme–questionnaire pour une enquête', *AÉSC* 23 (1968) 335–52. Cf. Emery, 'Second Council of Lyons', 271; idem, *The Friars in Medieval France. A catalogue of French mendicant convents, 1200–1550*, New York and London 1962, 3, 8, 18. For the proliferation of the Order of Preachers in Poland (without 'parallel in the long history of religious orders [there] prior to the partitions of the country'), see J. Kłoczowski, 'Dominicans of the Polish province in the Middle Ages', The Christian Community of Medieval Poland. Polish Historical Library, 2, Wrocław 1981 (repr. Kłoczowski, *La Pologne dans l'Église médiévale*, VIII, Aldershot 1993), 73–9.

28 'Ordres mendiants', 932 n. 4, citing Salimbene (ed. Holder Egger, 233, 236).

29 E. Fugedi, 'La formation des villes et les ordres mendiants en Hongrie', *AÉSC* 25 (1970) 966–87; John B. Freed, *The Friars and German Society in the Thirteenth Century*, Cambridge, Mass. 1977, 21–53.

30 The contribution of Alfredo Liquornik of the University of Montevideo, which Le Goff had hopes of in 1970 (*AÉSC* 25, 946), appears not to have materialised.

31 *Ibid.*, 941.

32 Thus V. Beltrán de Heredía, 'Examen crítico de la historiografía dominicana en las provincias de España y particularmente en Castilla', *AFP* 35 (1965) 195, 245.

33 Douais, 611–16, 618–56; Hernández, 'Primeras actas', 27–32; *idem*, 'Pergaminos', 13–17, 28–37, 44–59.

34 Cited in Le Goff, *AÉSC* 25 (1970) 930.

35 (Province of Braga): Astorga, Braga, Mondoñedo, Orense, Viseu; (province of Compostela): Avila, Coria, Lamego, Plasencia; (province of Seville): Cádiz, Silves; (province of Tarragona): Calahorra, Tarazona, Tortosa, Vic; (province of Toledo): Cuenca, Jaén, Osma, Segorbe, Sigüenza; (exempt sees): Cartagena, Oviedo.

36 Calatayud, Ribadavia, Santarém, Elvas, Guimarães (1275); Estella, Vitoria, Valladolid, Benavente, *Paniensis* (1281); *Cruniensis*, Pontevedra, Toro, Sangüesa, Játiva (1299).

37 For example, there is no mention in the 1250 *acta* of convents at either Vic or Gerona, though by that date there were Dominican bishops in both sees, nor of the Estella house until 1281. Linehan, *Spanish Church and the Papacy*, 78–9; see above, p. 12.

38 Douais, 611–16. The exception was the house at Santarém.

39 AHN, Clero 566/11–13 (January–November 1272).

40 *Litt. encyc.* 22–3.

41 AHN, Clero 1724/21 (31 January 1257).

42 On 20 January 1259 Alexander ordered the cancellation of various 'ordinationes vel statuta' that had been decreed against those electing burial with the Dominicans in the diocese of Palencia (AHN, Clero 1725/2).

43 J. González, *Reinado y diplomas de Fernando III*, i, Córdoba 1986, 398.

44 T. F. Ruiz, 'Expansion et changement: la conquête de Séville et la société castillane 1248–1350', *AÉSC* 34 (1979) 548–65.

45 J. A. García de Cortázar, *La sociedad rural en la España medieval*, 2nd edn, Madrid 1990, 198. For Ruiz's further thoughts on the subject, see his *Crisis and Continuity. Land and town in late medieval Castile*, Philadelphia 1994, 291–313.

46 Rodrigo Jiménez de Rada, *Historia de rebus Hispanie sive Historia Gothica*, IX. 17, ed. J. Fernández Valverde, Corpus Christianorum Continuatio Mediaevalis 72, Turnhout 1987, 299. See chapter five.

47 Peter Linehan, 'The *gravamina* of the Castilian Church in 1262–3', *EHR* 85 (1970), 730–54 (reprinted in Linehan, *Spanish Church and Society 1150–1300*, London 1983); *idem*, *Spanish Church and the Papacy*, ch. 8: suggestions developed by S. Aguade Nieto, 'En los orígenes de una coyuntura depresiva. La crisis agraria de 1255 a 1262 en la Corona de Castilla' in *De la sociedad arcaica a la sociedad campesina en la Asturias medieval. Estudios de historia agraria*, Alcalá de Henares 1988, 335–70.

48 E. Benito Ruano, 'La Iglesia española ante la caída del Imperio latino de Constantinopla', *HS* 11 (1958), 14–15.

49 A. Vauchez, 'Les stigmates de S. François et leurs détracteurs dans les derniers siècles du Moyen Age', École Française de Rome, *Mélanges d'Archéologie et d'Histoire* 80 (1968), 603, 607–8. Cf. Linehan, 'A tale', 82–3. For the destruction by flood of the new stone bridge over the Ebro at

🌼 🌼 🌼 🌼 🌼

Zaragoza (June 1261) see A. Canellas López, ed., *Colección diplomática del Concejo de Zaragoza*, Zaragoza 1972, no. 98.

50 *Reg. Inn. IV*, 2252, October 1246 (ed. A. Quintana Prieto, *La documentación pontificia de Inocencio IV (1243–1254)*, Rome 1987, no. 316); J. Goñi Gaztambide, *Historia de los obispos de Pamplona*, Pamplona 1979, i 633–5.

51 Linehan, 'A tale', 86–7.

52 The Franciscans had moved in 1260 from their church of S. Caterina to the new foundation of S. María de Miraglos nearby (L. Wadding, *Annales Minorum*, iv, Rome 1732, 158–9). In July 1263 Archbishop Juan of Compostela had licensed Bishop Suero to sell the site 'in utilitatem ecclesie Zamorensis' (*TB*, fo. 52^r).

53 ACZ, 1/4: '*Paci et quieti* . . . inhibemus ne aliquod monasterium de nouo in Camorensi ciuitate uel diocesi in locis ecclesie Camorensis subiectis auctoritate litterarum a sede apostolica obtentarum per quas non sit ius alicui acquisitum seu obtinendarum in quibus de presenti indulgentia expressa mentio facta non fuerit in uestrum preiudicium construatur . . .', (13 January 1261).

54 AHN, Clero 1894/16 (February 1265).

55 Appendix I. a: identical copies in Zamora, Archivo de Las Dueñas, and ACZ, 13/57 (= *TB*, fo. 27^v). *Doc. zamoranos*, no. 147.

56 R. F. Bennett, *The Early Dominicans*, Cambridge 1937, 138.

57 Appendix I. b: ACZ, 13/57b (26 March 1264).

58 *TB*, fo. 28^v.

59 'perpendentes etiam quod prefatus locus honori pocius quam utilitati nobis existat, attendentes etiam debita quibus nos dictus episcopus propter procuratam utilitatem nostre ecclesie tenebamur' (*ibid.*). Cf. ACZ 13/46, cited in Linehan, *Spanish Church and the Papacy*, 144.

60 Appendix I. a.

61 *TB*, fos. 27^v–8^r: 'Quod si forte, casu aliquo contingente, talis uobis uiolencia inferatur cui nos resistere non possimus . . .'.

62 *Ibid.*

63 'ut possessiones ac alia bona mobilia et immobilia exceptis feudalibus que personas liberas sororum vestrarum ad monasterium vestrum e seculo convolantium et professionem facientium in eodem si remansissent in seculo ratione successionis vel quocumque alio iusto titulo contigissent et illa potuissent libere aliis erogare, petere, percipere et retinere libere valeatis sine iuris preiudicio alieni' (*Devotionis vestre*, ACZ, 13/64 (2 July 1265)).

64 'Promittimus inquam saluis supradicti ordinis institutis ita quod in monasterio nostro uisitatio et institutio et destitutio fiat secundum instituta ordinis fratrum predicatorum, sicut alie domine eiusdem ordinis fratrum predicatorum uisitantur et priorisse in eodem ordine instituuntur et destituuntur . . .' (Appendix I. b).

65 'Nichilominus tamen concedimus quod episcopus Zamorensis qui pro tempore fuerit habeat uisitationem et correctionem in monasterio nostro' (*ibid.*).

66 'Quidam zelatores animarum induxerunt quasdam mulieres malae vitae quo

33

ad fornicationem ut relicto peccato congregarentur in locum unum ubi, mutato habitu saeculari et vano, agerent paenitentiam, ita tamen quod possunt si vellent accipere viros, et hae dicuntur paenitentes sive filiae Dei' (*Sermones*, Venice 1603, pt i, *sermo* 51).

67 'Una est a clausura. Alia a societate, quia nulla audet etiam ad fenestram loqui extraneo sine socia ad hoc deputata quae omnia audiat. Alia est de fratribus deforis curam earum habentibus' (*Sermones*, pt i, *sermo* 48). Cf. William of Saint-Amour's denunciation of 'illae mulieres quae vocantur Beguinae': 'Item, dixit quod mulieres existentes in saeculo, mutantes habitum suum in viliorem causa religionis, peccant graviter; et quae tondent capillos suos, existentes in saeculo, credentes hoc facere causa religionis, peccant: et debent istae et illae excommunicari' (E. Faral, 'Les "Responsiones" de Guillaume de Saint-Amour', *Archives d'histoire doctrinale du Moyen Age* 18 (1950–1) 344).

68 *Bullarium Ordinis Fratrum Praedicatorum*, i, Rome 1729, 481–2; Grundmann, *Religiöse Bewegungen*, 296.

69 D. L. Douie, *The Conflict between the Seculars and the Mendicants at the University of Paris in the Thirteenth Century*, Aquinas Paper no. 23, London 1954, 16–17.

70 Faral, 340, 344, 348–9.

71 *Ibid.*, 353.

72 B. Tierney, *Religion, Law, and the Growth of Constitutional Thought 1150–1650*, Cambridge 1982, 60–65. See also Y. M.-J. Congar, 'Aspects ecclésiologiques de la querelle entre mendiants et séculiers dans la seconde moitié du xiiie siècle et le début du xive', *Archives d'hist. doctr. du M. A.*, 36 (1961–2) 35–161.

73 *The Making of Europe. Conquest, colonization and cultural change 950–1350*, Harmondsworth 1994, 258.

74 For the controversy in its later stages see P. Glorieux, 'Les polémiques "contra Geraldinos". Les pièces du dossier', *Archives d'hist. doctr. du M.A.*, 6 (1934) 5–41; *idem*, '"Contra Geraldinos". L'enchaînement des polémiques', *ibid.*, 7 (1935) 129–55; S. Clasen, 'Tractatus Gerardi de Abbatisvilla "Contra adversarium perfectionis Christianae"', *AFH* 31 (1938) 276–329; 32 (1939) 89–200.

75 Cf. V. Beltrán de Heredia, *Cartulario de la Universidad de Salamanca (1218–1600)*, i, Salamanca 1970, 83–99, 604–6.

76 Linehan, *Spanish Church and the Papacy*, 257, 293, 301–3.

77 'Cum ab eodem rege ecclesia nostra multipliciter sit grauata tum quia ter a nobis exegit de prouentibus nostris decimam et percepit a paucis temporibus citra tum etiam quia propter exactiones huiusmodi prouentus nostri sunt adeo diminuti quod uis [*sic*] ex eis possumus sustentari . . .' (ACZ 4/3 (28 November 1266)). For the occasion of the latest papal grant to the king, see *Reg. Clem. IV*, 890; Linehan, *Spanish Church and the Papacy*, 175 n. 4 (where the reference ACZ 1/3 is incorrect), 207.

78 'per potenciam laycalem' (ACZ, 4/3).

79 R. A. MacDonald, 'Law and politics: Alfonso's program of political reform'

34

in R. I. Burns, ed., *The Worlds of Alfonso the Learned and James the Conqueror. Intellect and force in the Middle Ages*, Princeton 1985, 173ff.

80 *Ibid.*, 191–2; E. S. Procter, *Curia and Cortes in León and Castile 1072–1295*, Cambridge 1980, 137–8; T. F. Ruiz, 'The transformation of the Castilian municipalities: the case of Burgos 1248–1350', *Past & Present* 77 (1977), 3–32; *idem, Crisis and Continuity*, 239–48.

81 See M. González Jiménez, 'Alfonso X y las oligarquias urbanas de caballeros', *Glossae* 5–6 (1993–4), 195–214.

82 Ruiz, 'Transformation', 14. Cf. *idem*, 'Two patrician families in late medieval Burgos: the Sarracín and the Bonifaz' (*The City and the Realm. Burgos and Castile 1080–1492*, vi, Aldershot 1992).

83 Linehan, 'A tale'.

84 AHN, Clero 1874/3 (1 October 1274).

85 The only available volume of the Zamora documentation – *Documentos zamoranos* – stops short at the year 1261. For details of that 'published' by M. Sánchez Rodríguez, but not made available to the public, see J.-L. Martín, 'Fuentes y estudios zamoranos', *Primer Congreso de Historia de Zamora*, III. *Medieval y moderna*, Zamora 1991, 11–12.

86 '. . . e que furon en esta possesión fasta que yo metí un juyz en Çamora que iudgasse' (J. I. Coria Colino, 'El pleito entre cabildo y concejo zamoranos de 1278: análisis de la conflictividad jurisdiccional. Concejo, cabildo y rey', *Primer Congreso* (as n. 85), 291).

87 *Ibid.* The king's letter is dated 10 September 1278. The cortes was due to assemble at Michaelmas (Procter, *Curia and Cortes*, 133–4). Cf. Peter Linehan, *History and the Historians of Medieval Spain*, Oxford 1993, 460.

88 Coria Colino, 'El pleito', 287, 292–6.

89 *Ibid.*, 294; Juan Gil de Zamora, *De preconiis Hispanie*, ed. M. de Castro y Castro, Madrid 1955, 234.

90 Linehan, *Spanish Church and the Papacy*, 117; J.-L. Martín Rodríguez, *Campesinos vasallos del obispo Suero de Zamora (1254–86)*, Salamanca 1981. For a more favourable estimate see M. A. Sánchez Rodríguez, 'La diócesis de Zamora en la segunda mitad del siglo XIII', *Primer Congreso de Historia de Zamora*, III. *Medieval y moderna*, Zamora 1991, 147–71, containing much detail to supplement what follows.

91 P. Scheffer-Boichorst, 'Zur Geschichte Alfons X von Castilien', *MIöG* 9 (1888) 248. He was there again, in November 1258, witnessing Guy de Dampierre's homage to Alfonso (C. Duvivier, *La Querelle des d'Avesnes et des Dampierre jusqu'à la mort de Jean d'Avesnes, 1257. Les Influences françaises et germaniques en Belgique au XIIIe siècle*, ii, Brussels 1894, 531).

92 ACZ, 12/14 (see below, chapter three).

93 'Item, quando primo ad episcopatum ueni meum detuli completum apparatum de meo in equitaturis que fuerunt fere quadraginta. Non enim aliqua inueni in introitu episcopatus mei nisi unam azemelam de uno pede claudicantem' (*TB*, fo. 165^r). (The whole occupies fos. 162^r-5^v of the *Tumbo Blanco*.)

94 His predecessor, D. Pedro, had recorded his own more modest

achievements in a memorial dated 3 January 1255 (*Doc. zamoranos*, no. 147).

95 *TB*, fo. 162^r. The king's grant in April 1256 was occasioned 'por grant sabor que he de façer onrra et bien et mercet a don Suero mio criado, obispo de Zamora, por muchos seruicios que me fizo bien et lealmientre' (*ibid.*, fo. 86^v).

96 *Ibid.*, fos. 151^v–2^r, surrendering 'las dos partes delos diezmos delas tercias que el bispo ha enlas eglesias de Peniella cerca Toro' in exchange for real estate at Villamor (December 1271).

97 E.g. 'Item melioraui et feci multas domos in episcopatu predicto, utpote turrem multum sumptuosam quam feci Zamore cum appendiis suis' (fo. 162^r); [Fontesauco] 'Feci obtimum palacium. Item feci ibi multa loca populari et populatores aliunde abstraxi multis beneficiis ad ecclesiam Zamorensem' (fo. 163^v).

98 'Item detuli mecum, feci et emi multos bonos libros, tam in iure quam theologicos. Et hec omnia bona feci de bonis que habebam cum essem in notaria domini regis et in ecclesia Hyspalensi et Toletanam [*sic*] dignitatem archidiacon[alem] habebam, et in Compostellana et Legionensi et Salamantina et Siluensi et in quibusdam aliis ecclesia [*sic*] alia quamplurima beneficia pinguia' (fo. 165^r). Cf. Sánchez Rodríguez, 'La diócesis', 150–1; Linehan, *History and the Historians*, 519.

99 'Priuilegia Zamorensis ecclesie que prius erant antiquata sigillis de cera ad instanciam meam de gratia speciali dominus rex confirmauit multum complete et perfecte cum sigillis plumbeis, omni conditione excluda[*sic*]. Quam gratiam nulli alii ecclesie facere uoluit' (fo. 164^v). In fact, the practice preceded his pontificate (ACZ 12/10 (December 1254)).

100 Evidence of his chancery training occurs on various royal letters in the chapter archive. ACZ 15/33, for example, a sealed confirmation ('inspeximus') of a royal charter of October 1262 relating to his dispute with the *concejo* of Toro concerning jurisdiction over Villamor, is endorsed with the distinctive registration mark employed by both the papal and the royal chanceries at this date.

101 *Ibid.*, fos. 163^v, 164^v, 165^v.

102 E.g. '. . . et capitulum noluit partem habere delucro nec de danno, nec quicquam uoluit capitulum refundere pro expensis' (fo. 164^r); 'me recolo summa pecunie expendisse . . . nec in aliquo istorum usque ad hec tempora adiutorium aliquod a capitulo habuisse' (fo. 165^r).

103 The possibility that he was a native of the place (see note 104) is strengthened by the fact of his otherwise unaccountable presence at the diocesan synod of Badajoz in 1255 (A. García y García, *Synodicon Hispanum*, Madrid 1981– , v. 14. For Bishop Suero was no *aficionado* of synods. He was there, presumably, gathering his goods and chattels for the journey north to his new see.

104 'Et ad complendum legata supradicta mando quod totum meum hereditamentum quod in badalloz et aliis locis inuentum fuerit et totum meum mobile tam in labris et apotecis quam in donariis et bastitis distrahantur et uenalia disponantur. Nam mobile quod nunc habeo in

disposicione mea est quia quando ueni ad episcopatum non inueni ibi mobile usui cotidiano necessarium. Non enim recepi aliquid, uas argenteum nec equitaturam nisi unam açemilam claudam nec linteamen nec puluinare nec ornamentum lecti ubi possit capud suum etiam simplex clericus declinare. Et hec omnia per inuentarium inde confectum et per socios ista omnia sunt omnibus satis nota. Quando ueni ad ecclesiam multa uasa argentea et scutellas non modicas et equitaturas fere .xl. auxi et apparatum non modicum detuli in omnibus aliis sicut est omnibus manifestum' (ACZ, 12/14).

105 'Et sciendum quòd de bonis eciam propriis et cum inhereditate et aliis pro seruicio ecclesie expendi et distraxi fere quinque milia morabitinos legionenses, exceptis possessionibus ad opus ecclesie emptis et ecclesie reunitis. Et utinam successor aliquam remuneracionem faciat inde familie mee pro seruicio illi facto' (*ibid.*). As suggested above ('A note on money values', p. ix), in his 1285 recollections of his early-1260s expenditure D. Suero was playing to the gallery of history by manipulating the exchanges. In the early 1260s sums of the order of 5,000 and 6,000 maravedís were mighty sums.

106 'Item mando quod biblia maioris uoluminis et liber sermonum Innocentii dentur episcopo et successoribus futuris ut studeant per eosdem quia magnum deffectum inueni in hiis similibus quando ueni ad ecclesiam Zamorensem' (*ibid.*). Cf. M. A. Vilaplana, 'El Tumbo Negro de Zamora' (*Homenaje a D. Agustín Millares Carlo*, i, Las Palmas 1975, 82).

107 *Litt. encyc.* 121; Douais, 631. See below, chapter five).

108 Guadalupe, 'El tesoro', 171.

109 *Ibid.*, 169–70; ACZ, 39/5.

110 Guadalupe, item 80.

111 Una casula viridis que dicitur del Cardenal et alia de baldoquin que fuit magistri Fernandi' (*ibid.*, 179).

112 A. Pérez Martín, 'Estudiantes zamoranos en Bolonia', *Studia Zamorensia* 2 (1981) 34–7; *idem*, 'El Ordo iudiciarius', *Historia. Instituciones. Documentos* 8 (1981) 260–6, 418–23 (list of works cited); R. Filangieri, *I Registri della Cancilleria Angioina*, x (Naples, 1957) 91 ('Mag. Fernandus archidiaconus Zamorensis', nuncio of Alfonso X at Florence, June 1272/3).

113 Cf. Linehan, *Spanish Church and the Papacy*, 233–5.

114 'Hec sunt constitutiones quas nos S. episcopus Zamorensis edimus apud Taurum cum consilio archidiaconi et archipresbiteri eiusdem et beneplacito capituli clericorum' (*TB*, fos. 191ᵛ–2ʳ (ed. García y García, *Synodicon Hispanum*, iv. 431–3)). Datable perhaps to the summer of 1266, after the dean of Compostela's arbitration of the bishop's differences with the clergy of Toro (ACZ, 6/1), the five constitutions were concerned with lay (not clerical) concubinage, the payment of tithes and the acquisition of property by the religious orders. A similar practical rather than pastoral emphasis is apparent in the selection of constitutions of the Compostela council (1259/60) which immediately precede them in *TB*, fo. 191ʳᵛ. Cf. Linehan, *Spanish Church and the Papacy*, 172; García y García, i. 267.

115 On 13 May 1286, soon after his death, the dean (Alfonso Pérez) and chapter enacted the following constitution: 'Si ad presens vel posterum aliquis de capitulo factus fuerit episcopus Zamorensis non possit se excusare ab observacione singulorum et omnium predictorum dicendo quod tempore quo hec constitucio seu ordinacio fuit edicta vel ordinata non erat ipse· episcopus Zamorensis' (ACZ, *Liber constitutionum* (10 bis/4), fo. 8ra).

116 'rumpendo sibi cartas et frangendo eorum sigilla, non audiendo eum in iure suo, et sine causa': ACZ, 4/2.

117 *Litt. encyc.* 51.

118 ACZ, 13/63. The addressees of the papal mandate (31 October 1272) were the archdeacons of Cea and of Valderas and the treasurer of León. In the summons they issued on 31 January 1273 the first and the third of these are identified as 'M.' and 'Magister Gundisaluus'.

119 ACZ, 13/58a (= *TB*, fos. 28^v–9^r), 25 February 1273.

120 ACZ, 13/59a (the bishop's *supplicat*, Zamora, 19 October 1273); 13/59d, 59b (two exemplars of the prioress's *supplicat*, of the same date, the former containing the scribal error 'In *die* nomine Amen'; the latter including corrections and continuing after the dating clause with the words 'Et ut de premissis' deleted) = *TB*, fo. 29^{rv}.

121 Thus both add the word 'Amen' to the opening invocation and emend 'nullum priuilegium' to 'nullumque priuilegium'; see Appendix I. b below.

122 ACZ, 13/59b ('conuentus monialium monasterii sancte Marie Zamorensis ordinis sancti Dominici'). In an undated acknowledgement of obedience to the bishop 'segundo que se contien enlas cartas que auemos conusco' (but always 'saluo elos establecimientos de nostra orden'), Doña Elvira, as prioress, had described the community as 'de la orden de San Domingo' (*TB*, fo. 28^v).

123 ACZ, 13/59 (Zamora, 2 March 1274).

124 The bishop of Cádiz, Juan Martínez OFM, and the elect of Avila, fr. Aymar OP (ACZ, 13/59c) (Burgos, 'in domo domini episcopi ipsius ciuitatis', 22 March 1274). The see of Burgos was vacant at this time. Cf. Linehan, 'A tale', 94–5.

125 Procter, *Curia and Cortes*, 135–6.

126 ACZ, 11.ii/6 (May 1269).

127 ACZ 1/5 ('auctoritate domini pape et de ipsius speciali mandato viva voce oraculo nobis facto'), 2 May 1273.

128 'Item melioraui conditionem ecclesie Zamorensis in facto ecclesiarum que a militibus conferebantur pascalibus temporibus annuatim, in quarum collatione exponebantur uenales et contrahebatur hinc inde symonia . . .' (*TB*, fo. 164^v; Sánchez Rodríguez, 'La diócesis', 159). For the survival in western Spain of practices outlawed by Gregory VII, see R. A. Fletcher, *The Episcopate in the Kingdom of León in the Twelfth Century*, Oxford 1978, 169; Peter Linehan, 'The Church and Feudalism in the Spanish Kingdoms in the Eleventh and Twelfth Centuries', *Atti della dodecisima Settimana internazionale di studio, Mendola, 24–28 agosto 1992*, Milan 1995, 303–31. Fletcher, *loc. cit.*, suggests that the world of the 1140s which he describes

'was a world whose end was approaching'. But the bishop of Zamora's report indicates that a century later that end had still not arrived.

129 'las duennas de Caleruega donna Maria e Eluira Perez fiyas de Pedro Fernandez cauallero de Villa Lube' (ACZ, 13/68 (28 August 1274)). For the establishment of the Caleruega convent in June 1270, see J. Loperráez Corvalan, *Descripción histórica del obispado de Osma*, iii, Madrid 1788, 207–9.

130 ACZ, 13/68 see above, p. 14.

131 ACZ, 13/67 (10 September 1274). If the girl chose not to join she was to have two hundred maravedís as dowry.

132 fr. Pedro de Roma had also witnessed the transaction of late August (ACZ, 13/68).

133 'quod est valde indecens et etiam periculosum in mulieribus. Unde videtur expediens quod nulla religio mulierum fieret nisi haberet unde quoquo modo posset sustentari in domo sine huiusmodi discursu': *Opusculum tripartitum*, ed. Edward Brown, *Appendix ad Fasciculum rerum expetendarum & fugiendarum . . . sive tomus secundus*, London 1690, 224.) Cf. Grundmann, *Religiöse Bewegungen*, 335 n. 32.

134 Douais, 623–4; Hernández, 'Pergaminos', 21, 24.

135 Douais, 620, 623; Hernández, 'Pergaminos', 17–19, 23–4.

CHAPTER TWO

> What men call gallantry, and gods adultery,
> Is much more common where the climate's sultry.
> (Byron, *Don Juan*, canto I.LXIII)

SOME TIME between Lyons and León the affairs of the Ladies of Zamora took a new turn, and on visiting their convent in July 1279 a bishop not conspicuous for personal piety himself declared their conduct to have become a matter of public scandal.

While working in the archive of Zamora cathedral in 1966 I chanced on the record of what the bishop and his colleagues were told on that occasion and in 1971 provided a summary account of it.[1] Since then some readers of that account, and not only readers in Spain, have asked for more. Since 1971, however, developments in Spain itself had led me to expect that sooner or later a Spanish scholar would undertake the task. In view of the recent renaissance of interest in the history of the Spanish past, and especially in the history of those regions which had previously been accounted provincial, it seemed inevitable that before long the bishop of Zamora's visitation record would be published, possibly in a full buckram numbered edition, even perhaps that there would be an international congress assembled to do the subject full justice.

In the event, none of this has happened. As mentioned above, the publication of the contents of the cathedral archive has come to a full stop at the year 1261. What instead has occurred is a rare example of the phenomenon of colonisation preceding reconquest, of ideological colonisation, indeed, of the as yet uncharted past, with the still unpublished episcopal visitation record being recruited to the cause of historiographical modishness and the ladies themselves being sacrificed to the pitiless imperatives of the dialectic. As to the ultimate usefulness of the intuition that has prompted that endeavour – with its presentation of the friars' reported violation of the nuns' enclosure as a symbolic act of penetration (an insight which has already shed so much light on the events of the year 711), its deployment of such fashionable categories as 'religious space' and the rest, and the suggestion that the whole story was a put-up job and a male plot – it would doubtless be prudent to leave others to judge. What is attempted here is less ambitious. Yet even to present the facts of the case so far as they can be ascertained may still prove a worthwhile exercise – and not least because in the snippets of evidence which she has released Dr Bueno Domínguez (who must be unaware of what I published in 1971 since nowhere does she cite it) reveals an understanding of the language in which the activities of the Ladies of Zamora were recorded scarcely less tenuous than that of the ladies themselves regarding the rule of life to which they were formally committed.[2]

Back in the late 1270s, it is sufficiently clear from the bishop's visitation record of July 1279 what had been going on. The fomenting of conventual discord was a grave matter, though, according to the nuns' rule, contumacy and rebellion were worse, and 'incorrigibility' the most serious defect of all. And the community of Las Dueñas was afflicted by all three conditions. It was split down the middle, between those of its members who had remained loyal to the bishop and his jurisdiction (or who said they had) and those who to a greater or lesser degree had opted for 'incorporation' with the friars. In the words of one of the nuns who gave evidence on that occasion, 'the group who favoured the friars sought to free themselves from the bishop's jurisdiction and to submit themselves to that of the friars'.[3]

Altogether less clear is the chronology of events over the previous decade. Although the bishop's authority had first been challenged and flouted as early as 1271 or 1272, and the rift within the community may well have commenced by the spring of 1274, with the two factions led by the prioress Doña Stefanía and the sub-prioress (and co-foundress) Doña Jimena, it is nevertheless impossible to determine where at this stage the two ladies' respective sympathies lay. As will be seen, in 1279 they were both ranged against D. Suero; indeed they were identified as the principal anti-episcopal activists.[4] Yet if it was during the mid-1270s, against a background of frequent vacancies in the Roman Church and mounting political crisis within Castile, that the pro-mendicant party secured that measure of control over the affairs of

42

Las Dueñas which was remarked upon by the nun María Vicéncez in 1279 [8], in 1274 the rift within the community had not yet developed into schism. If there were already cracks in the cloister by then they were not yet such as to prevent D. Suero from having dealings with Doña Jimena, who had succeeded to the office of prioress by the August of that year.[5]

It is not known for certain how long Doña Jimena remained in office. In the only surviving record of these years, a further reaffirmation of the nuns' obedience to the bishop, the prioress does not identify herself by name. Moreover, the date of that act of reconciliation is itself uncertain. To whichever year it belongs, however, 1277 or 1278, the members of 'the Order of Saint Augustine who wore the habit of the Preachers', as they chose to describe themselves, again acknowledged that it was from D. Suero that they had received both their habit and their order ('elos habitos que trahemos e ela orden que tenemos').[6] They renewed their pledge to him, though always 'saluos los establecemientos dela orden delos frades predicadores', and begged him to provide them with confessors and the sacraments, services which he had been withholding after papal privileges had been obtained prejudicial to his jurisdiction. These privileges the prioress and convent now renounced, disavowing any promise or undertaking that any of the ladies may have made or given to the friars – not that they were prepared to concede that any commitments of the sort had in fact been entered into.[7]

Because those of the ladies who sided with the bishop obviously had no reason for seeking to extenuate the actions of their wayward sisters, that final disclaimer strongly suggests that for all its professions of obedience to the bishop the 1277/8 declaration was in reality wholly pro-mendicant in character. If so, it was neither the first time nor the last that D. Suero was deceived by the friars' friends within the convent[8] – or for that matter by those without, notably that Pedro Pérez whose intimate involvement in the Ladies' affairs was shortly to be revealed, and whose namesake (unless indeed it was the rabid pro-mendicant himself) acted as witness in 1277/8.

We know that by July 1279 María Domingo was styling herself prioress, for it was in that capacity that at the eleventh hour she offered D. Suero further assurances; also, from the evidence of the bishop's inquiry, that she was a member of the mendicant party,[9] and that she had supplanted María Martínez, the lady appointed by D. Suero at the time of his previous visitation.[10] After that earlier intervention the convent had remained in a state of turmoil [5], causing the bishop to send the letter banning the friars from the place, which, when it was read there, led to a total breakdown of order and the systematic persecution of María Martínez [6, 17].[11] Piecing together these stray indications suggests that it was on the occasion of that first visitation that the nuns had proffered their latest simulation of submission, the undertaking with the confusion in its dating clause. Further, the fact that it was not until the end of 1279 that the bishop again referred the matter to Rome may indicate that that first visitation occurred later rather than earlier, in September 1278 rather than September 1277.[12]

At any event, although trouble had long been brewing at Las Dueñas and the ladies had been excommunicated and the convent under interdict on and off for at least seven years, the events which were described when the bishop revisited Las Dueñas in July 1279 must all have been very recent. Moreover, contrary to what the local Dominicans were later to allege, even now D. Suero had no quarrel with the ladies either on account of their membership of the 'Order of Saint Augustine' or in relation to their wearing of the Dominican habit. Neither matter was contentious. It was in these very terms indeed, in strict accordance with the agreement of fifteen years before, that he described the community to whose battle-scarred precincts he returned in that month.[13] It was the observance of this 'rule' and their adherence to this 'constitution' that the ladies were now lined up to be quizzed about. That, and their care for the rule of silence. But the bishop was not there because of reported breaches of their rule of silence. In 1279 there was a larger issue to be confronted, the issue which had been fudged in 1264 and which since then had become urgent, the issue of how they were to reconcile their assumption of the Dominican habit with their duty of obedience to him and to the church of Zamora.

Clearly though that was the issue, however, it can hardly have been much easier for the bishop and his four colleagues[14] then than it is 700 years on to make clear sense of the evidence presented or to discern the loyalty networks and identify the rifts within a community so deeply divided by 'conflict and discord'.

That said, now as then, the principal culprits are readily enough identifiable. As is so often the case, silence was fatal. The ladies with the least to say in answer to the bishop's questions evidently had the most to hide. The sullenness of these thirteenth-century predecessors of the pleaders of the Fifth Amendment, the unsworn contingent whose tight-lipped telegraphic testimony comes at the end [18–33],[15] is as eloquent as the total recall of those prepared to name names. The first witness on the stand showed the way. On being asked who had released María de Sevilla and María de Valladolid from the stocks, the sub-prioress said that 'many had'. Asked who in particular, 'she did not reply but said that they had left the convent of their own volition'. María Alfónsez of León did even better. Her performance under cross-examination was an object lesson in the art of obfuscation. On being requested to identify 'the many who disobeyed María Martínez and the sub-prioress and misused the prioress shamefully and dis-honoured her with disgraceful language', she answered: 'those of them who favoured the friars and threatened her' [11]. Of course. *QED*.

One of those who might have said more than she did, as well as declining to give evidence on oath, was Doña Caterina de Zamora[4]. Doña Caterina admitted to a technical, albeit venial, breach of the rule. It was true, she admitted, that she had sold wheat outside the convent. That was not all that was true, however. She failed to mention that while doing so she had been accompanied by the cleric Pedro Pérez and that this Pedro Pérez was her lover. It was others – Doña María the sub-prioress, Arnalda Eiménerez, Doña Margarita de Benavente, María Martínez the prioress, and Sol Martínez [1, 9, 12, 14, 16] – who provided the details of that sin of the flesh of hers which the rule castigated as the most abhorrent offence of all, recall-ing how Pedro Pérez had come to the convent by night with Doña Caterina 'et cum baronibus', and announced to their confederates within that the ladies were now 'incorporated' into the Dominican Order and that they should take the prioress captive. Likewise, it is from the testimony of others that it emerges that incorporation into the Dominican Order did not imply stricter observance of the rule, or indeed the observance of any rule at all, and least of all of the rule forbidding engagement in commercial enterprise and the retention of private property. The moral of that piece of tale-telling is plain. In the eyes of the pro-episcopal faction the pro-mendicant nuns had been having it both ways, enjoying the benefits of incorporation while con-tinuing to avail themselves of the worldly advantages which Clement IV had conferred upon them in their pre-mendicant period.[16]

William of Saint-Amour would not have been amused – but he would not have been surprised either.

Was it on that same hectic night that María de Sevilla and María de Valladolid were released from the stocks where the prioress had put them? We are not told. And who had let them out? Even at the time there was widespread uncertainty on that point. Marina Rodríguez's recollection [5] was that Elvira Pérez 'and many others' were responsible. Marina Reináldez [7] named other names. But she failed to mention what Xemena Pérez remembered [15], that she herself had played a leading part. Memory can play odd tricks.

Such odd tricks indeed that before proceeding further something needs to be said about the objective value of all these nuns' tales. Historians have to be on guard. They are all too liable to be taken advantage of, especially by lawyers. A measure of scepticism is necessary, especially in a case such as this in which the record is forensic in nature *and* derives from a community of possibly vindictive women. 'Casta est quam nemo rogavit' ('There's none so chaste as she who's ne'er pursued' (Ovid, *Amores*, 1.8.43)). And none more warped than those who get no post, especially in a place like Las Dueñas, where the postman seems always to have knocked twice, other than for those for whom he never knocked at all because no one ever wrote to them – or even spoke to them (the forbidding Doña Sancha de Toro, for example [34], who said she had seen nothing going on between the friars and the nuns, because the friars had steered clear of her). Faced with material as unstable as this, even historians of medieval Spain may be capable of misdirecting themselves.

They need to have their methodological wits about them, especially when (as in the present case) circumstances favoured not just the piecemeal fabrication of evidence but even deliberate and wholesale falsification in favour of the bishop, the bishop's prioress and his prioress's friends, with the purpose of blackening the reputation of the friars and *their* friends by means of conspiracy, collusion and a show trial of a sort. Dr Bueno Domínguez comes close to suggesting that that is what we are dealing with here. As she observes, at the heart of the matter was an issue of jurisdiction. In her view it is 'very possible', therefore, that the whole scandalous episode was an invention designed to put the friars in their place and discredit a community of independent-minded women of private means whom the local bishop was otherwise incapable of controlling.[17]

Having brought his readers thus far, needless to say the present author does not share these suspicions. Even if he did, he would not regard the exercise as invalidated. For there are facts for the historian in fantasy too. As the late J. H. Mundy remarked of similar allegations of sexual profligacy brought against the abbot of Lézat to the south of Toulouse in the years 1253–4, the possibility that they contain 'a mass of perjured and dishonest testimony trumped up . . . to defeat the abbot . . . in no way harms the testimony's value for the purpose of . . . study'. What was of interest to Mundy was 'not so much what the abbot of Lézat actually did, but rather what his contemporaries thought of what they said he did'. 'The abbot's guilt or innocence (and whether or not such concepts are applicable) are surely to be decided only by the deity', Mundy concluded.[18]

These are secondary considerations, however. The main problem about Dr Bueno Domínguez's scepticism is not this. It goes deeper than that. It is that it is not itself sufficiently sceptical about its own credentials. True, there was overlap between the testimonies of the various ladies in July 1279. But overlapping evidence cannot be treated as evidence of conspiracy to deceive. A conspiracy-theory hypothesis which depends for its plausibility upon the degree of corroboration discernible in the testimonies presented is logically flawed. For if corroboration is to be treated as tantamount to an admission of conspiracy to deceive, then we shall soon be driven to the conclusion that the most credible evidence available to the historian is uncorroborated evidence – or better still, the absence of any evidence at all.[19]

Anyway, what is really striking in the case of the enquiry of 1279 is not the degree of corroboration observable in the various nuns' tales. What is striking is the extent of discrepancy as to crucial particulars. For example, while the variety of opinion expressed on the question whether the excommunicated nuns had received the sacraments may be attributable to a desire to confirm or conceal the fact of the matter [2, 3, 7], no such explanation will account for the differing reports of the circumstances surrounding the release of the mutineers from the stocks. The witnesses of the incident (and they were numerous) were united in their profession of outrage at the deed. And no one remembered other than it was María de Sevilla and María de Valladolid who had been freed. As to the identity of those responsible for freeing them, however, there was widespread disagreement. Such discrepancies are reassuring. The lack of certainty amongst the witnesses

47

of the convent's recent disorders regarding this and other memorable incidents is the surest indication of the substantial plausibility of their depositions. In the tale it contains of 'complex allegations and counter-allegations', the story of the Ladies of Zamora belongs to a genre with which all students of medieval Europe, and not least those of medieval Spain, ought by now to be generally familiar.[20]

Not everyone was prepared even to admit that the convent had experienced a collapse of discipline. Doña Perona de Zamora apart, however [10], something of the sort was generally conceded. The excommunicated insurgents had besieged the chapel in order to view the sacrament [2] and had set up their own altar [6]. They had also told the bishop's prioress that she was the daughter of a heretic and not their prioress but Saint Augustine's [15, 12]. (So much for the Augustinian veil in which as recently as a year or two previously the prioress had shrouded her community.)[21] But the full flavour of life with the ladies is most authentically conveyed in their own words, starting with those of the lady whom the bishop had left in charge:

[14] On oath and under interrogation María Martínez stated that neither the rule nor the constitutions are observed. Nor is silence. Sometimes the nuns received letters and gifts from the Dominicans brought in by women or passed through holes in the wall. The women had these messages written on their fingers. The reason why the nuns lived in a state of discord was that the friars frequented the convent and engaged in dissolute activities with the nuns there. She herself had asked brother Diego to prevent the friars from visiting them. The community was divided, with some nuns favouring the friars and others remaining obedient to the church of Zamora. As to dissolute activities, the friars used to strip themselves naked in the presence of the nuns. While Doña Xemena was at the lavatory one of them took her tunic and covered himself with it. The divine office was either not celebrated or was celebrated at the wrong time. The friar who put Xemena's tunic on made up a rhyme about Ines Domínguez. Also they rose up against the prioress (that is herself) saying that she was not prioress and that whoever said she was was in a state of mortal sin, because she was not prioress – except of three of them. They said disgraceful things about her. They threatened her, and deprived her of the office of prioress. The ringleaders were Doña Xemena, the sub-prioress, Doña Stefanía, Marina Rodríguez and the others who were in league with the friars. It was these who had aided and abetted the group who deprived her of office. Doña Perona and María de Sevilla took possession of the hangings from over the altars, though later they returned them to her. But the relics, which Doña Xemena took, were not returned. Nor had she had back the

keys which they took from her. Doña Xemena never obeyed her as prioress, though she had required her to do so by virtue of her obedience. And there were others who disobeyed her and ignored the penance she prescribed. The cleric Pedro Pérez came to the convent and said that the nuns were incorporated into the Dominican Order and that they should take María Martínez captive. And he said this in order to make her leave. Otherwise she would be taken, shackled and killed. Caterina left the order and was taken in by friars nearby. Pedro Pérez came to San Frontis and took her with him round the villages and was seen selling wheat with her at Montamarta. Then the nuns who favoured the friars and Caterina wrote to the prioress saying that she should leave the convent. Asked who was fit to be prioress, she named Doña Orobona. Arnalda and María Garcés and her daughter and many others had sung songs against María Martínez when she was prioress. Perona Franca had struck her and locked her up with some other nuns. María Reináldez laid hands on her and in defiance of her authority approached the convent grille. Miorovida had a row with another nun after compline, and when María Martínez went to separate them Miorovida squashed her between two doors and made her bleed. Regarding the letters thrown into choir and the *Te Deum* she answered like the rest. Doña Stefanía besmirched the honour of the prioress's mother, and her grandmother's, and all her family's, and vilified her, and refused to eat at table in the refectory with the other nuns, insisting instead on taking her meals in a private room, which, when she was prioress, María Martínez deprived her of. And Doña Stefanía received a letter, the upshot of which was that María Martínez was badly knocked about in the dormitory. When she had imposed a penance on Elvira Pérez, Elvira had insulted her, giving her the evil eye[22] and ignoring her summons when she was called to chapter.

As another Doña Stefanía described it, the place was liberty hall, with every nun doing her own thing, though it was not she, of course, but her namesake who had caused the *Te Deum* to be struck up when the letters had been 'thrown into choir' – the letters announcing that the nuns had been incorporated with the Dominicans following the appeal they had made, 'on the advice and instructions of the friars' [13]. There was general agreement regarding the incident of the letters – except that in Marina Rodríguez's account [5] it was not letters that had been thrown, but stones. Presumably these were the letters which the nameless prioress of 1277/8 had been so eager to disavow.

Billets-doux pushed through holes in the convent wall, some of them on wax tablets (a use of the medium apparently unfamiliar to students of the medieval wax tablet);[23] messages written on hands (a practice still common amongst female undergraduates); all manner of irregularities, in short. Everything other than bagpipes. But shocking as this was, worse immediately followed as first Xemena Pérez and then Sol Martínez and Doña Caterina de Benavente took the stand.

[15] On oath and under interrogation, Xemena Pérez stated that the rule, the constitutions and silence [were not observed]. The trouble in the convent stemmed from the presence of the friars there. Brother Munio said that he would strip Doña Orobona of her habit. [The nuns and the friars had paired off and taken lovers:] María Reináldez with brother Bernabé, Ines Domínguez with brother Nicolás, Marina Domínguez de Toro with brother Juan of Aviancos who bared himself in the convent in the presence of the nuns, and Teresa Arnáldez with brother Pedro Gutiérrez who entered the convent and went to the kitchen where he spent some time and then came out, and for fear of him the nuns locked themselves in the oven and suffocated. Would to God that the friars did not come to the convent! They were their lovers. All the nuns who took the friars' part were opposed to the prioress María Martínez. They vilified her and called her the daughter of a heretic. When some of the postulants were walking through the town they encountered two Dominicans on the bridge, and one of these pinched one of the girls on the leg. (She had this from the girl herself.) Ines Domínguez had two lovers amongst the friars, brothers Nicolás and Juan de Aviancos. And brother Juan sat on a bed in the infirmary with her and said: 'My little angel-nun, don't you love that boy. Love old me. A good old'un is worth more than a bad young'un.'[24] And when he came to preach he moved through the choir, saying 'there's my little nun'. Doña Stefanía took off brother Gil's clothes – and later put them back on him. Ines Domínguez and María Reináldez did the same with brother Domingo Yuáñez. It was these carryings-on that caused all the scandal. Ines Domínguez, Elvira Pérez, Doña Juana and María Reináldez cut compline and went off drinking (without permission), saying 'Let the prioress María Martínez recite compline with the cleric-mongers.' But for the friars the convent would be a far better place than it is. The friar-group were intent on liberating themselves from the bishop's jurisdiction if they could. Perona Veya, María de Sevilla and Miorovida said that they would beat the bishop up; the witness reports this on hearsay. Regarding the letters thrown into choir and the *Te Deum* she answered like the rest. Marina Románez, M. Giráldez, Elvira Pérez, Doña Juana, Ines Domínguez and María Reináldez released María de Sevilla and María de Valladolid from the stocks and went to the church with candles lit. The sub-prioress was fit for the office of prioress.

[16] On oath and under interrogation, Sol Martínez stated that the rule and the constitutions were not observed. Nor was silence. The root of the problem was that the friars wanted to deprive the bishop of his jurisdiction over the convent and give it to themselves. She and some others were

against this. The friars came frequently to the convent and had talks with the young nuns privately. Brother Munio threatened those who took the bishop's side that he would have them taken and chained up for ever. Some of the friars gave the nuns who were their lovers girdles sewn with silk, and the nuns returned the compliment with gifts of handkerchiefs and *superzonas*.[25] Brother Juan de Aviancos stripped off in front of the nuns. Brother Martín Picamillo and another brother held conversations in the nuns' dormitory with young Perona Franca and María Reináldez. Brother Domingo Yuáñez and brother Gil were in the dormitory too, and also bared themselves, after which the girls dressed them, and Doña Stefanía and María Reináldez and various others girded them [did them up?]. Doña Stefanía said that she had brother Gil's trousers and kept them with her by night for love of the said friar. In defiance of the bishop's instructions, Doña Jimena, Doña Stefanía, Doña Perona and various other nuns opened the great gate to the friars and spoke with them there. Brother Juan Yuáñez surveyed the convent and said: 'This would make a fine love-nest for brother Nicolás.' And then and there he and Ines Domínguez made love. Meanwhile brother Pedro Gutiérrez was on the loose. For fear of him the girls hid themselves in the oven. Also, brother Juan de Aviancos was roaming the convent looking for nuns. All this was the cause of the scandal. And she said that all those who favoured the friars were disobedient to the prioress María Martínez and said disgusting things about her. And María Reináldez and Perona Franca roughed her up and said to her: 'You traitor, you sent out false letters.' And many other vile things they said about her, which are not to be repeated. The friar-group was intent on liberating themselves from the bishop's jurisdiction. Its principal ringleaders were Doña Xemena and Doña Stefanía. Miorovida and María de Sevilla, wielding clubs, and Perona were intent on battering the lord bishop. Almost all the nuns had their own property. Caterina had letters through holes in the wall from the cleric Pedro Pérez whose mistress she was and is believed still to be. Regarding the letters thrown into choir and the *Te Deum*, she answered like the rest. María de Sevilla and María de Valladolid wanted to put María Martínez in chains when she was prioress. When they were excommunicated they celebrated the divine office aloud.

[17] On oath and under interrogation, Doña Caterina de Benavente stated that the rule and the constitutions were not observed. The root of the trouble was the friars. Some of the nuns favour the friars, others the church of Zamora. Ines Domínguez, Doña Juana, M. Reináldez and Perona Franca had friars for lovers and washed their clothes for them. And when the friars had gone away they processed solemnly through the cloister, attributing the names of the friars to each other and singing a chant as though they were accompanying a corpse to its grave. The friar-group had threatened the party of the church of Zamora and said that any supporter of the church of Zamora would be locked up for ever on account of the

letter from the bishop that had been read out in the chapter to the effect that the friars were not to come to the convent again. Once when the witness was lighting the lamps the nuns ragged her in a bad way because when she had been prioress María Martínez had imposed a penance on Elvira Pérez. The said Elvira Pérez together with Sancha Garcés had risen up against the prioress. They had gone about giving her the evil eye and chanting to the prioress: 'You are false and are possessed by the devil because you have had the friars removed from here on account of the clerics.' Perona Franca called the prioress 'Merina, bacallar, caraça, asnal',[26] and said that Gonzalo Pérez was false because he had delivered the bishop's letter, and that the bishop's letter was also false. The friar-group were disobedient to the prioress. María Reináldez roughed up the prioress María Martínez. María de Sevilla roughed her up too. Elvira Pérez had repeated what she is already stated to have said. The nuns who had been excommunicated threw stones at the church door and closed it. 'It is as well for you, Madam,' they said, 'that Doña Xemena is in there with you. Otherwise you would never come out. You would stay there and starve.' The friar-group were intent on shaking off the bishop's jurisdiction and submitting to the friars. Regarding the letters thrown into choir and the *Te Deum* she answered like the rest. The sub-prioress was fit for the office of prioress.

Since so many of the principal malefactors remained defiantly silent in July 1279 and loyal to their confederates, it is difficult to judge how far within the convent membership of the rebel group extended. Plainly the prioress María Martínez was totally discredited. Only one of the ladies, Arnalda Eiménerez [9], considered her fit to remain in office. The majority (twenty-three of the thirty-four nuns questioned, each of whom had two votes) opted for the sub-prioress – a lady whom Doña Perona [3] identified as Doña María, which of course leaves her identity uncertain.[27] But what was her position? Although one of her supporters was the Xemena Pérez who exclaimed 'Would to God that the friars had never come to the convent!' [15], and another, María Alfónsez of León [11] twice in her evidence claimed Doña María to have been an ally of María Martínez during the troubles, according to María Martínez herself the 'subpriora' had belonged to the pro-mendicant group [14]. By the following spring, moreover, (if not sooner), one of the two ladies whom the sub-prioress recommended for office, Marina Rodríguez [5], had joined that group too.[28] More tellingly still, her supporters amongst the Adullamite group, whose perfunctory testimony comes at the end, included both the formidable María de Sevilla [25] and the emotionally involved Teresa Arnáldez [26][29] – suggesting that the sub-prioress Doña María may have been less than fully committed to the episcopal cause in July 1279, and that the community of Las Dueñas was divided not into two groups, but three: a pro-episcopal party; a hard-line pro-mendicant party, many of whose members had already left the convent by then [3]; and a group of closet mendicant-sympathisers of whom the sub-prioress was the leading light.

But not much of a light. In the view of 'Domina Xemena', who attested jointly with Marina Rodríguez de Toro and Doña Stefanía and nominated themselves for the office [27–29], the sub-prioress was 'good but weak'. A complication arises from the fact that the community contained as many as three ladies of the same name: this one, another 'Domina Xemena' [2], and the Xemena Pérez whose memories of excursions to the oven and the infirmary have already been mentioned [15].[30] As to the identity of the laconic 'Domina Xemena', however, the 'Domina Xemena' whose disobedience the embattled prioress singled out for special mention, the evidence allows of only one conclusion. The proprietory manner in which she was reported to have seized and retained the convent's relics, and the anecdotal evidence that but for her presence as hostage the pro-episcopal nuns under siege in the chapel would have been left to starve to death there,[31] indicate that she was none other than the co-foundress, Doña Jimena Rodríguez.

As well as Doña Jimena Rodríguez, eleven ladies were named by one or more of the witnesses in 1279 as having played a leading part in the persecution of the prioress, and in their testimonies most of them said virtually nothing other than to propose one or other of themselves for the office of prioress. These were Doña Caterina de Zamora [4], Elvira Pérez de Zamora [24], Doña Stefanía, Ines Domínguez [21], Doña Juana [33], María Reináldez [7], María de Sevilla [25], Marina Domínguez de Toro [18], Miorovida de Toro [23], Doña Perona, and Teresa Arnáldez [26].[32] Again problems of identification confuse the issue. For example, which (if either) of the two ladies both called 'Domina Stephania' [13, 29] was the ex-prioress of that name?[33] Which (if not both of them) was it who had so rudely addressed the prioress and so tenderly undressed brother Gil?[34] And which was the 'domina Esteuania Fernandez' whom Doña Sancha de Toro [34] regarded as prioress material? Then there is the proliferation of Peronas. Various ladies in 1279 gave graphic accounts of the exploits of possibly as many as three nuns of this name – 'Perona ueya' (old

Perona), Perona Franca (who to judge by the attention paid to her was far from old),[35] and just plain Perona (though sometimes she was called Doña Perona) [12, 14–17]. The last of these was presumably the Doña Perona who held María Martínez responsible for all the trouble and who told the bishop to his face that she was not pleased to see him there [3]. But for how much of what had happened was Doña Perona de Zamora responsible, the lady who claimed that disobedience to the prioress had been minimal [10]?

The ramifications of the loyalty network were so extensive as to defy analysis. For example, the beleaguered María Martínez's choice of successor was Doña Orobona, the nun whom brother Munio had threatened to strip of her habit. Yet Orobona, it was reported [1], was the sister of that Marina Rodríguez who had been one of María Martínez's chief tormentors.[36] In order to discover the realities behind the Betjemanesque cadences ('Elvira said Xemena did it . . .') and to establish which nun was whose friend when, the assistance of a sophisticated computer program would be required. Pending that assistance, it is already evident, however, that mendicant–episcopal polarity was not the only determinant of alignments amongst the ladies on the occasion of the bishop's visitation.

The immediate consequence of that visitation was D. Suero's reappointment of the almost universally regretted María Martínez as prioress. Then the story moved on. In October 1279, two of the papal judges-delegate appointed by Gregory X, the archdeacon of Cea and the (new) treasurer of León, at long last blew the dust off their Las Dueñas file. In view of recent events their access of energy was understandable – but, for the same reason, so too was the alacrity with which they immediately referred the case to the cantor of Avila.[37] Presumably on account of the cat-and-mouse game that the nuns had been playing with him over the previous seven years, D. Suero had not pressed the matter. But now, armed with his new and sensational material, and judging no doubt that fresh momentum was required, he initiated a fresh action. Thus it was that on 1 December 1279 a further enquiry into the ladies' activities was set in train. In response to the bishop's complaint that after visiting the convent and admonishing the prioress and certain of the senior nuns, the ladies had flouted his authority and in defiance of his sentences of excommunication and interdict had continued in rebellion 'for a year or more', Nicholas III ordered the prior of Valladolid to investigate. Yet the new papal mandate was virtually indistinguishable from Gregory X's of 1272, in common form and containing no allusion to recent developments at Las Dueñas.[38] Six years later, when the friars were the accusers and the bishop the accused, the narrative of Honorius IV's mandate to the archbishop of Toledo would be far more circumstantial. It can hardly have been that the papal chancery in 1279 would have regarded the revelations from Zamora as run-of-the-mill. The explanation must be that the chancery was as yet unaware of them.

Even so, with the damning evidence he had in his possession, a fresh mandate and a new judge, D. Suero might now hope for results at last. And indeed, in the spring of 1280, the prior of Valladolid, Master Gil, summoned the rebel ladies to a hearing of the complaints against them 'in crastino Quasimodo' – exactly as the Leonese ecclesiastics had done in January 1273, though this time at Valladolid. Up to a point, history was repeating itself. As in 1273, so on 29 April 1280 the ladies failed to appear. But this time the matter was not allowed to rest. After giving them ten days' grace, the prior duly ordered the bishop's sentences to be published far and wide.

As will be seen, little was to come of D. Suero's latest initiative either, not least because one effect of the ladies' continuing recalcitrance was to ensure that the 1279 evidence was never written into the record. Nevertheless, the prior of Valladolid's judgement is of considerable interest – principally because it names the rebel nuns and identifies their leader. The summons which he had sent in March, and which had been ignored, had been addressed to 'Doña Xemena who calls herself prioress and to the other nuns who were with her in her rebellion'.[39] The rebel leader, sometime co-foundress of Las Dueñas, now moves into the limelight, and with her so do her confederates, all thirty-one of them. Comparison with the prior's list of names with those of the principal troublemakers identifiable and still in residence in 1279 provides an indication of the consequences of D. Suero's decision to leave the luckless María Martínez in charge.[40]

The results of that comparison can have given the bishop little cause for satisfaction (and it is only he who can have supplied the prior with details of the delinquents). Of the earlier list of twelve, only one name is absent from the prior's inventory – that of the multiple Perona, who unless she had elected to return to a cloistered existence under episcopal supervision, or opted for the more peaceful conditions of the outside world, may have expired, exhausted by a conventual regime which consisted of raucous sing-songs and prioress-pummel-ling sessions interspersed with tours of duty at the gate, letting friars in at all hours, washing their clothes, and making herself agreeable to them in other ways. But Perona's defection or disappearance in 1280 was more than compensated for by the addition of two of the previously indistinguishable Stefanías, as well as of a further fifteen recruits to the cause, concerning whom there had only been second-hand reports at the earlier date, presumably because in July 1279 they had already left the convent.[41] In short, it appears that there had been as much coming and going across the lines in recent months as there had previously been both over the wall and through the gate.

By the summer of 1281 those 'almost forty ladies' who would later be represented to Honorius IV as innocent victims of episcopal aggression driven from their cloister and condemned to roaming the countryside 'for many years',[42] had settled 60 kilometres away at Benavente, the northern point of the Zamora–Toro–Benavente triangle of Dominican houses within D. Suero's diocese. This we know from a letter which María Martínez wrote to a cardinal in Rome at the time. Since the reinstatement of María Martínez as prioress of Las Dueñas, the convent had ceased to be a taboo subject within immediate earshot of D. Suero. Only recently the dean, Pedro Yáñez, had felt able to make a bequest to the nuns ('a las doñas dalan rio') without fear of offending him. (Not so another in favour of the local Dominicans however: his fifty maravedís bequest to them was only to be paid 'if it please my lord bishop'.)[43] But the fact that the nuns on the run had found sanctuary at Benavente was another matter. For Benavente was an ecclesiastical Gibraltar, by a quirk of ecclesiastical geography exempt from D. Suero's jurisdiction and subject to that of the bishop of Oviedo, whose home territory was far away to the north – and who, to make matters worse, in 1281 was a Frenchman, and not only a Frenchman, but also an officious Frenchman. Fredulus of Oviedo had been intruded into his see to act as collector of ecclesiastical revenues for the benefit of Alfonso X, a task which he performed with such ruthlessness that even Nicholas III felt constrained to rebuke him. A representative of all that Alfonso X's increasingly disenchanted old guard liked least about Alfonso X's Castile in the early 1280s, it was by this *arriviste*'s permission that the Dominicans had been installed at Benavente in 1277.[44] And now the rebel nuns of Zamora were there too, sheltering on the bishop of Zamora's very doorstep, though (courtesy of a pushy foreigner who had risen on the current of the king of Castile's imperial fantasies) just beyond his reach. Memories are made of this. In the spring of 1282 continuing soreness on this account doubtless helped to push the bishop of Zamora across Castile's political divide.

Meanwhile, in the summer of 1281, the prioress of Las Dueñas wrote her letter to the Leonese cardinal bishop of Tusculum, Ordoño Alvarez.[45] It read as follows:

> To the honoured father and lord D. Ordoño, cardinal of the Church of Rome, we María Martínez, prioress of the monastery of S. María de Zamora of the Order of Saint Augustine and convent of the said place kiss your feet and hands. We wish you to know, my lord, that the monastery in which we are was once the property of the bishop of Zamora and that the sisters who originally asked the bishop to grant it to them promised both for themselves and for their successors that they would receive the habit which we wear from him, be obedient and subject and reverent to him and his successors in the church of Zamora, live strictly according to the rule of Saint Augustine, and receive the bishop's visitation and correction. And all this they promised in good faith, committing themselves under oath never to break that promise. And all this we, too, have promised, many times, and as often as we have done so, we have sworn to remain true to our undertakings.
>
> But, my lord, the nuns being thus bound, friars of the Order of Preachers took to coming here, more and more frequently, almost every day, and every day from first thing till siesta-time and from siesta-time till night. And often they would even spend the night here. And sometimes there were as many as twenty of them here at a time. And they came right into the convent and created great disorder, entering the enclosure with the young nuns and behaving with them disgracefully, embracing them and making free with them and saying such things to them as men of their cloth ought not to say; and even stripping themselves of their garments, and parading around the place naked as the day they were born, and dressing up in the sisters' clothes and dressing the sisters up in theirs, and also doing other wicked things which we cannot bring ourselves to describe.
>
> And all of this was tolerated by Doña Xemena, who was prioress at the time, and by the nuns who were here and who are now at Benavente, having departed from the convent without permission. And apart from all the other things they did, brother Munio and the Dominicans often told the nuns not to observe the promises they had made to the bishop, D. Suero, but instead to join forces with the nuns who had gone to Benavente. And this did great damage and caused much distress in the convent, harming its reputation and creating disruption therein.

And, my lord, observing that the things that were happening were to the disservice of God, as well as perilous to the convent, we were much grieved. But when we urged them – the friars and the nuns – to cease their activities, they used us exceeding ill. And although we reported it to our lord bishop, and although he warned them to desist from what they were doing, they did not desist. Rather, in defiance of their promises, they continued, and they beat us, often, and treated us very badly.

Wherefore, my lord, with tears streaming from our eyes, we urge and implore you to take pity on us, and to intercede with the pope so that we may be spared further menaces and misery at the hands of the friars of the Order of Preachers and not be made to suffer further in our convent. And we beseech you of your mercy that you secure the pope's confirmation of what we promised our lord the bishop of Zamora, which we believe and trust to be for the salvation of our souls and the proper conduct of our lives that we should do.

Dated at Zamora in the said convent, 13 July *era* 1319 [AD 1281].

Seventy years ago the youthful Américo Castro published the text of the prioress's plaintive appeal, and, having done so, never again returned to it. Despite the title he gave his piece,[46] its interest for Castro in 1923 was not moral but morphological. There is also another sort of moral here, one to be drawn by researchers. Just as students are enjoined to inspect the books on the shelf in the vicinity of the volume they have been sent to consult, so also ought their seniors always to check both right and left. For although in the case of the prioress's letter the *signatura* in the archive of Zamora cathedral is no longer what it was at the beginning of the century,[47] nevertheless next to it then, as it still is now, was the record of D. Suero's visitation. But this was in Latin, so presumably Castro did not look at it – presumably, because had he done so he could hardly have failed to appreciate its interest. Had the author of *España en su historia: Cristianos, moros y judíos* inspected the visitation record, he would have encountered there, *inter alias*, that lady of the south, Doña María de Sevilla. And had he done so, he must surely have found use for her in that celebrated account of his, published in 1948, of the development of 'Spanishness' in the land of the three religions which kept Spain's medievalists so harmlessly occupied during the long years of General Franco's rule.

But he did not. What instead happened was that, almost as soon as it was published, his discovery was appropriated by Doña Mercedes Gaibrois de Ballesteros. In 1923 Doña Mercedes had been invited to contribute to the great Heinrich Finke's seventieth birthday volume.

It is not difficult to guess why. She had been invited to do so because in 1920 her forthcoming study of the reign of Sancho IV had recently been awarded a prize. The award of 'el Premio del Duque de Alba' marked Doña Mercedes out. To one of the organisers of the *Festschrift*, Germans and Catalans mostly, it must have occurred that in a volume in which such scant references as there were to Castile were on the whole depreciatory the inclusion of a token Castilian contribution would be desirable.[48] Hers was the one Castilian piece in a volume of thirty-one contributions. True, Finke's Spanish focus had been Aragonese. Even so, as Primo de Rivera was beginning to take control of Spain, it was not inappropriate to pay a perfunctory tribute to the Castilian past.

So the up-and-coming Doña Mercedes was called upon to represent Castile. And at a time when Spain was lurking at the periphery of European affairs, the subject of her piece for the Finke *Festschrift* was well chosen. Within her period, Munio of Zamora OP was one of the very few Castilians to have made anything of a mark in the wider world. Doña Mercedes would, therefore, provide an account of the career of the Dominican friar from Saint Dominic's own homeland who, in preference to the usual Italians and Frenchmen, had been elected Master General of the Order in 1285. The fact, as unaccountable as it was unfortunate, that six years later the Spanish friar had also been ignominiously hounded from office was nicely balanced by the German honorand's long-standing interest in the history of the Dominican Order.[49]

What she had discovered in Sancho IV's fiscal records had provided Doña Mercedes with adequate new material for an article on the Castilian king's relationship with the Spanish Master General. What she learned on reading Castro's contribution to the *Bulletin Hispanique*, therefore, when the preparation of her piece must already have been well advanced, can only have come as a bombshell. Her consternation may be imagined. For the reference in the prioress's letter to 'brother Munio' in relation to the sordid escapades in the Zamora nunnery appeared at last to provide the explanation of the circumstances, hitherto wholly mysterious, surrounding the Spanish Master General's removal from office in 1291.

Seventy years on, appreciation of the extent of Doña Mercedes's discomfiture at this moment requires an effort of imagination. For the benefit of a generation of historians unfamiliar with the labours of finessing with the typewriter it is perhaps necessary to stress the seriousness of the implications of Castro's five pages in the year 1923. Packed with dynamite as it was, Castro's squib blew a gaping hole beneath the water-line of Doña Mercedes's text – of her *typewritten* text. This was an emergency, requiring emergency procedures. The drill in such cases was well understood. Footnotes first. In accordance with established procedures, therefore, Doña Mercedes attended to the sequence of her footnotes. That assured,[50] the text itself could be adjusted, as indeed it must have been, substantially. And in the little niche in which she enshrined it, for almost half a century Castro's discovery remained undisturbed. Until 1971 no significant attention was paid to the activities of Brother Munio prior to his disgrace.[51]

As in 1925 and 1971, so in 1281 the scandals from Zamora were proclaimed to the wider world. In 1281, however, the response was rather more immediate. In the next chapter we will return to María Martínez's letter and the tremors it produced. Meanwhile, however, other aspects of the administration of Las Dueñas were being subjected to outside scrutiny. On 5 December 1279, just four days after the prior of Valladolid had been recruited to bring the insurgent nuns to book, the dean of Salamanca was ordered to investigate yet another report that had reached Rome regarding the Ladies of Zamora. Now, it seemed, at last the pace was hotting up.

For as well as themselves and their paramours (it had been reported to Rome), the Ladies had been engaged in divesting their house of its corporate assets. It had come to the attention of the authorities there that the prioress and community, and their predecessors before them, had been alienating the convent's property wholesale. Tithes and lands, houses and vines, meadows and pastures, woods and mills, sundry rights and properties had been made over to clergy and laity, either on fixed leases or in perpetuity. Some of the recipients had even contrived to secure papal confirmation of their ill-gotten goods. Or so it had been alleged.[52]

Now allegations of this sort did not ordinarily merit the pope's personal attention. Massive peculation was not a matter for the pontiff. Moreover, in accordance with Nicholas III's own recent reform of chancery procedure, the rescript addressed to the dean of Salamanca would have been issued without being read before the pope.[53] So the fact that it is dated just four days after the mandate requiring the prior of Valladolid to investigate the ladies' other activities does not mean that the pope would have made the connexion. It does not even imply that he was so much as aware of the existence of Las Dueñas. But the coincidence can hardly have been entirely accidental. Someone at Rome was on the *qui vive*. There was someone there intent on bringing the nuns to book and on ensuring that a judge was appointed competent to investigate the issue of the illicit conveyances without delay. As it was, the judge appointed, the dean of Salamanca, Pedro Pérez, displayed a truly Zamoran sense of urgency. Almost nine months passed before he summoned Alfonso Garcés de Carvajal, knight of the diocese of León, to appear before him at Salamanca on 12 November 1280.[54]

We do not know what, if anything, transpired there. If he knew his business, the convent's proctor presumably prayed in aid the privilege the nuns had had from Clement IV in 1265 entitling them to make free with their possessions 'as they might have done had they instead remained outside the cloister'. Then the debate would presumably have turned on the meaning to be attached to the papal exclusion clause. In 1265 the ladies had been assured of free disposal of all their moveable and immoveable goods 'exceptis feudalibus'.[55] What did this mean? Did it apply to the alienations of property recently complained of, to some with 'a life interest' ('ad vitam'), to others for 'a longer term' ('ad non modicum tempus'), to others again 'in perpetuity at farm or for an annual rent' ('perpetuo ad firmam vel sub censu annuo')? Did the fact that since 1265 the ladies had been incorporated (in some sense) into the Order of Preachers affect the issue? In 1280 these were questions admitting of no clear answers. From the case of the Poor Clares of Allariz it is clear that nothing was clear about the status of the female communities attached to the principal mendicant orders.[56]

Had he been aware of it, would Nicholas III have been shocked to learn of the dispersal of the corporate endowment of the Ladies of Zamora? Would he have been scandalised had he known that transactions of the sort had been effected with the full knowledge and consent of their bishop? As we have seen, it had been with D. Suero's express approval that in 1274 the *cantor* of his cathedral, Pedro Johan, had purchased the convent's water-mill at Matarranas.[57] Property speculation on such a scale may have been deprecated at Rome. For the bishop of Zamora and the members of his cathedral chapter, however, it was the most natural thing in the world. For it was not only the bishop who was engaged in increasing his patrimony during these years. So too were the canons and dignitaries of his chapter. The *cantor* of Zamora stood for a group of possessive individualists only recently enfranchised.

With the prior and guardian of the local Dominican and Franciscan convents in attendance (such were the ambiguities of the age), in May 1266 bishop and chapter had put what they hoped would be an end to their long-standing differences by doing what most other Spanish churches had done long before. They had proceeded to an 'amicable' division of their corporate endowment.[58]

As well as privatising the previously shared resources of the church of Zamora, in an attempt to achieve amity between the parties, in 1266 the dean of Compostela, Fernando Alfónsez (himself one of the century's most heroic pluralists) had gone so far as to authorise the repudiation of papal provision to benefices within the cathedral. In the same spirit, the dean and chapter had on the same occasion pre-scribed severe penalties against anyone using the capitular seal in support of petitions to Rome for advancement anywhere within the diocese[59]. With the economically liberated dignitaries of the cathedral church extending and rationalising their newly acquired estates, however, the much desired era of peace and concord came to nothing. After D. Suero's death further measures were necessary in order to counter episcopal circumvention of the 1266 settlement.[60] And even before that, throughout the 1270s the city and diocese of Zamora was a hive of capitalist enterprise.

Members of the cathedral chapter had long been subject to severe censure for neglecting to cultivate the capitular vineyards before the beginning of May. More recently access to their *bodegas* had been a perennial cause of contention with the local *concejo*. Like the English knightly class of the age, the thirteenth-century canons of Zamora were increasingly devoting themselves to estate management. It was in accordance with the rhythms of the agricultural round rather than the imperatives of the liturgical calendar that their accounting year ran from October to September.[61] And as well as a hive of enterprise, of course, city and diocese were also one great battlefield. At Fermoselle the *concejo* of Zamora did 4,000 maravedís'-worth of damage to episcopal property, as well as destroying vines and (accord-ing to the royal loss-adjusters' calculations) sixty-odd trees, and when the king found in the bishop's favour fiercely contested both the issue of liability and the estimate for dilapidations.[62] In the case of Venialbo and Villamor, where the bishop was in dispute with the *concejo* of Toro, the king's judgment in the former's favour remained a dead letter, involving D. Suero in lengthy attendance at the royal court and ultimately reducing him to turn for assistance to the pope whose mandates of provision to benefices he and his chapter routinely refused to obey.[63]

Not that the pope's intervention proved any more effective than the king's. While in flagrant contempt of the king the *concejo* of Zamora persisted in giving aid and comfort to malefactors sentenced by ecclesiastical tribunals, and with his own chapter (led by the very man he had smuggled into the deanery) aligning with Suero's foes, open warfare continued across an area stretching from Pobladura to the north of Zamora to Venialbo in the south-east.[64] In May 1265, in the very choir of his own cathedral church, the chapter with the dean, García Núñez, at its head witnessed the memorandum of grievances against the bishop which the 'capitulum clericorum' of Toro, 39 individuals in 26 places, was forwarding to Rome.[65] Twelve months later the deposition submitted to the arbitration of the dean of Compostela listed no fewer than 144 members of the clerical proletariat of the town and its surrounding countryside.[66]

With Bishop Suero in conflict both with his chapter and with the municipality, widespread disaffection throughout the length and breadth of his diocese, and the king of Castile and his heir intervening on opposite sides of various overlapping disputes – in April 1271 Fernando de la Cerda undertook not to prosecute Garcí Velasco of Toro on account of the vendetta which he had been pursuing against the bishop's brother Johann Pérez; in August 1278, at the behest of María de Molina, Alfonso X commuted five of the six *servicios* due from the 'Cabildo delos clerigos de Toro'[67] – the complexity of the network of local alliances and loyalties was such that no pope in distant Viterbo could possibly appreciate the extent of their ramifications. Of this network the Ladies of Zamora were part.

It was a network sustained by hierarchical distinctions, social distinctions whose moral and religious delineaments especially perceptive contemporaries thought themselves capable of discerning. According to Humbert de Romans (who was perceptive), virginity went with lineage – just as sanctity did, according to that sociologically less literate member of Fernando III's entourage whose come-

63

uppance Gil de Zamora recorded in his Legend of the lowly Saint Isidore of Madrid.[68] But although lineage may have been a necessary qualification for virginity, it is clear from the case of Doña Stefanía that it was not also sufficient.

Noted for her attachment to Brother Gil and his trousers, Doña Stefanía was the former prioress of Las Dueñas who 'would not eat in the refectory with the other nuns', and whose insistence on taking her meals in her own room, like that of her companions on going off drinking together, was mentioned in July 1279 as an example of the contempt shown by the insurgent sisters for the ordinary rules of the common life. And just five years after Humbert of Romans had deplored the practice as a sign of the morally degenerate times through which the Church was passing, so it was.[69] But that was not all it was. Behaviour such as that of the incorrigible Doña Stefanía – or of Doña Caterina de Zamora in giving her evidence early in the proceedings rather than at the end together with the tight-lipped contingent with whom she plainly belonged – also betokened a whole complex of aristocratic attitudes: attitudes shared by Salvador Pérez, who, when recording the nuns' tales, was assiduous in ensuring that those of them who really were *domine* ('Doñas') had that mark of their rank duly acknowledged.[70] Whatever else they may have sacrificed, the Ladies of Zamora were not to be allowed to lose their social status.

For ladies such as these, the Rule's requirement that they should manage without things of their own ('sine proprio uiuere'), as the Order's novices were required to promise to manage,[71] was likely to prove arduous. And so indeed the record relates. 'Almost all the nuns had their own property', Sol Martínez asserted [16]. 'They had and retained private possessions', Arnalda Eiménerez confirmed [9]. If they were not prepared even to eat together, moreover, they were hardly likely to consent to have their hair cut and washed or be bled by rote,[72] or tolerate the prioress and her acolytes searching their beds for such little treasures as they had squirrelled away there[73] (a pair of friar's trousers, for example), or on being found out submit gracefully to the discipline of systematic social ostracism and the indignity of kneeling bare-breasted and being flogged by the rest of the community[74] – or (least of all) when they were at death's door, to having the entire community in attendance and the priest in full canonicals, when what they most wanted, then of all times, was that degree of privacy to which by upbringing they were accustomed.[75]

The importance to them of questions of rank and hierarchy their use of seals personal confirms. In March 1264 the foundation charters of Las Dueñas had been sealed by three Cistercian abbots because Doña Jimena and Doña Elvira had no seals of their own. So matters remained in February 1273 when Jimena as sub-prioress used the convent's seal to authenticate the latest truce with D. Suero. In August 1274, however, just as the mendicants were coming to dominate the ladies' affairs, as it happens, when authenticating the conveyance concerning the water-mill at Matarranas, Doña Jimena used a seal of her own as well as the conventual seal. Likewise in September 1278. Finally, on the occasion of the truce of July 1279, María Domingo dispensed with the conventual seal altogether (or perhaps the bishop had confiscated it) and employed her own.[76] On the face of it, the prioresses of Las Dueñas had come a long way in fifteen years. In fact, they had reverted to type.

In another detail of María Domingo's belated pact with D. Suero a further glimpse of the social pretensions of the prioress of Las Dueñas and of the social stratification that was in evidence at Zamora, just as it was at Allariz,[77] is provided in what is no more than a textual detail. As already mentioned, after all that had recently passed between D. Suero and the ladies, so perfunctory was María Domingo's regard for the bishop that in July 1279 she was content merely to repeat the text of Doña Jimena's submission of six years before. In 1273 Jimena had referred to the Cistercian abbots who had confirmed the ladies' original agreement with the bishop as having done so 'a peticion e a Ruego de nos' ('at our petition and request'), which was indeed what had occurred in 1264. On reaching this phrase in 1279, María Domingo hesitated in her labour of repetition, and rightly. But rightly for the wrong reason – as the formulation she adopted ('a peticion e a Ruego de mi e del Conuento') tellingly reveals. Plainly, 'a Ruego de nos' no longer applied. Because the prioress in 1279 had not been party to the 1264 agreement, either the whole phrase needed to be recast or the word 'nos' required changing to 'del Conuento'. But evidently it was not these considerations that troubled the prioress when her eye fell upon 'a Ruego de nos'. To judge by the solution she adopted, what troubled her about the phrase was the failure of the collective pronoun 'nos' to indicate that distinction between a prioress and her community which social propriety required.[78]

The prioress's emendation of these four words, even as the bishop

65

was hammering at the convent gate, speaks volumes. If María Domingo was more of a snob than she was a textual critic, however, she was in good company. Indeed, she was in the very best of company, company such as mere historians are not ordinarily privileged to share. Like the Order of Santiago which she had decided against entering, the community which Doña Elvira had endowed sustained family relationships and harboured family groups of which the record leaves only the barest of traces: the pairs of sisters Marina Rodríguez and Orobona, and Doña Caterina and Doña Margarita de Benevento; Elvira Pérez and Sancha Garcés, the *consobrine* of Brother Munio; Marina Garcés and her daughter Marina Domínguez.[79] Though earlier historians of Las Dueñas were clearly mistaken in supposing that Doña Teresa, Alfonso IX's Portuguese queen, had been involved in the foundation of the place and her daughter the Infanta Sancha had taken the veil there, they were correct enough in their description of the convent as 'esta casa aristocrática'.[80]

Although girls of only thirteen were regarded as not 'notably young', and, provided they passed the compulsory pregnancy test, could be received into the order,[81] as to the age-structure of this *parador* of the well-heeled the record is silent. Yet while it therefore cannot be said how many members of the Zamora community may have chosen the 'status of widowhood' for the freedom that the order provided from the rule of priest or husband,[82] doubtless at least some of the merry widows resident there had both older and younger *brothers*. The first thing that the bishop was told by the first witness in July 1279 was that the insurgents had come by night 'cum baronibus'. Doubtless too, the bishop knew who these *varones*, these men, were. Regrettably, all too rarely are we able to share this knowledge or to discover the connexions of the bishop's adversaries.[83] We are as much in the dark as successive popes were at the time and as incapable as they were of discerning the family relationships that may have existed between (let us say) the forty ladies who slipped away from the convent of Las Dueñas before and after the bishop descended upon it in 1279 and (for example) the forty 'laymen of Toro and its region' whom the bishop had delated to Clement IV in 1265, merely a matter of months after establishing the Ladies of Zamora in their seminary of sedition 'de allende rrio'.[84]

❀ ❀ ❀ ❀ ❀

Notes

1 *Spanish Church and the Papacy*, 226–8.
2 M. L. Bueno Domínguez, 'Las mujeres de Santa María de las Dueñas de Zamora: la realidad humana' in *Las mujeres en el Cristianismo medieval. Imágenes téoricas y cauces de actuación religiosa*, ed. A. Muñoz Fernández, Madrid 1989, 237–45 (especially 241, 244); 'Las tensiones del episcopado de Palencia y él de Zamora. Siglos XIII y XIV', *Actas del II Congreso de Historia de Palencia. 27, 28 y 29 de abril de 1989*, ii, Palencia 1990, 401–11 (403); 'Santa María de las Dueñas de Zamora. ¿Beguinas o monjas? El proceso de 1279', *HID* 20 (1993) 85–105 (especially 92, 105). (Amongst this author's misreadings, 'comminatus' (for 'cominatus'; see below, p. 170) coincides with my own earlier lapse (*Spanish Church and the Papacy*, 224, n. 3).) Cf. M. Pardo, 'Le roi Rodrigue ou Rodrigue roi', *Imprévue* 6 (1983) 61–105 (especially 85).
3 'Grauis culpa est si qua cum aliqua lites habuerit . . . uel si qua in proclamatione iurgium fecerit'; 'Grauior culpa est si qua per contumaciam uel manifestam rebellionem maioribus suis inobediens extiterit, uel cum eis proterue contendere ausa fuerit'; 'Grauissima culpa est incorrigibilitas illius que nec culpas timet admittere et penam recusat ferre' ('Rule', 344, 345; ACZ, 13/61, witness 17, Appendix II (for ease of reference, the witnesses are there and hereinafter identified by number [1–34])).
4 See above, p. 26.
5 ACZ, 13/68, where her name appears as 'Xemenna Rodrigues'. In what follows the alternative Latin and Spanish forms of names (e.g. Xemena/Jimena) are usually given as they occur in the documentation but are ocasionally varied in the interests of clarity.
6 'Nos priora e el conuento delas duenas de santa Maria de Çamora dela orden de sant Agostin que trahemos el habito delos Predicadores' (ACZ, 13/58b – an (undated) notarial copy by Pedro Fernández 'notario publico del Rey en Toro' of a document dated 'Çamora enno monesterio sobredicho .vi. dias andados de Setenbrio [*sic*]. enna era de mill e ccc. e xvi. annos [i.e. 1278]. Anno domini M.CC.lxvii' [i.e. 1277]).
7 'Et renunciamos appellaciones, cartas e priuilegios ganados del papa e se furen ganados daqui enadelante por alguien prometemos a bona fe de non usar delos nen de hir contra estas cosas sobredichas e de guardarlas sienpre e de non uenir contra elas. Et se algun prometimiento o juramento a predicador o a predicadores fu fecho per alguna donna o donnas del monesterio sobredicho, elo que non creemos nin sabemos que fecho fusse, nos la priora e el conuento sobredicho quitamos nos delo e renunciamos lo. Et prometemos a bona fe delo non guardar' (*ibid.*).
8 Doña Jimena had done so in February 1273 (see above, p. 25) and when María Domingo repeated the exercise in July 1279, with one small but revealing exception (considered above, p. 65), she was content simply to repeat Doña Jimena's text – despite the fact that the bishop was at the gates (or possibly within them) at this time (ACZ, 13/58).

67

🌀 🌀 🌀 🌀 🌀

9 ACZ, 13/58 (7 July 1279; cf. Bueno Domínguez, 'S. María de las Dueñas', 92–3, whose misdating of María Domingo's act of submission both to 1273 and to 1277 makes nonsense of the events of these years). María Domingo testified at the end together with other members of the anti-episcopal hard core [22]. It is not clear whether the 'M. Dominici' who sang nasty songs ('turpes cantilenas') at the prioress [9] was this lady or that other active member of the pro-mendicant group, *Marina* Domingo de Toro [18] whose amatory and other exploits were mentioned by witnesses 1 and 15.

10 In July 1279 the witnesses Sol Martínez and Doña Caterina de Benavento [16, 17] both stated that *de facto* María Martínez had ceased to be prioress by then. This is confirmed by the episcopal record of the lady's own testimony [14] which refrains from describing her as prioress, thereby conceding the lawfulness of her deposition *de jure*: a tactical error.

11 See above, pp. 51–2.

12 See above, p. 54. Cf. Bueno Domínguez, *loc. cit.*, who fails to note the dating problem and assigns the visitation to 1277.

13 '. . . et desiderantes reformationem et bonum statum monasterii monialium Sancte Marie ordinis Sancti Augustini que portant habitum fratrum predicatorum' (Appendix II). Cf. *Reg. Hon. IV*, 147 (see above, p. 3).

14 M. abbot of Moreruela (presumably Abbot Martin, May 1269 × January 1279: (Rodríguez Fernández, *Los fueros locales*, 374, 377)) and Domingo Pérez, sometime abbot of Valparaíso, both Cistercian houses of the diocese, and two members of the chapter – M. Vicéncez (treasurer) and Pedro Benítez (*magisterscolarum* and D. Suero's successor as bishop of Zamora). M[artín] Vicéntez had clashed with the bishop in the past (Linehan, *Spanish Church and the Papacy*, 301–2). The canon Salvador Pérez did not authenticate the transcript; presumably he wrote it. If the ex-abbot of Valparaíso was the prelate who had testified for the foundresses in 1264, the bishop's involvement of him in 1279 was astute. The two monks, described in the bishop's record as 'nobis adiunctis', were evidently viewed as more central to the enquiry than the two dignitaries.

15 The circumstantial character of Doña Sancha de Toro's evidence [34] disposes of the suspicion that the cursory character of this part of the record is attributable to weariness on the part of the scribe.

16 'Ille que sunt exparte predicatorum . . . tenebant et habebant proprium scilicet denarios' [9]. Cf. above, p. 14; 'Rule', 345 ('Eodem modo penitere debet si qua, quod absit, in peccatum carnis lapsa fuerit: quod grauius ceteris puniri censemus et plusquam omnia alia abhominamur').

17 'Por tanto es muy posible que la incontinencia referida entre de lleno en una política de desprestigio iniciada por el obispo para influir en la sociedad zamorana e incluso en las jerarquías de la Iglesia, y mermar o eliminar el poder de los predicadores en la ciudad, atribuyéndoles a unos y otros comportamientos escandalosos que justificaran la acción del obispo, contra unas monjas que por proceder de ambiente elevados [*sic*] gozan de una formación que les hace difícilmente manejables' ('S. María de las Dueñas', 105).

18 *Men and Women at Toulouse in the Age of the Cathars*, Toronto 1990, 195. For details of the well-endowed Peter de Dalbs's (alleged) rampant sexuality and his numerous exploits up hill and down dale, see the depositions of the thirty-six witnesses for the prosecution (*ibid.*, 50–65).

19 Cf. J. H. Langbein's observation regarding the 'staple of Marxist argumentation for dealing with contrary evidence' which he calls 'the legitimation trick' – 'Evidence that cuts against the thesis is dismissed as part of a sub-plot to make the conspiracy more palatable to its victims, to legitimate it' (*'Albion's* fatal flaws', *Past & Present* 98 (1983) 114).

20 Cf. A. MacKay, 'A typical example of late medieval Castilian anarchy? The affray of 1458 in Alcaraz', in *Medieval and Renaissance Studies in Honour of R. B. Tate*, ed. R. Cardwell and I. Michael, Oxford 1986, 81–93; *idem*, 'Courtly love and lust in Loja', in *The Age of the Catholic Monarchs, 1474–1516. Literary Studies in Memory of Keith Whinnom*, ed. A. Deyermond and I. Macpherson, *BHS* Special Issue, Liverpool 1989, 83–94 (especially 84).

21 See above, p. 43.

22 'Cum digitis ad oculos'. Cf. J.-C. Schmitt, *La Raison des gestes dans l'Occident médiéval*, Paris 1990, 163, lower illustration (*c.* 1200), in which two fingers of the right hand of the man on the left are pointed at his adversary in the gesture still employed in parts of southern Europe. Cf. Saint Anne's two fingers pointing towards the genitals of her grandson, the infant Jesus, in the remarkable early sixteenth-century German woodcut discussed by J. Wirth, 'Sainte Anne est une sorcière', *Bibliothèque d'Humanisme et de Renaissance* 40 (1978) 449–80; Schmitt, 325.

23 'tabulas cereas', according to Alda Eiménerez [9]. The reference to messages on wax recalls the specific prohibition of 'Rule', 341: 'Item nulla mittat uel recipiat sine licencia litteras uel cedulam scriptam eciam sine sigillo, nec eciam scriptum aliquod in tabulis uel in cera nisi magistro uel priori prouinciali uel uicario.' For the (alleged) employment of the wax tablet in Alfonso X's *scriptorium*, see J. Gómez Pérez, 'Elaboración de la Primera Crónica General de España y su trasmisión manuscrita', *Scriptorium* 17 (1963), 234–6. Cf. R. H. and M. A. Rouse, 'The vocabulary of wax tablets' in *Vocabulaire du livre et de l'écriture au Moyen Age*, ed. O. Weijers, Turnhout 1989, 220–30; E. Lalou, 'Les tablettes de cire médiévales', *BÉC* 147 (1989) 123–40; *eadem*, 'Inventaire des tablettes médiévales et présentation générale' in *Les Tablettes à écrire de l'Antiquité à l'époque moderne*, ed. E. Lalou, *Bibliologia* 12, Turnhout 1992, 233–88, mentioning no Spanish examples. Cf. J. Trenchs Odena and M. J. Carbonell, 'Tablettes de cire aragonaises (xiie–xve siècle)', *BÉC* 151 (1993) 155–60.

24 It was not for purposes such as these that Elvira González had endowed the infirmary in 1274 with 'quanto e en Castro Nouo'. 'Que non sea metido enal saluo del allinar e del llaurar', she had stipulated (ACZ, 13/67).

25 Garments worn above the belt, presumably. According to the Rule, the giving and receipt of favours (*munuscula*) to and from men were specifically forbidden ('Rule', 341, 345).

26 *Bacallar*, 'sheep' (cf. *bellaco*: 'hombre de mala vida' (J. Corominas, *Diccionario crítico etimológico de la lengua castellana*, Madrid and Berne 1954, *s.v.*)); *caraça* (probably referring to her face rather than signifying the corollary of *carajo*, 'penis'); *asnal*, 'ass'. Similarly, Marina Rodríguez [5]: 'Turpia verba fuerunt prolata contra priorissam dicendo caraça o merina quod non habuerat bene prioratum'; Alda Eiménerez [9]: 'caraça et mastina'. The ladies' unladylike repertoire significantly extends the list of rude words culled from the *fueros* by H. Dillard, *Daughters of the Reconquest. Women in Castilian town society, 1100–1300*, Cambridge 1984, 170, where *aleusa* is described as 'often for men only' (cf. 'aleviosa' [6, 16]). María Alfónsez of León mentions 'bad and shameful songs' ('cantilenas malas et turpes') and Doña Margarita de Benavento one composed by Perona 'that enraged the prioress' [11, 12]. The Rule prohibiting 'turpem sermonem' ('Rule', 344) had not anticipated dirty ditties.

27 Nos. 2–5, 7–13, 15, 17–20, 25–30, 32. Cf. Bueno Domínguez's unaccountable statement, apropos the evidence of both Dª Perona and Dª Caterina de Zamora, that 'doña Gimena' was sub-prioress ('S. María de Las Dueñas', 97).

28 Might the sub-prioress perhaps be identified with Doña María de Valladolid, one of the ladies released from the stocks, or, more plausibly, because no one of this name was mentioned in July 1279, with Maria Geraldi, both of whom were in the rebel camp by 1280? (see below, note 40).

29 See above, p. 50.

30 See above, pp. 48, 52. There is the additional difficulty of separating the exploits of Marina Rodríguez [5] and the tight-lipped Marina Rodríguez of Toro [28].

31 See above, pp. 48, 51–2.

32 Jimena Rodríguez, receiving nine votes, including her own [21, 22, 27, 28, 29, 30, 31, 33, 34]; María de Sevilla four [21, 24, 31, 33]; Marina Domínguez de Toro three [23, 31, 33]; Marina Rodríguez one [24]; Stefanía Fernández one [34].

33 See above, p. 25.

34 See above, pp. 49, 50.

35 See above, p. 51.

36 See above, p. 48.

37 ACZ, 13/63 (11 October 1279); see above, p. 25 and note 118. The treasurer was now identified as 'F.'.

38 '... iustitia exigens quatinus ipse per annum et amplius animo indurato dampnabiliter contempserunt in animarum suarum periculo, plurimorum scandalum et dicti episcopi preiudicium et grauamen' (ACZ, 13/62 *Sua nobis* – the text of the executive summons, identifying the prioress as 'E[xemena]'). Cf. Peter Herde, *Audientia litterarum contradictarum. Untersuchungen über die päpstlichen Justizbriefe und die päpstliche Delegationsgerichtsbarkeit vom 13. bis zum Beginn des 16. Jahrhunderts*, ii, Tübingen 1970, 458, 524.

39 'a Doña Xemena que se dezia priorissa e estas otras monjas que eran con ella en su rebeldia (ACZ, 13/62 (31 March 1280)).

40 '. . . Stephanie Ferrandi, Dompne Marie de Ponte, Marine Roderiçi germane de Dompna Orobuena, Marine Dominiçi de Tauro, Elvire Dominiçi, Ygnes Dominiçi, Marie Sugerii, Stephanie Munionis, Dompne Velasquite, Marine Dominiçi de Çamora, Elvire Petri et Sançie Garssie consobrinis fratris Munionis, Marie Rinaldi, Marie Vincençii, Johanne Dominiçi, Teresie Arnaldi, Dompne Cataline de Benavento, Dompne Margarite eius germane, Dominice Johannis, Miorovida, Dompne Marie de Sevilla, Caterine de Çamora, Dompne Marie de Vallisoleto, Dompne Duriane, Marine Romani, Marine G[uter]ii, Marine Garssie et Marine Dominiçi eius filie, Marie Geraldi, Dompne Ysabel, Marine Johannis de Çamora, spiritum consilii sanioris . . .' (ibid.).

41 Domina Maria de Ponte; Ygnes Dominici; Marina Dominici de Çamora; Elvira Petri; Sançia Garssie; Dominica Johannis; *Doña Maria de Vallisoleto* [Valladolid]; *Doña Duriana*; *Marina Románez*; Marina Guterii; *Marina Garssie*; Marina Dominici; *Maria Geraldi*; *Doña Ysabel*; *Marina Johannis de Çamora*. (Names in italics are those of rebels delated by others in 1279.)

42 'sicque dicte sorores ejecte coacte sunt per plures annos extra dictum monasterium miserabiliter evagari' (*Reg. Hon. IV*, 147).

43 'se ploguer a mio sennor el obispo' (ACZ, 18/9 (April 1281)). The bishop kept a copy of the dean's will (*TB*, fos. 159ᵛ–160ᵛ).

44 AHN, Clero 3524/8 (Burgos, 16 April 1277); P. Madoz, *Diccionario geográfico-estadístico-histórico de España y sus provincias de Ultramar*, iv, Madrid 1846, 186. Both the Infante Sancho and the local *concejo* had actively supported the foundation. Since 1270 Franciscan communities of both men and women had also been established there under royal auspices (Fernández Duro, i. 455–7, 464). Cf. Linehan, *Spanish Church and the Papacy*, 213–15.

45 The grandson of Ordoño Alvarez de Asturias, *señor* of Noreña and in 1246 Fernando III's first *alcalde* of reconquered Jaén, and brother of Pero Alvarez de Asturias, Sancho IV's *mayordomo mayor*, Cardinal Ordoño was a member of one of the leading dynasties of the kingdom of León (Gaibrois, *Sancho IV*, i. 120, 125; S. de Moxó, 'De la nobleza vieja a la nobleza nueva', *Cuadernos de Historia* 3 (1969) 142–4). On account of his family's inclusion in Portuguese genealogies from as early as the 1280s (*Livros velhos de linhagens*, ed. J. M. Piel and J. Mattoso, Lisbon 1980, 27), however, and the fact that for almost three years before receiving the red hat from Nicholas III in March 1278 he had been archbishop of Braga, the cardinal continues to be accounted Portuguese (thus J. Veríssimo Serrão, *Portugueses no Estudo de Salamanca*, I *(1250–1550)*, Lisbon 1962, 25). But he had previously been abbot of the secular church of Husillos (Palencia). Moreover, there is no reason for supposing that he ever set foot in Portugal during the years of Afonso III's persecution of churchmen there (Linehan, *Spanish Church and the Papacy*, 294–5, where in accordance with historiographical tradition he is mistakenly referred to as 'Ordonho Alvares').

46 'Une charte léonaise intéressante pour l'histoire des moeurs', *Bulletin Hispanique* 25 (1923) 193–7.

47 Castro, who had copied it 'many years previously', refers to 'caj. D, leg. 3, n. 4'. It is now 13/60. Written in Spanish, it bears the same *signatura* as another letter of the same date from the prioress to the cardinal. This Latin letter is not a translation of the other. Though no less lachrymose, it is briefer. It states what the Spanish letter does not, that 'a certain prioress and nuns of her persuasion had previously petitioned Rome to have the convent placed under the friars' ('quod licet olim quedam Priorissa et alique moniales sibi in hac parte adherentes a sede Apostolica uoluerint obtinere Quod Monasterium nostrum subiceretur ordini fratrum predicatorum, ut uidelicet fratres predicatores in ipso monasterio uisitacionem, correctionem et alia secundum instituta sui ordinis obtinerent'), but that now, with the experience they had enjoyed of what that subjection involved, and in view of what the 'immoderate and intolerable excesses' of the friars' overstepping of the mark meant in terms of the safety of their souls, popular scandal, material loss and cost to their own reputation ('quia tamen pluribus exemplis et certis experimentis didiscimus quod sine periculo animarum et magno scandalo populi et rerum nostrarum dispendio et graui personarum infamia propter aliquorum fratrum predicatorum suos terminos transgrediencium inmoderatos et intollerabiles excessus'), they begged the cardinal to prevail upon the Holy Father to relieve them of that subjection. In this letter they would not particularise regarding the nature of these 'excesses'. Their proctor Gundisalvus Johannis had the details, as he did of other matters 'which for shame we dare not set down on paper' ('que propter pudorem scribere non audemus'). These 'details' (or some of them) are those contained in the letter translated in the text, the script of which is markedly rougher and more cursive than that of the Latin letter.

48 Cf. A. Jiménez Soler, 'La política española de Jaime II' in *Eine Festgabe zum siebzigsten Geburtstag ... Heinrich Finke* (Vorreformationsgeschichtliche Forschungen. Supplementband), Münster-i.-W. 1925, 184–6: an Aragonese critique referring specifically to the work of M. Gaibrois.

49 *Ungedruckte Dominikanerbriefe des 13. Jahrhunderts*, Paderborn 1891 – a work containing material for her subject which Gaibrois neglected to use.

50 'Fray Munio de Zamora', *Festgabe Finke*, 127–46, notes 57 bis, 58 bis. Cf. M. Gaibrois de Ballesteros, *Historia del reinado de Sancho IV de Castilla*, ii, Madrid 1928, 105.

51 Linehan, *Spanish Church and the Papacy*, 224–5. For Hinnebusch's allusion to the matter in 1965, see below, p. 106.

52 '... quod tam dilecte in Christo filie priorissa et conventus monasterii Sancte Marie Camorensis per priorissam soliti gubernari ordinis Sancti Augustini quam alie que in monasterio ipso processerunt easdem, decimas, terras, domos, vineas, prata, pascua, nemora, molendina, iura, iurisdictiones et quedam alia bona ad monasterium ipsum spectancia, datis super hoc litteris, interpositis iuramentis, factis renuntiationibus et penis adiectis, in

gravem ipsius monasterii lesionem, nonnullis clericis et laycis, aliquibus
eorum ad vitam, quibusdam vero ad non modicum tempus et aliis perpetuo
ad firmam vel sub censu annuo concesserunt, quorum aliqui super hiis
confirmationis litteras in forma communi a sede apostolica impetrasse
dicuntur. . .' (ACZ, 1/6, *Ad audienciam nostram*, 5 December 1279).

53 G. Barraclough, 'The chancery ordinance of Nicholas III, a study of the
sources', *Quellen und Forschungen aus italienischen Archiven und Bibliotheken*
25 (1933/4) 239, no. 16; P. Herde, *Beiträge zum päpstlichen Kanzlei- und
Urkundenwesen im dreizehnten Jahrhundert*, 2nd edn, Kallmünz 1967, 162–4.

54 ACZ, 1/6 (30 August 1280). Others too were ordered to present themselves:
Alfonso Garcés, Gonzalo Munionis and Rodrigo Rodríguez, knights of
Toro, and D. Miguel of Valladolid. They are named in a document issued
six days prior to the hearing in which María Martínez and the community
appointed García Pérez *clericus chori* of Zamora their proctor (ACZ, 13/65).

55 See above, p. 14.

56 See below, chapter six.

57 See above, p. 27.

58 *TB*, fos. 41ʳ–42ᵛ; ACZ, MS. 1415/10 bis, fos. 96ʳᵇ–97ᵛᵇ: the distribution
between the parties of rights of patronage to churches within the diocese
established by the arbitrator Fernando Alfónsez dean of Compostela 'post
multas et varias altercaciones'; Linehan, *Spanish Church and the Papacy*, 293;
Sánchez Rodríguez, 'La diócesis', 156–7.

59 'Item, diffinio quod nec episcopus per se uel capitulum per se aliquem
recipiant in socium uel in fratrem, siue proprio motu siue per litteras
apostolicas, nisi utrisque in capitulo congregatis . . .' (*TB*, fos. 42ʳ, 40ᵛ
(December 1268)); Linehan, Spanish *Church and the Papacy*, 260, 293.

60 *Ibid.*, fos 42ᵛ–43ʳ (?May 1286). Cf. 'Prestimonia annexa personatibus et
dignitatibus Ecclesie Zamorensis' (MS 1415/10 bis, fos 105ᵛᵇ–107ʳᵃ; Linehan,
Spanish Church and the Papacy, 260.

61 ACZ, *Liber constitutionum*, fos. 6ʳᵇ, 14ʳᵃ; Coria Colino, 'El pleito', 293.

62 *TB*, fos. 90ᵛ, 92ʳ ('et agora disso nos el obispo que dubdades se duuades
apreciar lo que ualian las casas quando gellas derribaron o quanto custarian
afaçer otras tales casas cuemo aquellas eran', May 1261); *Doc. zamoranos*,
nos. 157, 168, 171–2.

63 *TB*, fos. 71ᵛ–77ᵛ; ACZ, 15/33; Martín Rodríguez, *Campesinos vasallos*, 21–2.
Suero variously claimed to have spent two years and two months, and three
years and more (1263–6), in pursuit of justice 'per Romanam curiam et per
regem' (*TB*, fos. 163ʳ, 165ʳ; see also above, p. 22. In April 1265 Clement IV
issued five mandates addressed to the bishops of Astorga, León and
Salamanca, instructing them to enforce D. Suero's sentences on some forty
named 'laici de villa de Tauro et eius districtu' (ACZ, II.1a/3).

64 *TB*, fos. 14ᵛ–15ʳ (10 September 1272); ACZ, II.1a/13, II.1a/10 (mandates of
Nicholas III (*Sua nobis*, 1 May 1278) and Martin IV (*Conquestus est*, 7 May
1281), citing the nobleman Martín, son of Alfonso Tellez, of the diocese of
Palencia, 'super quibusdam domibus et rebus aliis ad mensam suam
episcopalem spectantibus').

65 ACZ, 4/2. Cf. Linehan, *Spanish Church and the Papacy*, 301.

66 ACZ, 6/1(a), 7 May 1266.

67 ACZ, 15/32; 9/15 ('por ruego de donna Maria Alfonso').

68 'Virgo quae Deum requirit non debet esse vulgaris, non debet esse in foro, non in plateis' (*Sermo* 52 'Ad puellas que nutriuntur cum mulieribus' (pt i, 53–4)); Linehan, *History and the Historians*, 517.

69 See above, pp. 49, 51; *Opus tripartitum*, 224. Cf. 'Rule', 344: 'Media culpa est si qua a . . . refeccione communi . . . ex causa minus racionabili remanserit.'

70 Thus too in the Lézat documentation 'a woman of any social level acting in a charter was normally described as "domina"' (Mundy, *Men and Women at Toulouse*, 37).

71 'Rule', 343.

72 Seven and four times a year respectively (*ibid.*, 341a).

73 'Priorissa cum duabus sororibus quas elegerit cum sibi expedire uidebitur sororibus absentibus scrutetur singulos lectos sororum, et si ibi inveniant aliquid . . .' (*ibid.*, 341b).

74 'denudata usque ad cingulum uapulet ad pedes singularum' (*ibid.*, 345a; cf. 345b, also the provisions in the constitutions of the sisters of Montargis, ed. Creytens, 'Les constitutions primitives', 78: 'denuo vapulet ad pedes singularum' – a very different proposition).

75 'Rule', 347–8.

76 ACZ, 13/58a, 13/68, 13/58b, 13/58. Seizure of their seal was one of the complaints made by the ladies in 1285 (see above, p. 3). Nothing of the sort had been alleged in 1279, however.

77 For Allariz see chapter six (pp. 137–40).

78 ACZ, 13/58.

79 Cf. Echániz Sans, *Las mujeres de la Orden de Santiago*, 60.

80 Fernández Duro, *Memorias históricas*, i. 428–30. Cf. Bueno Domínguez, 'S. María de las Dueñas', 102 n. 20. It was allowable for a convent of the order to exceed its number limits if the postulant's social standing was such that she could not be refused 'sine graui dampno uel scandalo' ('Rule', 342).

81 *Ibid.*, 342, 343. Cf. R. C. Trexler, 'Le célibat à la fin du Moyen Age: Les religieuses de Florence', *AÉSC* 27 (1972) 1342–4.

82 As alleged by Bishop Bruno of Olmütz in his 'Relatio' (1274), citing the Pauline prescription 'Let not a widow be taken into the number under threescore years . . . The younger widows refuse' (1 Tim.5.9, 11; Grundmann, *Religiöse Bewegungen*, 336 n. 33). The intuition of Bueno Domínguez that the younger nuns were recruited into rebellion by their seniors – 'que las que estaban en el movimiento de revuelta eran las dueñas más formadas y mayores y que empleaban la fuerza de las palabras y de los escritos entre las más jovenes porque eran las más indecisas a la hora de tomar posturas extremas de desobediencia' ('S. María de Las Dueñas', 97–8) – is indeed that writer's intuition.

83 As Graña Cid has had some success in doing in her analysis of the Clarissan communities of Córdoba and Seville: 'Las primeras clarisas

andaluzas. Franciscanismo femenino y reconquista en el siglo XIII', *AIA*, 2ª época 54 (1994) 694. See below, p. 162.

84 The distance from the cathedral to the convent takes fifteen minutes to cover downhill on a dry day, slightly more in the other direction, slightly less, presumably, for young nuns with friars in hot pursuit. I am assuming (with Represa, 'Génesis', 541 and map opp. p. 530) that the convent was situated in 1279 where it stands now, in the suburb of Carbañales to the south of the then new bridge, rather than (as the present community believes) a quarter of a mile further west at San Frontis. The convent established in 1264 was not at, but rather, was near ('iuxta') San Frontis. See Appendix 1.b.

CHAPTER THREE

These few short years make wondrous alterations
Particularly amongst sun-burnt nations
(Byron, *Don Juan*, canto I.LXIX)

*D*ESPITE continuing problems with the urban oligarchs of his cathedral city and the rural rebels centred on Toro, at the beginning of 1280 the bishop of Zamora ought at least to have felt confident that the rebels of Las Dueñas were in retreat. With the prior of Valladolid's investigation under way, the outcome was surely a foregone conclusion. Sex was bad, especially for women. That at least had been established. There was nothing more degrading to women than fornication, it had been said not long before – and said by the Dominican Master General himself, no less.[1]

A fortiori the friars who had dallied with the local ladies stood discredited too. Did not the findings of July 1279 provide the clearest possible evidence of that institutionalised hypocrisy for which the Dominicans' Parisian critics had been castigating them over almost three decades? Certainly, those findings had confirmed fears which Humbert de Romans had expressed as long ago as 1260. Urging the sisters to 'holy conversation', the Master General had beseeched them to avoid committing any act capable of bringing a posthumous blush to the founder's cheek. At the same time he had also reminded them of the risks associated with the 'immoderate reception of individuals'.[2] Now events at Las Dueñas (where in 1264 a community of twelve had been regarded as viable, yet by 1280 the insurgent party alone could muster some forty sisters) had confirmed that the one development was conducive to the other. The corollary of overcrowding, enunciated at the Barcelona General Chapter of 1261, was *familiaritas*.[3]

Just two months before the bishop of Zamora's descent upon Las

77

Dueñas, the brethren at large had again been alerted to the perils of undue familiarity: 'familiaritates incaute'. Thereafter barely a year went by without the issuing of a further solemn warning.[4] On no account were friars to enter convents of women, the Ferrara General Chapter decreed in 1290, 'except in cases of evident necessity'.[5] The prohibition was unequivocal. But when there was so little resemblance between the General Chapter's sense of 'evident necessity' and that by which brother Juan de Aviancos was driven in his late-flowering lust, it was also unenforceable. Moreover, in 1274 the General Council at Lyons had provided bishops from all parts of the Western Church with an opportunity to vent their collective spleen against the friars.[6] The ordinaries were in the ascendant, and the Ladies of Zamora and their paramours had been caught *in flagrante*.

Yet rather than receiving an exemplary penance, within seven years of the exposure of their activities, the Ladies of Zamora were being likened by the pope to the prudent virgins who had kept their lamps trimmed,[7] their paramours were being represented as the innocent victims of episcopal persecution, and the community whose infirmary, choir and oven had accommodated the scenes previously described was definitively incorporated into the Dominican Order. The 'prudent virgins' epithet was common form; it went with their admission to membership. In this case it was the admission to membership that was the miracle. But the miracle was one of those miracles that are assiduously striven for. It was none the less remarkable for that. Coming as it did so soon after the tradition of pontifical indulgence towards the rulers of Castile had been replaced by a policy of rigour and critical scrutiny, it was, indeed, all the more remarkable.

The earliest manifestation of the papacy's new approach belongs to the very year of the investigations at Las Dueñas. Although throughout July 1279 the attention of the city of Zamora may have been concentrated on the latest revelations from the local convent, elsewhere in the kingdom a rival and, for the kingdom's future, potentially more significant battle was being joined. For the first time since before 1212, a pope had set about bringing a king of Castile to book. Now that Alfonso X was no longer a contender for empire, Nicholas III was able to take him to task for the numerous and notorious liberties which, like his father before him, the king was accustomed to taking with the Castilian Church. In the previous March, a special nuncio, Bishop Pietro of Rieti, was dispatched to Alfonso X armed with a 'secret memorial' containing the Castilian bishops' denunciation of their monarch as a free-thinker manipulated by astronomers, augurs, soothsayers and Jews. Alfonso (they claimed) was committed to the systematic spoliation of their churches and of the Church itself. He had entrusted the sees of his kingdom to 'vile and idiot men'. Under his auspices illicit marriages were contracted. The 'keys of the Church' were held in contempt.[8] And the pope who earlier that year had forced Alfonso's son-in-law, Afonso III of Portugal, to a death-bed submission meant business. In 1279 Nicholas III was not to be fobbed off with verbal excuses. This time he was intent on establishing the real truth.[9] This time the pope was determined to get to the root of the matter.

Accordingly, on 29 July 1279, Alfonso wrote to his son the Infante Sancho from Seville, attaching a copy of the nuncio's articles of indictment together with their text in translation, and seeking the advice of those about the Infante who would have advice to give 'in a matter such as this'. Whereupon the advisers of the Infante, who two years later was to contract a marriage of the sort the bishops now told the pope so greatly offended their religious sensibilities (so far as we are aware without any of them registering a protest on this occasion) set about fabricating the sort of excuses which the pope had instructed their master not to attempt, made a singularly poor job of it, and in the version which has survived of their essay in prevarication abandoned the attempt altogether before reaching the really difficult part of the exercise.[10] Their inability to assemble a credible defence is not to be wondered at. As the prior and chapter of Osma protested when they were consulted on the matter in the autumn of that year, the fact was that what the pope said was true, and the king and the Infante Sancho knew it was.[11]

To the breakdown of the special relationship with Rome that had sustained the kings of Castile for generations there were now added the dire financial consequences of Alfonso's imperial adventures and the collapse of royal authority itself.[12] In the summer of 1279 the Infante Sancho appears still to have been providing his father with assistance. But that assistance was not to be forthcoming for much longer. With the face that masked his celebrated brain falling to bits,[13] the cancerous old king was finally cracking up and, with him, so was the government of his kingdom. In the spring of 1282 the son proclaimed open rebellion, attracting to his pseudo-cortes at Valladolid on 21 April all those elements of Castilian society with grudges against his father.

When, half-way through the ensuing civil war, the representatives of the endangered ecclesiastical species of bishops and abbots met at Benavente in May 1283 and gave voice to the various grievances which they had been harbouring since the beginning of Alfonso's reign, prominent in the list they presented were the 'molestations' which over the previous thirty years they had suffered at the hands of the mendicants.[14] The fact that when presenting Nicholas III with their *gravamina* in 1279 the same bishops had refrained even from mentioning the matter is an indication of their estimate of the influence wielded by the friars at both the king's court and the pope's.[15] Equally, their willingness to break their silence on the subject four years later suggests that the Infante's calculated rhetoric had persuaded them that that influence was about to be curbed.

It was an oddly assorted bunch of malcontents who assembled at Benavente and consoled themselves by harking back to the good old days of the Infante's grandfather Fernando III. And prominent amongst the gathering – soon to be swollen by that very embodiment of episcopal ineptitude, the bishop of Jaén, the extent of whose intellectual incompetence did not escape the choirboys of his cathedral[16] – and in the very city, moreover, in which the Ladies of Zamora had recently found refuge from him, was Zamora's bishop.[17] Hitherto usually a shrewd judge of the main chance, after almost thirty years in the service of Alfonso X, the king to whom he owed his entire advancement, the barometric D. Suero had attached himself to the rebel cause.

Possibly he had been thus predisposed ever since 1278, when the Infante had so decisively and, from the bishop's point of view, so satisfactorily intervened in his dispute with the *concejo* of his cathedral city.[18] If not, then the Infante's assurance at the Benavente assembly, 'that he would be true to him and help him and be with him against all the men of the world', and the grant to him of sums levied by Sancho on his church and his vassals, must have proved decisive.[19] The bishop of Zamora appeared to have timed his move to perfection. Admittedly, there was a price to be paid for insurgency, and in the following August this was stated, when Pope Martin IV eventually excommunicated the Infante and his adherents,[20] which had the effect of inhibiting D. Suero's litigation at Rome against the *concejo* of

Zamora, marauding noblemen[21] – and of course the Ladies of Zamora. But Martin IV was a creature of the mendicants anyway. Also, he was an old man. In opting for the young pretender, the veteran prelate whose Roman connexions dated back thirty years to the time of the *zamorano* Cardinal Gil Torres, and who was not without contacts of his own in the papal chancery,[22] doubtless persuaded himself that as usual he had chosen well.

But this time he had not. This time his judgement had deserted him. In common with all those others who read into the Infante's evocation of the golden age of his sainted grandfather a commitment to lifting the heavy yoke which Alfonso X had imposed upon them, D. Suero was soon to be disappointed. Already by the time of the Benavente meeting the Infante had given notice that the fiscal impositions upon churchmen itemised in 1279 were to continue *sine die*. As early as May 1282 he had been trading in ecclesiastical revenues, farming the *tercias* of the dioceses of Zamora, Salamanca, Ciudad Rodrigo and Coria to his *adelantado mayor* in Galicia, the layman Esteban Fernández.[23] Then, during the month of July 1283, just three months after the magnificent undertaking he had given to D. Suero, first he transferred to his wife María de Molina all the properties in Toro, Venialbo and Villamor which D. Suero had spent the previous thirty years accumulating, and then confiscated his property in its entirety.[24]

With Sancho's partisans in control of Zamora, Bishop Suero had moved as fast as most in the early weeks of 1282. On 4 May he was one of the six Leonese bishops and more than two dozen abbots who espoused the Infante's cause at Valladolid.[25] The signatures contained in all four margins of his copy of D. Suero's own copy of this declaration, and the remains of the thirty-three seals attached to it, testify to the press of newcomers clamouring to swell the ranks of the rebels whose names were listed in the text of the *pronunciamento* itself.[26] With his name inscribed in the text rather than the margins, the bishop of Zamora had moved fast, therefore. But the Ladies of Zamora – or rather the pro-episcopal rump of them – had moved faster still. On 10 April María Martínez and the convent had sent proctors to the Infante to seek his assistance in recovering the property which (they informed him) Doña Xemena and 'the other ladies who had left the convent' had prevailed upon Alfonso to appropriate.[27] The prioress's initiative is highly significant, both for what it tells of the actions of the pro-mendicant group since 1279 and for what it reveals of the remedies now being sought by their pro-episcopal opponents. By April 1282 the two sides within the Zamora community had followed the rest of the kingdom, polarising and attaching themselves respectively to the old king's fading regime and to his son's rising star. And in the process the bishop of Zamora had been bypassed, ignored and isolated.

Although D. Suero was not the only bishop to suffer at the hands of the new king,[28] he does seem to have suffered more than most. Why this was is far from clear. In view of the Infante's partiality for his old chancery colleague Ferrán Pérez, the dean of Seville notable for his addiction to conspiracy, sodomy and the hunt, it can hardly have been the bishop of Zamora's chancery background that gave offence.[29] Nor can it have been his earlier association with Alfonso X,[30] for, as we have seen, he had abandoned the old king sooner than most. It may have had something to do with D. Suero's long-running disputes with relatives of Sancho's queen, María de Molina.[31] But, whatever the reason, the new king's antipathy to the bishop knew no bounds. He found him insufferable. As he later admitted, it was 'on account of his hostility towards the bishop' that he had pronounced judgment against the bishop's church, and 'on account of the things the bishop had done' that he had deprived him of his estates at Fermoselle.[32]

On the occasion of his first visit to Zamora as king in October 1284 D. Suero was made painfully aware of the extent of his fall from favour. When Sancho assembled his closest associates around him the bishop of Zamora was not present. Now that Sancho was king he had no need of the bishop to whom as infante he had promised 'to be true . . . and to help . . . and to be with . . . against all the men of the world'. D. Suero had been spurned. In his own cathedral city, the hammer of the mendicants was not of the party. But the prior provincial of the Dominicans, Brother Munio, was.[33]

The sidelining of Bishop Suero was an ominous development for bishops generally, and over the following weeks the omens were confirmed. By the end of 1284 Sancho IV had fully restored the apparatus of oppression which the bishops who had supported him at Benavente had supposed that he was intent on dismantling. Payments had been authorised towards the costs of the Parisian education of a nephew of that hated symbol of the old regime, Fredulus, the former

82

bishop of Oviedo,[34] and the friars who had already received various marks of Sancho's favour were again basking in the affection in which they were held by every branch of Castile's divided royal family.[35] It seemed to be an invariable rule that, however the royal family divided, the mendicants emerged on the winning side.

For the convent of Las Dueñas, therefore, a favourable outcome to their dispute with the bishop was now only a matter of time. The election of Honorius IV in April 1285 settled the matter and sealed the bishop's fate. For while the new pope, yet another firm friend of the friars, offered the Zamora Dominicans a ready ear, the now ageing D. Suero was still prevented from reactivating the proceedings concerning the ladies which had been pending at the papal curia since 1272. As late as May 1281 he had been represented there by the formidable (and pricey) Aragonese proctor, Berengarius de Azanuy[36]. It was only in November 1286 that Martin IV's sentences against Sancho's recent partners in crime were lifted, on the grounds (cause gone, effect fails) that the former criminal whose rebellion had occasioned the former pope's sentences was now king of Castile.[37]

Though had he been aware of it (cause gone, effect fails), the pope's reasoning would have afforded D. Suero scant consolation. Having suffered all the effects of insurgency and enjoyed none of its rewards, all that was left to him in 1285 was to observe the mendicants' inexorable advance. In the autumn of that year, with the friars' account of recent events at Zamora prevailing at Rome, he was summoned there to explain himself. The archbishop of Toledo, Gonzalo Pérez, to whom the pontiff had entrusted the inquiry into the friars' grievances, was closely attached both to the Order and the king. His own metropolitan, the new archbishop of Compostela appointed by Honorius IV in May 1286, was yet another Dominican (though it might have been worse, it might have been Munio).[38] The bishop of Zamora had no hope of a fair hearing in Castile. By this stage, his only hope was Rome or death. By mid-May 1286 he was dead.[39]

Both the form and the content of the will he had drawn up on 11 May 1285 leave little doubt as to his state of mind during the last year of his life. It states no place of issue: a lapse wholly uncharacteristic of a man of Suero's chancery training. Describing himself conventionally enough as sound in body and mind ('corpore incolumis, mentis mee compos et in bona mea uoluntate'), in May 1285 D. Suero was 'in exile' from Zamora, apparently at or near Fermoselle and contemplating the prospect of being buried, not in the tomb he had constructed 'by the door of the chapel of San Nicolás' in his cathedral, but there in the place on which he had spent so much money and effort, had protected from his 'persecutors', and which he now adjured his successors and the chapter for ever to defend against the 'threats and terrors of princes and others'. These sentiments come at the end of what is in effect a great rambling diatribe with a couple of bequests added, which have very much the appearance of an afterthought. Though he had made an earlier will, more than four years before,[40] there was no mention of it in the 1285 testament. This has an urgent, almost hectic quality. Its pace is breathless, rather as if written on the road or while under siege – as perhaps it was. With the end approaching and time running out, D. Suero remembered Roncesvalles and the services he had received from Pedro Molasquid and his mother María Fernández.[41]

In a document of over 4,000 words, the bishop recapitulated many of the grievances which he had already recorded in his 'Inventory of improvements', refighting old fights and giving fresh vent to ancient resentments.[42] 'The moveables I have are mine', he insisted. Rancorous to the end, he could not mention any place within the diocese without being reminded of some slight or misprision from decades before. Thus the specification of property at Morales to pay for the oil for the lamps which were to burn in his memory in the cathedral served as cue for an extended *tour d'horizon* of the chapter's supine refusal to contribute to the fighting fund he had established at the very beginning of his pontificate for the recovery of Zamora's tithe income at Villardefrades from D. Alfonso de Molina,[43] and the recollection of the 300 maravedís he had spent on the case, this time remembered in old (that is to say 'good' money), all of thirty years before.[44]

While reliving the past, D. Suero nevertheless found time to provide for his own future in the hereafter and for the present welfare of those for whom he still cared. There were numerous anniversaries endowed, for himself chiefly, for his mother (but not his father), for Alfonso X whom he had betrayed (but not the son who had betrayed him),[45] for various *cofradías* (with a marked and characteristic preference expressed for the warrior Santiago), for his brother Juan Pérez and his brother's wife Maria Velasci, for innumerable servants and hangers-on, and notably for the Cistercian houses of Valparaíso,

Moreruela and San Miguel del Monte – notably because it was the abbots of these three monasteries who had attended the establishment of the Ladies' foundation and two of them who had been present at the inquiry in July 1279.[46] Inevitably the Ladies themselves were less favoured, as indeed were all Zamora's other mendicant communities. Even if they came to his funeral, there would only be a pittance for them,[47] while the Ladies themselves were set a further test – though in the excitement of the moment (if not for some other reason) the scribe's command of the Latin language failed him, leaving the Ladies lost both as to where they were and as to where their bishop wanted them, whether in or out of salvation.[48]

Regarding his own salvation the bishop had made prior arrangements with the principal religious orders, the mendicant orders included. In accordance with practices which seem to belong to the early eleventh century rather than the late thirteenth, his agents were to traverse the province of Compostela and mobilise the prayers and activate the grace which by their letters the monks and friars had previously promised.[49]

He had secured the future then, as best he could. But he had not protected his back. He had failed to allow for the possibility of a coup from within the chapter, which is what seems to have occurred some time before mid-March 1285 when García Pérez, canon of Zamora, is recorded as operating in Zamora as Suero's vicar.[50] The signs are that D. Suero had been displaced by a royal coup and that García Pérez had been put into the see to act as informal coadjutor until Suero either died or could be otherwise spirited away. As Bishop Martín González of Astorga demonstrated by the part he played in the downfall of the archdeacon of Oviedo Ferrán Alfonso two years later, there was no shortage of accomplices, even episcopal accomplices, willing to assist the process.[51]

Although the name of the bishop's vicar in the spring of 1285 is known, his identity remains uncertain. For there were two clerics named García Pérez active in Zamora in these years, both Bologna-trained and to that extent both beneficiaries of D. Suero's commitment to the education of the clergy of his church. The senior of them, who was present in the Italian city in June 1262, was already a canon of the church by that date, so cannot have been the same person as the García Pérez 'clericus çamorensis' who was there in the winter of 1268–9.[52] It was the canon of that name who sold the *aldea* of

Ricobayo to D. Suero in November 1276, and the 'clericus chori' whom the prioress María Martínez and the convent of Las Dueñas appointed as their proctor at the dean of Salamanca's hearing four years later.[53] There is no knowing which of these two was the 'García Pérez canonigo' who appeared before the rebel Infante's judges in January and April 1283 as proctor of the bishop and chapter,[54] or which of them it was who within two years of that had thrown in his lot with the king and supplanted the bishop. And in the bishop's will there was no legacy for either of them.

There were too many men of this name active in Sancho IV's chancery to enable the renegade's subsequent career to be traced.[55] No such uncertainty surrounds the identity of Bishop Pedro II, don Suero's successor in the see of Zamora, however. As the will he made in July 1302 reveals, he was Pedro Benítez, the *magisterscolarum* of the church whom we have encountered more than once already in the course of this narrative, the nephew both of Suero's predecessor, Bishop Pedro I, and of Master Esteban (abbot of Husillos, Palencia, and himself the nephew of Cardinal Gil Torres).[56] Bishop Pedro II's promotion to the see, therefore, represented a reversion to Zamoran type, a reassertion of local connexions after its thirty-year occupation by that stormy man from the south. Fifty years earlier the career of this cleric of many uncles had been launched by powerful patrons at the court of Innocent IV.[57] In 1259 it had been he, already *magisterscolarum*, who had refused Rodrigo Peláez's request for the return of his wife, Doña Elvira the co-foundress of Las Dueñas, and twenty years after that had been a member of the episcopal commission which had investigated the convent's affairs.[58]

So Bishop Pedro II had a complete knowledge of local affairs, and of the affairs of the Ladies of Zamora in particular. But as well as that he was a man of wide horizons. In 1302 he left 500 maravedís to the church of Palencia (D. Suero would have deeply disapproved), as well as 200 to S. María la Mayor at Toro for a commemoration on the feast-day of San Antolín, Palencia's patron saint (a symbolic act if ever there was one), another 200 to the secular abbacy of Husillos in that diocese, and a further 1,500 to the church of Salamanca.[59] The intellectual tastes of the youthful scholar whose 'merita scientie' had been lauded by Innocent IV fifty years before were very different from those of his predecessor. They embraced medicine as well as law[60] (the speciality of that Master Gil who had been *cantor* of Zamora before joining the Dominicans, and was yet another of his uncles).[61] D. Suero's library had been a library of books of law and theology. His will – and it is to be noted that in 1281 as in 1285 alone amongst the major dignitaries of the church the name of Pedro Benítez is missing from his list of executors – had been written in Latin. Pedro II's was in the vernacular. Don Suero Pérez died at the cusp of a new age and his vendetta against the ladies died with him.[62]

Thus the tale that the pope might have heard from the man to whom it is difficult to warm but with whom it is impossible not to sympathise remained untold. Instead, in August 1286, Honorius IV definitively incorporated the Ladies of Zamora into the Dominican Order and committed them to the friars' care.[63]

There was one last formality to be attended to. It was stipulated that the ladies' incorporation required the bishop's consent.[64] The outcome was never in doubt, of course. Even so, *Affectu sincero* had been retrospectively abrogated, and its provisions silently reversed. As D. Suero had always insisted, and the lists of convents recorded at the Bordeaux General Chapter in 1277 confirmed,[65] the Ladies of Zamora had not been incorporated earlier, after all. In 1286 the episcopal position was preserved and D. Suero posthumously vindicated. Honorius IV did not endorse the convent's status. He conceded it *de novo* to a community which claimed already to be voluntarily observing certain of the Order's rules and now wished for formal association,[66] and he did so subject to the granting of approval by the local bishop. In the circumstances, the granting of approval was, of course, no more than a formality. In view of the accord between pope and king, in this case there can have been no question of assent being refused.

Even so, bishop and chapter did what they could to limit the damage. At the urgent insistence of Sancho IV (who was in the vicinity at the time), in mid-February 1288 they duly surrendered to the friars the 'care and burden' of the sisters. They did so, they stated, 'of their free will'.[67] But they took care to retain undiminished the rights of the church of Zamora as well as tithes and other payments due from those parishes in which the convent had possessions. Pressured though they were, on this point bishop and chapter were insistent, and their insistence constitutes a further tribute of a sort to the prelate whom the ladies had outmanoeuvred. For although the deed of 1288 was indeed an act of capitulation, its inclusion of a reference to Innocent IV's decretal *Volentes* made it an altogether more professional piece of work than the original agreements which had led to all the trouble. To no one in 1264 had it occurred to invoke *Volentes*, with the assurances that that measure granted the ordinaries in their dealings with exempt communities.[68] Its inclusion in the settlement of 1288 is not the only evidence that survives from these years of the greater familiarity and increasing facility with the canon law that the canons of Zamora had acquired in the course of the career of the worldy-wise prelate who had sent them to school.[69]

None the less, capitulation it was. And thereafter the ladies flourished. In August 1290 – a year after the archdeacon of Zamora, Pedro Anays, had felt able to bequeath the modest sum of 10 maravedís 'alas doñas de allende rrio' without fear of offending his bishop[70] – Sancho IV took the convent of Las Dueñas under his protection. Out of consideration for the prioress of the place (his cousin, *cormana*, Doña Blanca who, such were the complications of his family relationships, was also his sister-in-law), the king granted the sisters a wide range of fiscal privileges and confirmed Honorius IV's licence to them to receive and retain property contrary to the custom and statutes of the Dominican Order.[71] In 1297 the young Fernando IV confirmed his father's privilege, and in 1315 Alfonso XI (also young at the time) did so too.[72] In July 1302 Bishop Pedro II bequeathed 'the friaresses across the river' the sum of 50 maravedís.[73] 'And with this', according to the Order's seventeenth-century historian, 'the differences which the nuns and the convent of Saint Dominic had had with the bishops [*sic*] and chapter of the church of Zamora came to an end'.[74]

As so they did. But the settlement of February 1288 was far from being the end of the story.

Notes

1 'Circa has autem notandum quod inter omnia genera peccatorum nullum est quod ita vilificet mulierem sicut peccatum fornicationis. Item nullum est adeo damnosum, quia per istas mulieres innumerabiles animae capiuntur a diabolo' (Humbert de Romanis, *Sermo* 51 (Venice 1603, pt i, 52)).
2 *Litt. encyc.* 57.
3 *Ibid.*, 59.
4 *Ibid.*, 114, 118, 132.
5 *Acta cap. gen.*, 257.
6 *Litt. encyc.* 96–100; Emery, 'The Second Council of Lyons and the mendicant orders', 257–60.

7 'Apostolice sedis benignitas prudentes virgines que se parant accensis lampadibus . . .' (*Reg. Vat.* 43, fo. 156ʳᵛ (*Reg. Hon. IV*, 600)).

8 Peter Linehan, 'The Spanish Church revisited: the episcopal *gravamina* of 1279', in B. Tierney and P. Linehan, eds, *Authority and Power. Studies on medieval law and government presented to Walter Ullmann on his seventieth birthday* (Cambridge 1980), 127–47 (reprinted in *Spanish Church and Society*).

9 'non verbalem tantummodo set realem . . . veritatem' (*Reg. Nich. III*, 739). Cf. Almeida, *História da Igreja em Portugal*, i. 194–8.

10 Linehan, 'Spanish Church revisited', 133 n. 27, 137.

11 'Que bien sabien el Rey e don Sancho que lo que el Papa dizie que verdat era e derecho' (Burgo de Osma, Biblioteca del Cabildo, cód. 8, fo. 201ᵛ (*ibid.*, 138)).

12 'Agora fago uos saber que es mester muy grand auer pora estos fechos grandes en que so, et senalada mientre pora esta guerra delos moros que es tangran seruiçio de dios e tan grand onrra e pro de nos e de toda nuestra terra', Alfonso wrote to the *concejo* of Toro in August 1279 (ACZ, 9/15). Cf. M. A. Ladero Quesada, *Fiscalidad y poder real en Castilla (1252–1369)*, Madrid 1993, 62.

13 M. E. Presilla, 'The image of death and political ideology in the *Cantigas de Santa Maria*' in *Studies on the 'Cantigas de Santa Maria': Art, Music, and Poetry. Proceedings of the International Symposium on the 'Cantigas de Santa Maria' of Alfonso X, el Sabio (1221–1284) in commemoration of its 700th anniversary year – 1981* (New York, 19–21 November), ed. I. J. Katz and J. E. Keller, Madison, Wisc. 1987, 403–57, especially 433–40; R. P. Kinkade, 'Alfonso X, *Cantiga* 235, and the events of 1269–1278', *Speculum* 67 (1992), 284–323.

14 'quod adhibeatur remedium super molestationibus predicatorum et minorum quas cotidie inferunt ecclesiis et clero et monasteriis, iura eorum contra suum ordinem indebite usurpanda' (*MHE*, ii. 96).

15 The 'new order or religion' complained of on that occasion ('Item instituit auctoritate propria novum ordinem seu religionem quod esse de iure non potest, cuius occasione ecclesie multipliciter aggravantur' (Linehan, 'Spanish Church revisited', 145)) seems to have referred to the military order of S. María de España (*idem, History and the Historians*, 514–15).

16 *Idem, Spanish Church and the Papacy*, 235; see above, p. 24.

17 *MHE*, ii. 97.

18 Coria Colino, 'El pleito', 292–6; Procter, *Curia and Cortes*, 143; see above, [p. 20].

19 Coria Colino, 'El pleito', 297 (10 April 1283); Hernández, *Rentas* i. 473 (18 March 1283).

20 A. Ballesteros y Beretta, *Alfonso X el Sabio*, Barcelona 1963, 1026 ff. When in January 1283 Alfonso had asked him to send a legate to Castile, the pope had refrained from intervening because he was still awaiting information from the Castilian bishops (*Reg. Mart. IV*, 300).

21 On 7 May 1281 Martin IV had instructed Geraldus Laurentii (archdeacon

of Neiva, Braga) to compel the *concejo* of Zamora to comply with the Infante Sancho's September 1278 arbitration of their differences with the bishop and chapter, and on the same day had brought the nobleman Martín Alfonso to book (*Sua nobis* (ACZ, II, 2a/10)); see above, note 64 to chapter two.

22 Linehan, *Spanish Church and the Papacy*, 294–5, 302–4. For the papal scribe *Bernardus Zamorensis* (*fl.* 1276–8), notable for the fineness of his calligraphy, see *ibid.* 295 n. 6; G. F. Nüske, 'Untersuchungen über das Personal der päpstlichen Kanzlei 1254–1304', *Archiv für Diplomatik* 20 (1974) 185–6; B. Barbiche, *Les Actes pontificaux originaux des Archives Nationales de Paris*, ii, Vatican City 1978, 496; W. Hilger, *Verzeichnis der Originale spätmittelalterliche Papsturkunden in Osterreich 1198–1304*, Vienna 1991, no. 497; T. Schmidt, *Die Originale der Papsturkunden in Baden-Württemberg 1198–1417*, Città del Vaticano 1993, 622.

23 For three years at 60,000 *maravedís* per annum (AC Toledo, O.12.B.I.9). For the *tercias* and the abuse of royal appropriation since the reign of Fernando III, see Linehan, *Spanish Church and the Papacy*, 111–12, 121.

24 'ala reyna donna Maria todo lo que el obispo de Camora auje en Toro e en Venjaluo e en Villamaor e los lugares desu termino asi de çelleros commo de pan e de uino' (Gaibrois, *Sancho IV*, i. p. cxlix); 'Johan Rroyz juiz de Camora auie a recabdar las rentas delos çelleros e todos los otros derechos dela mesa del obispo de Camora' (*ibid.*, p. clxxv).

25 *Cronica de Alfonso X*, 61a; *MHE*, ii. 68–9.

26 ACZ, 13/23.

27 ACZ, 13/66: letter empowering Pedro Pérez and Alfonso Eanes 'pora pedir a nuestro Senor el Inffant don Sancho merçed e restitucion delos bienes et delos heredamientos que tomaron a nos e a nuestro monesterio por cartas de nuestro Senor el Rey et ... pora pedir esta merçed e esta restitucion a nuestro Senor el Inffant ... e pora recibirla e pora monstrarle elos grauamientos elos danos e elos menoscabos que nos e nuestro Monesterio recibimos por rraçon delas cartas que dona Xemena por si et por las otras donas que saliron del dito monesterio gano de nuestro Senor el Rey ... et otros danos e otros males que recebimos nos e nuestro monesterio por cartas de nuestro Senor el Rey' (Zamora, 10 April 1282).

28 In August 1283 the episcopal rents of the vacant see of Salamanca for the period Easter 1283–Easter 1284 were farmed to Diego Pérez, the Infante's *escriuano*, for the sum of 30,000 *maravedís* (AC Toledo, I.4.O.I.80).

29 Linehan, *Spanish Church and the Papacy*, 230–31.

30 As suggested by Gaibrois, 'Fray Munio de Zamora', 142 n. 61.

31 The 'nobilis vir Martinus natus nobilis viri Aldefonsi Tellii Palentini diocesis', with whom D. Suero had been in dispute in May 1281 (see above, note 64 to chapter two), was María's maternal uncle (Gaibrois, *Sancho IV*, i. 29). In the mid-1250s, as he recalled in May 1285, Suero had been locked in combat with Alfonso de Molina concerning tithe income in the area bounding the dioceses of Zamora and Palencia. As usual, he had had no assistance from his chapter who had been overawed by 'regalis potestas' (see

above, p. 84). But in view of what was to come, the chapter of Zamora was well advised not to get involved in the bishop's battles. For as well as being his great uncle, by 1284 Alfonso de Molina was also Sancho IV's father-in-law.

32 'por sanna que auya al obispo don Suero'; 'por cosas que fizo' (Gaibrois, *Sancho IV*, i. 128; iii. no. 422).

33 The record of the occasion was published in garbled form by T. Rymer, *Foedera*, I. ii, London 1816, 649 ('frater Diurno fratrum ordinis praedicatorum in regnis Hispann' prior provincial' . . . Actum simor' die Martis, decimo Octobris, anno domini MCCLXXXIV').

34 *Ibid.*, p. clxxvi. This was Jofré, archdeacon of Ribadeo (Oviedo). See above, p. 56. By 1284 Fredulus himself had been translated to the see of Le Puy.

35 Gaibrois, *Sancho IV*, i, pp. clvi–clvii, iii, nos. 16–18 (Salamanca OP, Béjar OFM, Zamora O.S. Clare). While at Zamora in October 1284 Sancho confirmed all the privileges of the Franciscans of the province of Santiago (M. Rodríguez Pazos, 'Privilegios de Sancho IV a los franciscanos de la provincia de Santiago (1284) y de Castilla (1285)', *AIA*, 2ª época 36 (1976) 533–4).

36 ACZ, 11/10; Peter Linehan, 'Spanish litigants and their agents at the thirteenth-century papal curia', in S. Kuttner and K. Pennington, eds, *Proceedings of the Fifth Congress of Medieval Canon Law . . . 1976*, Vatican City 1980 (reprinted in Linehan, *Past and Present in Medieval Spain*, Aldershot 1992), 497.

37 'attendentes quod cessante causa si etiam affuisset cessare debet effectus' (*Reg. Hon. IV*, 808).

38 For the appointment of Rodrigo González de León, see *Reg. Hon. IV*, 536. See below, note 46. to chapter four

39 See above, p. 3, and note 115 to chapter one. The copy of the September 1285 mandate in the papal register (Reg. Vat. 43, fo. 41^r (*Reg. Hon. IV*, 147)) has the words 'S[uggerius] ep[iscopus]' inserted between the words 'ven. f. n.' and 'Zamorren'. The reason for this may have been a concern on the papal registrator's part not to make Suero's successor responsible for Suero's alleged actions. (Registration might occur as much as three months after issue of a letter (E. Pásztor, 'Contributo alla storia dei Registri Pontifici del secolo XIII', *Bullettino dell' "Archivio Paleografico Italiano"*, 3rd ser. 1 [1962] 73.))

40 ACZ, 12/16, recording the agreement of 'P. Johannis decanus, Alfonsus Petri cantor, Sthephanus Petri archidiaconus, Martinus Vincencii thesaurarius' to act as his executors (Toro, 23 January 1281). The same 'exequtores et deffensores testamenti mei' are invoked *ex officio* in 1285: 'decanum, cantorem et archidiaconum de Thauro et thesaurarium et eorum successores' (ACZ, 12/14).

41 'Volo insuper et mando quod si contingat me in hoc exilio decedere reponatur corpus meum in ecclesia sancti Romani que est in castro de Fremoselle. Et nec ipsum castrum nec corpus meum capitulo Zamorensi uel alicui uiuenti traditur nisi episcopo Zamorensi uel electo canonice

confirmato [. . . et] castrum ipsum traditur et corpus meum sepeliendum in
monumento meo que est fabricatum in ecclesia cathedrali. Et quia castrum
de Fremoselle cum uilla et cum aliis circumadiacentibus possessionibus
acquisiui et hedificia quantum potui consumaui multis laboribus et espensis
et ibidem cum dei auxilio a persecutoribus deffendi me et iura ecclesie
Zamorensis, et in posterum periculosis temporibus [uolens] ecclesie
refugium et congruam deffensionem et priuilegiorum et aliorum bonorum
conseruationem habere idcirco protestor et contestor coram deo et angelis
et omnibus sanctis suis quod successores et socii propter minas uel terrores
principum seu aliorum predictum castrum nunquam alienent sed semper
munire et dominio ecclesie penitus conseruent et faciant fideliter custodiri.
Item mando duo milia morabitinorum et diuidantur per illos qui alias
remuneracionem uel legatum aliud non habuerunt. Hec autem diuisio inter
eos fiat secundum deum et merita et seruicia personarum. Item lego .L.
morabitinos hospitali roscideuallis conuertendos in aliquibus possessionibus
uel refectionibus loci sui apud Taurum. Item mando Petro Molaquid .C.
morabitinos et Marie Fernandi matri sue .L. morabitinos' (*ibid.*). For the
connexions between Roncesvalles and Zamora and Roncesvalles'
encomiendas at Zamora and Toro, see M. I. Ostolaza, *Colección diplomática
de S. María de Roncesvalles (1127–1300)*, Pamplona n. d., 373–4.

42 See above, pp. 21–2.

43 ACZ, 12/14: '. . . ego condolens in ipsa nouitate promocionis mee de
occupacione huiusmodi uiolenta significaui capitulo Zamorensi quod si me
uellent expensis et aliis adiuuare laborarem pro uiribus ut dicta tercia
pontificalis a Palentina ecclesia extraheretur et ad ius et proprietatem
Zamorensis ecclesie perueniret. Videntes autem maiores et seniores capituli
negocium esse magnum et aduerssarios nimis diuites et potentes
responderunt quod de tam ardua causa nolebant se intromittere cum
dictam terciam Palentina ecclesia tanto tempore retinuisset quod iam
uidebatur quondam perscripsisse, nec uolebant esse participes honeris uel
honoris, maxime cum iam tenerent dictam terciam per regalem potenciam
confirmatam. Ego autem in domino confidens adgressus sum negocium
meis sumptibus et expensis non minimis et cum dei auxilio et romane
ecclesie iusticia et cum fauore domini Regis in dicta causa obtinui
antequam ad Zamorensem ecclesiam uenirem nec reditus perciperem de
eadem. Et ut in pace dictam terciam retinerem et cum ecclesia Palentina et
cum domino Alfonso de Molina, qui tunc temporis dictam terciam per
Palentinam ecclesiam detinebat, scandala in posterum non haberent et ut
uexaciones redimerem solui eisdem multam peccunie quantitatem.'

44 *TB*, fos. 164ʳ, 186ʳ (Dec. 1255); cf. *Doc. zamoranos*, no. 154.

45 ACZ, 12/14: 'Pro anniuersario domini Regis Alfonsi domini F. illustris Regis
filii, patris domini Sancii, in crastinum Sancti Clementis faciendi'. The
failure to describe 'dominus Sancius' as king is notable but may not be
deliberate, any more than was the failure to correct the date of Alfonso X's
commemoration (24 November) from that of his birth (23 November), as in
the earlier will presumably, to the anniversary of his death. In 1295 Sancho

IV was more punctilious, vindictively perhaps, choosing to confirm Alfonso X's grant of Fermoselle (to the income of which Suero had charged the royal anniversary) on 23 November (*TB*, fos. 95^v–6^v).

46 'Item lego alios ducentos morabitinos monete de la guerra monasterio Vallisparadisi ad emendum aliquid pro pitancia danda in festo sancti Bernaldi pro anniuersario matris mee. Item mando quod dentur pitancie tempore obitus mei monasterio de Morerola et monasterio Vallisparadisi et monasterio sancti Michaelis de Monte' (*ibid.*). Cf. pp. 13, 44 above.

47 ACZ, 12/14: 'Item mando quod dentur pitancie ... conuentui fratrum minorum et conuentui fratrum predicatorum si ad sepulturam meam uenerint. Et conuentui minorissarum ...

48 'Et conuentui monialium sancte Marie ciuitatis Zamorensis si ad ecclesiam Zamorensem redierint ab salute [*sic*].'

49 'Item mando quod deputentur aliqui fideles clerici uel laici cum sufficientibus expensis qui discurrant per episcopatus regni Legionis et per alios de Castella et de Portugalia qui sunt de prouincia Compostellana et per maiores ordinum Cisterciensium, premonstratensium, predicatorum et minorum tam in regno quam extra ut beneficia et oraciones pro me deo sollicite exsoluant. Sic idem ordines pro me tamquam pro fratribus suis per suas litteras exsoluere liberaliter promisserunt' (*ibid.*).

50 Ostolaza, *Colección diplomática de Roncesvalles*, 380.

51 'Credendum est potius suggestionibus callidis emulorum per subreptionis astutiam quam ex deliberatione uestri consilii manauisse', Cardinal Jordan de Ursinis wrote to Sancho on this occasion concerning certain royal letters directed against the archdeacon: see Linehan, *Spanish Church and the Papacy*, 231–2; idem, *History and the Historians*, 473. Sancho IV's court was notorious for its rumour-mongering and smear campaigns. See Gaibrois, *Sancho IV*, i. 88–114.

52 I. da Rosa Pereira, 'Livros de direito na Idade Media', *Lusitania Sacra* 7 (1964–6) 26; *Chartularium Studii Bononiensis*, VIII. 149. For other references to 'Garsias Petri clericus çamorensis' in 1268–9 see Pérez Martín, 'Estudiantes zamoranos en Bolonia', 37–8, whose conflation of the two men produces a single individual active for an improbable span of sixty-six years. 'Garsias Petro canonicus çamorensis' was at Bologna again in July 1273 (Pérez Martín, 57).

53 ACZ, 16/14, 13/65.

54 Coria Colino, 'El pleito', 298, 300.

55 Gaibrois, *Sancho IV*, iii, pp. ccclxxvi, cdlxxv. For 'Garçi Perez de Zamora', recipient of revenue from the Badajoz *judería* in 1290, see F. J. Hernández (ed.), *Las rentas del rey. Sociedad y fisco en el reino castellano del siglo XIII*, i, Madrid 1993, 369.

56 ACZ, 12/15. His bequests included anniversaries in the church of Palencia 'por el obispo don Pedro nuestro tio' – one of them on 5 March, perhaps the day of his death – and another for himself in the church of Husillos. Two of the anniversaries he established for himself were on the feast-day of Saint Benedict. His colleague as co-executor of the Spanish cardinal's will

had been the future Pope Nicholas III: see Linehan, *Spanish Church and the Papacy*, 217n. (J. M. Ruiz Asencio, *Colección documental del Archivo de la Catedral de León*, VIII *(1230–1269)*, León 1993, no. 2276), 278.

57 Quintana Prieto, *Documentación pontificia de Inocencio IV*, nos. 727, 735.

58 See above, p. 4, note 14 to chapter two.

59 ACZ, 12/15.

60 'Mandamos quelas degretales que ffuron del abbade Mestre Esteuan que empresteymos a Fernand Alfonso nuestro sobrino que ffuron estimadas en çient marauedis delos coronados que dey los çient marauedis o las degretales. Et la Summa de Grauffedo [*sic*: the work referred to is Goffredus de Trano, *Summa super titulis decretalium*] e los liuros dela mediçina que y acharon que los uendan e senon achegaren las degretales e la summa e los liuros dela medicina a seysçientos marauedis que los cunplan delo nuestro' (*ibid.*).

61 In his memory he endowed three anniversaries in the cathedral from the proceeds of the houses which Master Gil had bequeathed to him. See above, p. 5.

62 Cf. the record of the July 1279 proceedings itself in which, in addition to rendering terms of abuse in the vernacular, the scribe is inconsistent in respect of the conjunction 'or': *o* or *uel* [4, 24].

63 'ut sub magisterio et doctrina magistri et prioris [Yspanie] predictorum qui pro tempore fuerint debeatis decetero permanere, illis gaudentes priuilegiis que ordini predicto ab apostolica sede concessa sunt uel in posterum concedentur' (Reg. Vat. 43, fo. 156^{rv} (*Reg. Hon. IV*, 600)).

64 'dummodo venerabilis fratris nostri . . . episcopi Zamorensis loci diocesani accedat assensus' (*ibid.*).

65 These mentioned just two in the Spanish province, Madrid and Caleruega. By 1303 there were four more (Chelas, Lisbon, Zamora, Segovia) (Quétif-Échard, *Scriptores*, i. pp. i, iv).

66 'Cum igitur sicut ex parte uestra fuit propositum coram nobis uos incluse corpore in castris claustralibus mente tamen libera deuote domino famulantes de institutionibus ordinis fratrum predicatorum illas que uobis competunt laudabiliter hactenus duxeritis obseruandas, et committi . . . magistro et . . . priori prouinciali yspanie ipsius ordinis affectetis. . .' (Reg. Vat. 43, fo. 156^{r}).

67 Zamora, Archivo de Las Dueñas, dated 'XV kal. marcii anno domini M.CC.LXXXVII' (Appendix III). In February 1287 the see of Zamora was still vacant (M. Férotin, *Recueil des chartes de l'abbaye de Silos*, Paris 1897, 286; Gaibrois, *Sancho IV*, i. 174; iii. nos. 179–85).

68 Appendix III; Spanish summary in J. López, *Tercera parte de la Historia General de Sancto Domingo y de su Orden de Predicadores*, Valladolid 1613, 240–1. There is a mystery about this record which is a photograph bearing a certificate, issued by the *notario del obispado de Zamora* in November 1981 at the request of the convent, stating it to be a true copy of the 'original'. Where this original had come from, and where it is now, no one can say, or has said. Two years later the nuns did not even know the name of the

Dominican friar who had produced it (Dr Francisco Cantelar to the Author, 9 March 1983). Moreover, in 1987, only the photograph of the document's dorse could be found (Dr Heath Dillard to the Author, 12 May 1991). And my own visit to Las Dueñas in September 1996 proved equally fruitless. However, from the photograph of the *face* of the photograph kindly procured for me by Dr Cantelar in 1983 it is clear that the original is (or was) an authentic instrument. Regarding the 'decretalis novella de privilegiis que incipit *Volentes*' (VI 5.7.1 *de privilegiis*; Friedberg, ii. 1082–3), see S. Kuttner, 'Die Konstitutionen des ersten allgemeinen Konzils von Lyon', *Studia et documenta historiae et iuris* 6 (1940) 118–19.

69 In striving against clerics and laymen litigating against it, the chapter of Zamora had taken account of the provisions 'in decretali *de postulando* qui incipit "Cum sacerdotis"' [X 1.37.3 (Friedberg, ii. 211)] (ACZ, *Liber constitutionum*, fo. 2ra (December 1268)). Cf. A. Pérez Martín, 'Estudiantes zamoranos en Bolonia', *Studia Zamorensia* 2 (1981) 31–40.

70 ACZ, 18/10 (31 August 1289).

71 'Por fazer bien e merced a dona Blanca nuestra cormana priora del monesterio de las duenas de Çamora dela orden delos predicadores e a todo el conuento desse mismo logar', the king exempted the *heredades* of the nuns from liability for payment of all taxes and tribute other than 'moneda forera' (Huete, 20 Aug. 1290: Zamora, Archivo de Las Dueñas). Doña Blanca was the sister of Maria de Molina (A. Benavides, *Memorias de D. Fernando IV de Castilla*, i, Madrid 1860, 681). López, 237, states that she had taken the habit there. Cf. the pope's provision: 'Liceat uobis redditus et possessiones recipere ac ea libere retinere, non obstante contraria consuetudine uel statuto ipsius ordinis [OP] confirmatione sedis apostolice uel quacumque firmitate alia roboratis' (Reg. Vat. 43, fo. 156r).

72 Zamora, 4 October 1297; Burgos, 11 October 1315: Zamora, Archivo de Las Dueñas.

73 'A las ffrayras de alende Rio cincuenta moravedis' (ACZ, 12/15). Similar sums were left to the local Franciscans and Dominicans, and 100 maravedís to the Clarissas.

74 López, 241.

CHAPTER FOUR

There is a tide in the affairs of women
Which taken at the flood leads – God knows where.
(Byron, *Don Juan*, canto VI.II)

SOME TIME in the late 1280s knowledge of the events that had pre-ceded their incorporation into the Dominican Order, and of the role in those events of one individual in particular, began to seep into the public domain. Within just a few months of the bishop and chapter's acceptance of the inevitable, the Ladies of Zamora were casting their shadow across a wider stage.

History does not record the fate of those of the ladies of Las Dueñas who had remained loyal to the bishop through the tempestu-ous 1270s. It will be remembered, however, that in July 1281 their leader, the embattled María Martínez, had provided Cardinal Ordoño Alvarez with a graphic account of their recent tribulations and had begged him to intervene with Pope Martin IV to ensure their deliver-ance from 'further menaces and misery at the hands of the friars of the Order of Preachers'.[1]

In her tearful recollection of 'the things that brother Munio and the other Dominicans did', María Martínez had mentioned just one name – that of Brother Munio. And from her manner of referring to him it is clear that there was no possibility of any uncertainty as to which Brother Munio she meant. There was no danger of mistaken identity because there was only one Brother Munio of Zamora: the Brother Munio who at the Florence General Chapter just seven weeks before María Martínez wrote her letter had been elected prior of the Spanish province of the Order.

Having taken the habit in 1257 at the age of twenty, in 1281 Munio of Zamora had been a Dominican friar for twenty-four years.[2] So when the troubles began in earnest at Las Dueñas the 'frei Nunno' who had been one of the many Dominican witnesses of Doña Elvira's profession of obedience to Bishop Suero in April 1264 was in his early thirties, and therefore qualified both to hear confessions and to preach.[3] The part he played in later developments there was remembered by more than one of those who had witnessed them. 'Brother Munio threatened those who took the bishop's side that he would have them taken and chained up for ever', Sol Martínez reported. 'Brother Munio said that he would strip Doña Orobona of her habit', Xemena Perez could clearly recall.[4] In 1280 the prior of Valladolid found it helpful to refer to Elvira Pérez and Sancha Garcés, who had regularly been in the thick of things together, at both the drinking session and the stocks episode, as 'consobrinis fratris Munionis'.[5] And whatever the term *consobrine* may have meant in that context, whether nieces or relations of an unspecified sort, these are not the only indications of brother Munio's connexions with the place or of the personal nature of those connexions. As late as August 1294 the will of the archdeacon of Zamora, Pedro Anays, recorded a debt of 563 maravedís owed him by *frey* Munio and the prioress jointly.[6] If, as a decree of the León provincial chapter of 1275 may imply, attempts had recently been made to prevent knowledge of developments at Zamora reaching the wider world,[7] in 1281 the prioress's letter will have broken the conspiracy of silence. In addressing the cardinal on that July Sunday there can have been no doubt in her mind what the effect would be of her mentioning Brother Munio by name.

We know that the new prior provincial was present at Valladolid in the following April when the Infante Sancho declared against his father, but not how he reacted on being called upon by the bishops of Burgos and Palencia to witness their protest on that occasion at having their names associated with the rebel cause.[8] Nor do we know what his movements were during the war of 1282–4 – though his attendance on Sancho IV in October 1284 suggests that unlike his confrères within the episcopate he felt no compunction about abandoning the old king when the tide turned against him.[9]

Be that as it may, at the Bologna General Chapter in May 1285, Munio of Zamora was elected Master General of the Order and – whether or not he is to be regarded as the first Spaniard to be so honoured, as Castilian historians of the Order used once to assert[10] – his election certainly appeared to augur well, in the words of the most recent historian of the Order, seeming 'to promise years of capable administration and a determined holding of the line against infractions of obedience'.[11] Nor was the Order itself the only beneficiary of Munio's advancement. Another was the king of Castile. For Sancho IV Munio's election was both propitious and timely. With so many Castilian sees lacking bishops,[12] an influential presence at the papal curia was more than ever desirable in order to ensure that the king's wishes in the matter were not neglected. But of even greater interest to D. Sancho must have been the part that Munio might play in the matter of the royal marriage. For the royal marriage was uncanonical to an unusual degree, and so long as it remained unregularised the royal succession itself was in jeopardy. A dispensation was urgently needed and, as will be seen, there were no lengths to which Sancho IV was not prepared to go in order to secure it.

The issue had doubtless been on the agenda at the Zamora meeting which Brother Munio had attended in the previous October. Also present on that occasion had been 'Magister Aço decretorum doctor': Master Azo de Lambertazzi, the noted Bolognese practitioner whom Sancho IV sent to Rome on his behalf in the following month.[13]

With business of this importance to be transacted, communication with Rome was essential. But to the extent that there were also confidences to be kept, and rumour to be suppressed, such comings and goings between Castile and the papal curia were also risky. For example, on his mission Master Azo must necessarily have encountered and traversed a complex network of relationships. Of most of these, of course, we have no knowledge 700 years on. But we do know that in December 1281, just five months after the prioress had written to Cardinal Ordoño, Pedro III of Aragón had been in correspondence, amiable correspondence, with the cardinal, too. (The king was anxious to do something for the cardinal's brother.)[14] What we do not know is whether in May 1285, when he had every reason for wishing to inconvenience Sancho IV, the wicked uncle who had deprived his La Cerda nephew of his just inheritance, and no reason for welcoming the election of a Castilian as Dominican Master General, the king of Aragón acted upon what he may have known. Nor can we be sure that on reaching Rome Master Azo called on Cardinal Ordoño, though since as well as being Sancho IV's only empurpled subject the cardinal was also the brother of the king's *mayordomo mayor*, it would be surprising if he had not done so. And if he did, perhaps it was then that Master Azo picked up the Roman gossip about the new Master General, and perhaps from Master Azo that the king discovered that word had reached Rome regarding Munio's murky past. We do not know. The capillaries of communication are closed to us.

But so in the year 1285 were they closed to Sancho IV, and since there was no means of knowing who knew what, all that could be done was to seek to stem and divert the fountain-head of rumour and speculation. By whatever route knowledge that tongues were wagging against the Spanish Master General may have reached him, in May 1285 Sancho IV would certainly have appreciated the consequences that such murmurings were bound to have for the cause that mattered to him most. The Master General might not be able to secure the problematic dispensation. But if the Master General who had only just been elected were to be incriminated, then the securing of it would certainly prove more difficult still.

On 8 June 1285, the king authorised a payment of 30,000 maravedís to Cardinal Ordoño.[15] There may be other explanations for this transfer of funds, of course. (It may have been the cardinal's birthday, for example.) But if it was the price of silence, or of active discretion, then the king's large outlay was surely justified – or would have been if the cardinal had survived long enough to be effective. Unfortunately however – unfortunately for the king, that is – by the end of 1285 the cardinal was dead.[16] And meanwhile word was continuing to spread. To those in the know ('Brother Munio said that he would strip Doña Orobona of her habit') the extreme unctuousness of the new Master General's first encyclical, with its pious injunctions about not allowing 'incautious familiarity' to tarnish the Order's brightness,[17] would have rung especially hollow, while the promulgation of his new Rule for the men and women of the Third Order, the *Ordo de Penitentia*, with its emphasis on the reverence due to bishops ('Brother Munio threatened those who took the bishop's side that he would have them taken and chained up for ever') and its prohibition on excursions into town,[18] must have proved particularly difficult to stomach.

In March 1288, a month after the completion of the incorporation-process at Zamora, Munio's concession of extra mattresses to keep the nuns of Caleruega warm at night in Saint Dominic's birthplace was likewise accompanied by much sententiousness on the subject of the particular need of the weaker sex for strict enclosure.[19] By then, however, the whispering campaign had reached the French convents.

At the Bordeaux General Chapter in 1287 certain brothers had been reported to have 'sharpened their tongues in derogation of the venerable father's reputation'. Under the venerable father's chairmanship the chapter imposed severe sentences upon the culprits.[20] And by now word of the Master General's seamy past had reached the German sisters, too, occasioning the intervention of the German provincial.[21]

The calumnies he was having to bear testified to their victim's heroic qualities, the German provincial assured the sisters.[22] But then, in May 1290, even before the agenda item had been reached which forbad friars to enter convents where there were women,[23] the proceedings of the Ferrara General Chapter were dramatically interrupted by a communication from Pope Nicholas IV ordering the Master General's immediate removal from the office in which he had laboured 'no little time'. The 'honesty and utility' of the Order required it, the assembly was informed.[24] No reasons were given.

The effect of the pope's intervention was electric. Not only had no charges been brought for the Master General to answer; worse, the pontiff had appointed two Dominican cardinals, Hugues de Billom and Latino Malabranca, to execute the sentence under general powers to deal with members of the Order 'of whatever condition', and the cardinals in turn had chosen not to confront the General Chapter themselves but instead had appointed four other members of the Order to act for them. Moreover, the Chapter was directed to persuade the Master General to tender his resignation, and if he refused to do so was instructed to depose him 'in as honest a manner as may best be done so as to avoid the need to proceed by means which might redound less to the honour of the said Master General'.[25]

The reaction was volcanic. The course of action prescribed was 'contrary to the rule of law', the Chapter declared, 'contrary to the Order's privileges',[26] and, as the assembly's encyclical informing the Order at large of their appeal to the pope emphasised, prejudicial not only to the Order's freedom but also to truth itself. Saint Augustine was prayed in aid. Novel procedures were not to be tolerated, even on grounds of utility. There were many brothers who would sooner die than accept them.[27] By refraining from stating what the matter was, and by attempting to bundle Brother Munio off-stage without a scene, the Franciscan pope had precipitated the gravest constitutional crisis in the history of the Dominican Order.

The Chapter's reason for refusing to allow Munio to submit his cause to public examination, therefore, was not any lack of confidence in one whose reputation for abstinence (from meat) was legendary. Such faults as might be imputed to him were no more than peccadilloes, trivial lapses of the sort 'without which life was not to be lived', lapses which the Rule itself tolerated, it was claimed. No, the Chapter's reason was its determination not to acquiesce in a breach of the Order's own rules for the correction of its members, and 'even its Master', since to do so would be to collude with those intent on reducing the Order to servitude.

'We are made slaves ('facti servi')', the cry went up at Ferrara when the news broke.[28] And in the following September the same cry was taken up by the provincial chapter of Provence at Pamiers. The friars at Pamiers were aghast at what they had heard, stupefied and in shock.[29] Again, they were in no doubt regarding Brother Munio's virtues, fitness for office and excellence in every regard.[30] What had taken their breath away, they sought to impress upon the pope, and what particularly exercised them, was not the *ad hominem* issue but rather the appointment of the two cardinals to regulate the Order's affairs. This was the nub of the matter. This was sinister – sinister and detrimental not only to law and reason but also to the order of their profession.[31]

No doubt these were exceptionally hard words to address to the supreme pontiff. But, as their exposition reveals, in the estimation of the friars assembled at Pamiers they were fully justified, for the times through which their Order was passing were exceptionally hard, too.

For who, pray, had ever heard of an order of regulars being subjected to a cardinal, it was asked – or, worse, to *two* cardinals? And here the friars had recourse to corporation theory, appropriating to their Order the characteristics of the Church itself and conjuring up the spectre of a body with two heads. To make a religious order subject to a cardinal was bad enough. To subject it to two 'would seem to be contrary to nature'. What if the two of them were in disagreement, for example? Stranger things had happened. And consider. At present the cardinal bishop of Ostia and cardinal priest of Santa Sabina were both Dominicans. But what if their successors in title, not being regulars, contrived to retain the functions that had been assigned to them? What then? Then the body with two heads might have two *secular* heads, with a body of one 'condition' and its heads of another, which would be 'monstrous' – 'as you are aware', they reminded the pope, who, as a former Minister General of the Franciscans himself, ought surely to be capable of appreciating the enormity of having seculars established in authority over mendicants.[32]

As professed religious, they were subject to the Master General to whom they had sworn obedience in accordance with the privileges of the Order which successive popes, most recently Nicholas himself, had confirmed. To require them to honour undertakings of obedience which they had not made would be to breach the law that knew no law, 'preter communium iurium observanciam', to undermine the principle of obedience itself and promote subversion everywhere.[33] So they, too, would opt for death rather than servitude. If the pope remained committed to the course of action upon which he had embarked, they would transfer to other orders.

The pope's commission to the two cardinals was the child of conspiracy, the offspring of 'suggestio falsitatis' and 'suppressio veritatis' regarding the Order's good estate and religion.[34] This charge repeated the protest voiced at Ferrara: 'Princes were often told lies', the provincials had observed in their response to the cardinals.[35] They were threatened with a body with two heads because the Master General had been slandered by men with two faces. In his encyclical to the Order on the same occasion, the Master General had hinted as much himself: 'We have been exposed to the shafts of our detractors, set up as a target for their arrows, made a spectacle to the world and to men.'[36]

From this and from other expostulations of the year 1290 the modern historian of the Order concluded that the Master General's principal detractors were none other than the two Dominican cardinals themselves. According to Fr. Mortier, it was this pair of scandalmongers, friars in name but long removed from the mendicant regime, who had poisoned the mind of the friar-pope. (He failed to add that one of them was himself noted for his interest in ladies' skirts.)[37] And the friar-pope had been easily duped. Long removed from the mendicant regime himself, in his pontifical isolation Nicholas IV was prey to certain purveyors of curial tittle-tattle who had lured him into proceeding against the blameless *frey* Munio.[38]

At this point in his narrative, admittedly, Fr. Mortier's readers are left unsure whether it is Mortier's intuition of what the Provençal friars had in mind in 1290 that they are being presented with, or what was in Mortier's own mind at a time when French society was in the grip of virulent anticlericalism, diplomatic relations with the Holy See were suspended, and rumours of sexual escapades involving senior prelates were legion.[39] But whosesoever the intuition was, it is unsupported by anything approximating to evidence. And in Mortier's case this is unusual. For, as G. G. Coulton (in customarily generous vein) acknowledged, Mortier's History is 'as objective [a work] in its conclusions as can fairly be expected from a distinguished and devoted member of the Order'.[40] On the matter of Munio of Zamora, however, Mortier's mind was made up from the outset. Munio of Zamora was the sacrificial victim of hostile forces, a Master General more sinned against than adept at public relations.

Just as the Order itself did at Ferrara in 1290, so the historians of its Masters General have assumed that Munio was entirely innocent of the unspecified charges against him and, also just as the Order did, have suspected skulduggery at every turn. Over the years only the supposed identity of the villains has altered. For the Castilian author, Pedro Fernández de Pulgar, in the 1680s, it was France's inveterate hostility to his countrymen that was responsible. For the French friar, P. Mortier, in 1905, it was curial scheming. The particular apprehensions of the ages in which they wrote pervade their respective accounts of the matter.[41] Whence the frequent asides in Mortier's otherwise scrupulous narrative of the events of 1290–2. 'On se demande pourquoi toutes ces hésitations', he remarks apropos of the extended series of commissions from the pope downwards prior to the Order receiving the dread tidings.[42] Why, he enquires, did the belling of the cat have to be so extended a process? 'One wonders about all this toing-and-froing.'

The technique is effective. One does indeed begin to wonder. The implication that Mortier draws from Munio's reported demeanour, that he was the innocent victim of a campaign of character-assassination, serves to justify the spirit of scepticism in which Mortier addresses his task. There had been mischief afoot in 1290. But looking back from 1905 to the year 1290 one was at least able to recognise one's friends. It was at least possible to distinguish between those two of the cardinals' emissaries who had refused to be suborned and had 'resolutely' attested the appeal from the cardinals' sentence to the pope, on the one hand, and on the other those of their colleagues, whose failure to protest revealed that they 'lacked the same dignity of character'.[43] Far from being merely a perfunctory gesture, the customary prayers for the pope and the Dominican cardinals prescribed at Ferrara demonstrated Brother Munio's commitment to the evangelical precept to love one's enemies.[44] When the Master General, under sentence but still adamant that he would not resign, waited upon Nicholas IV later in 1290, did he not carry in his heart the evidence of his conscience, Mortier asks – meaning, of course, the evidence of his *clear* conscience?[45]

The possibility has of course to be allowed for that Mortier's conviction as to Brother Munio's innocence was soundly based, or at least no less soundly based than his identification of Brother Munio's detractors. It has also to be allowed that his refusal to resign provides confirmation of that innocence – notwithstanding the prioress's letter to the cardinal which, were it the only evidence against him, might be accounted the act of a vindictive woman with a grudge against the Dominicans, whose only reason for singling out Brother Munio was that Brother Munio himself had recently been singled out by his order. For it *was* only Brother Munio that María Martínez mentioned, and her motive for doing so in 1281 may indeed have been his recent elevation.

But that is not the only possible interpretation of the prioress's particularity in the matter. Nor is it the most plausible one. For as to the facts about the friar which may have been known to the pope in 1290, rather than conjectures regarding the prioress's psychological state nine years earlier and the cumulative effect of female fantasising earlier still, it is also the case that in 1279, well before he had achieved that wider prominence, Brother Munio had been delated to the bishop of Zamora – along with Brother Bernabé, Domingo Yuánez, Pedro Gutiérrez, Brother Nicolás, Brother Gil, old Juan de Aviancos and all – as one of the ringleaders of the group who had converted a convent of nuns into a bawdy-house.

There is, of course, no knowing whether Nicholas IV had access to that information. There is no knowing *what* information Nicholas IV had access to, who his informants were,[46] or indeed what other events at this time may have influenced his judgement. For example, when in November 1289 his rescript was issued regarding the reported alienation of property from the Order's Madrid convent, was he any more aware himself of the matter than Nicholas III had been in December 1279 in respect of similar alleged developments at Las Dueñas? Is the fact that the two rescripts are virtually identical attributable solely to the office routines of the papal chancery?[47] We cannot say, not least because Nicholas IV exercised complete discretion, maintained total silence, and revealed absolutely nothing. The Order laboured hard to draw him into the open, and on failing to do so concluded that since there was nothing that the pope was prepared to reveal, then the Master General had nothing to hide. Even *in extremis*, the pontiff refused to be drawn, with the consequence that he has received a bad press from posterity, and especially from Dominican posterity.

Ever since 1290 the motives of the pope who revealed nothing to anyone have been suspected by those who have claimed an interest in the matter, with those considerations of confidentiality which the twentieth century finds so difficult to credit proving equally implausible to the historians of the Order. As details of the Zamora affair have emerged, historians of the Order have been reluctant to acknowledge their import. Although, of course, Mortier himself is beyond reproach in this respect, since in 1905 no student of the subject was yet aware of the Ladies of Zamora and their associates, after Castro published his piece in 1923 they might have been, after Gaibrois published hers in 1925 they ought to have been, and when he published his History of the Order in 1965 Fr. Hinnebusch unquestionably was. Yet regarding the prioress's incriminating letter, all that Hinnebusch reported was that the prioress 'mentioned Provincial Munio in her appeal, whether or not he was personally involved'. This is strange. For, whether true or false, on the issue of Brother Munio's personal involvement in the Zamora affair María Martínez's allegations were at least unequivocal.[48]

An alternative explanation for the Master General's refusal to resign needs to be considered, therefore, namely that his refusal stemmed not so much from an untroubled conscience as from a supreme confidence in his own ability to brazen it out. After all, what were the demonstrable facts of the matter? What had become of the letter to the cardinal? – or rather, what did Brother Munio think had become of it? Had not Sancho IV paid the cardinal good money? Had not all that furore been stifled, together with María Martínez and her harridans? Was not Las Dueñas incorporated into the Order? Did not it, and he, enjoy the king's special favour? And, with promises of 'magnificent provision', had not that same king ensured – as no previous ruler had done – that the next General Chapter should be held at Palencia on the Master General's home territory?[49] Surely Munio of

106

Zamora would be safe in Castile. Now in his mid-fifties, he may well have reasoned thus as he ran before the storm to what seemed a secure haven.

In vain, however. For the storm followed him. Nicholas IV was adamant too. Not to be outfaced, he dispatched a mandate to the General Chapter decreeing the Master General's removal from office at the conclusion of the proceedings at Palencia. He dispatched it. But it never arrived, for as the pope's *cursores* approached Palencia they were ambushed and robbed of their letters. In the land in which hanging the herald was not uncommon practice, and where at about this time the dean of Burgos and others of his senior colleagues set upon the agents of a curialist who had come to take possession of a benefice there and all but drowned them in the river (with Sancho IV's connivance, it was believed), Nicholas IV plainly had his suspicions as to where responsibility for the Palencia hijack rested.[50] (Palencia was dangerous territory. This was the second such incident recently reported from those parts. In January 1291 the pontiff and the ineluctable Cardinal Latino had both commissioned the archbishop of Toledo to investigate an incident there involving the robbery and murder of Ventura Jacobi de Assisio and his companion.)[51] Moreover, unlike Fr. Hinnebusch, Nicholas was persuaded that Munio was well aware of the contents of the intercepted letters, and intimated as much in August of that year when he finally dismissed the Master General from office 'on account of various causes that have recently emerged' ('certis emergentibus causis')[52] – though still he did not reveal what those causes were. In August 1291, still the mystery remained.

And even after Mortier's careful consideration of the case,[53] unsolved it has remained down to the present century. In an age in which 'it was best to be French', Brother Munio's nationality was not to his advantage, Mortier suggested.[54] But that was not the explanation of his downfall, he conceded. Nor was the Franciscan pontiff's antipathy to the Dominican Order, though it was part of it, he suspected. The reasons for Nicholas IV's vendetta against Munio of Zamora were 'altogether personal',[55] but the context of that vendetta was inter-mendicant rivalry, and in particular the pope's resentment of Munio's designs on the 'third order'. By means of the Rule which he had issued in 1285 (and which Honorius IV had confirmed) Munio had appropriated a tradition of lay piety whose origins and inspiration were essentially Franciscan. It had been this act of 'usurpation' that had predisposed the pope to 'condemn an innocent'.[56] And in Mortier's estimation that at least was certain: Brother Munio was an innocent, and his private life was irreproachable.[57] Had it been otherwise, would Nicholas have offered him the see of Compostela on the occasion of their meeting in 1290, he asks?[58]

That particular rhetorical question was not well judged. Despite a venerable tradition to that effect, Nicholas IV did not in fact offer Munio the see of Compostela in 1290, for in 1290 the see of Compostela was not vacant. According to Ptolemy of Lucca, it was Honorius IV who had done so in 1285, soon after Munio's election as Master General: an offer which Munio had declined 'out of reverence for his office of Master'.[59] That misunderstanding apart, Mortier's observations are not without force. Munio's *Ordo de Penitentia* was indeed part of the problem. But it was not the reason for his downfall. Although it may have contributed to the dossier against him, it was not itself the cause.

Rivalry between the Franciscans and the Dominicans was everywhere in evidence during the late 1280s. Whereas at the beginning of that decade the two orders had still stood shoulder to shoulder against the ordinaries, carefully scrutinising papal communiqués regarding places of which they knew little, concerning issues for which they cared much,[60] by 1287 Franciscans and Dominicans were on opposite sides of various episcopal barricades – at Strasburg for example, as Munio knew to his cost. In a postscript to his 1288 encyclical the Master General had particularly stressed the importance of extending 'fraternal charity' to the other mendicant order.[61]

If it was necessary to issue a reminder on the subject of fraternal charity, then the knives were well and truly out. And with a Franciscan in charge at Rome, that signalled danger for the Dominicans – whether or not their Master General was a Spaniard, and whether or not he had a past. And Munio of Zamora did have a past. Quite how knowledge of the contents of María Martínez's letter to Cardinal Ordoño found its way to the pope, as that lady had intended that it should, we may never know. But in the circumstances of the late 1280s it was inevitable both that it should and, when it did, that the disclosures would shake the Order to its foundations.

By 1292, moreover, as the Dominican Order was beginning to adjust to recent events, it appears that it may also have been coming to terms with Brother Munio's earlier history. Despite Mortier's assurances, on the evidence which Mortier himself assembled, it would seem that by 1292 opinion within the Order itself was shifting. At Ferrara two years earlier the Order had closed ranks. But by 1292 that solidarity was showing signs of strain. On the usually impassive face of the record, in 1292 a flicker, the merest suggestion of a nervous twitch, is momentarily discernible.

In order to superintend the election of Munio's successor as Master General, Nicholas IV had directed the next General Chapter to assemble in Rome. Accordingly (although by then the pope was dead and the Roman see vacant), at Whitsun 1292 the friars assembled in their great church of Santa Sabina. As its first act the Chapter elected Stephen of Besançon as Master General. A hard man, according to tradition Stephen ruled the order with a rod of iron. And the first to feel his force was the hapless Munio, there present and summarily dispatched to his Castilian Siberia, with his successor's taunts ringing in his ears: 'It was your duty to strengthen ('munire') the Order', he chided him, playing on the etymology of his name, 'not weaken it.' Or so Sebastián de Olmedo reported in the mid sixteenth century.[62]

'Non mollire debuisses.' But 'not weaken' is a polite translation. 'Ecce qui mollius vestiuntur', William of Saint-Amour had exclaimed forty years before: 'they that wear soft clothing are in kings' houses' (Matthew 11.8). In the 1250s William had had the friars in mind, and those with ears to hear in 1292 may have recognised the allusion, if allusion it was and the words really were spoken.[63] We cannot be sure that they were. The Spaniard Olmedo, who was one of those inclined to attribute Munio's downfall to his Spanish origins,[64] did not reveal the source of Stephen's remark. Even so, we may be sure that, whatever form it took, the new Master General's reprimand will have been the object of exhaustive exegesis in the buzzing corridors of Santa Sabina in the early summer of 1292. In the early summer of 1292 'mollities' meant womanising, illicit socialising, rather than the solitary vice.[65] It was in this changed climate that the two Dominican cardinals who had been cast as the villains of the piece at Ferrara were vindicated at Rome. On the basis of information which it regarded as both 'certain' and 'firm', in 1292 the General Chapter acknowledged that the cardinals had indeed acted from the best of motives and out of a desire to ensure the Order's welfare. Likewise, in his first encyclical the new Master General chose to stress the need for a return to a rule of purity, modesty and chastity.[66] And in his next, and last, he again harked back to the recent voluptuary past.[67]

Certainly there was something of a Stalinist flavour about these proceedings. The Order of Preachers had finished with Munio of Zamora. In 1292 he had been condemned to the perpetual obscurity of a Castilian cell. The historian Ptolemy of Lucca, otherwise so attentive to the comings and goings of the Masters General of the order of which he was himself a member, remained totally silent on the subject of the Spaniard's downfall.[68] But history itself had not finished with Munio of Zamora. Nor, for that matter, had the king of Castile.

Notes

1 See above, pp. 57–8.

2 *Litt. encyc.*, 154. Details in D. A. Mortier, *Histoire des Maîtres Généraux de l'Ordre des Frères Prêcheurs*, ii, Paris 1905, 171 ff.

3 *TB*, fo. 28ᵛ; Douais, 617 (Hernández, 'Primeras actas', 41).

4 See above, pp. 50, 51.

5 ACZ, 13/62; Appendix II. Cf. Caterina of Benavento's testimony: 'Hec Elvira Petri et Sancia Garsie insurrexerunt contra priorissam eundo cum digitis ad oculos dicendo priorisse 'Falsa et demoniada quia fecisti fratres predicatores expelli a monasterio propter clericos.' See also witnesses 7, 12, 15. The pair [24, 30] had been vocal enough earlier but were unforthcoming when the bishop called.

6 'Ffrey Monio e la priora de alen rrio' (ACZ, 18/20 (published J. J. Coria Colino, 'Clerigos prestamistas. El mundo de los negocios en una ciudad medieval: Zamora (siglo XIII–XIV)', *El pasado histórico de Castilla y León*: Actas del I Congreso de Historia de Castilla y León, I, Burgos 1983, 353–8, misdated 1284)).

7 'Item, quod priores nullo modo audeant impedire aliquem quod scribat libere priori provinciali seu vicario; et contrarium facientes severius puniantur' (Douais, 620 (Hernández, 'Pergaminos', 19)). In view of the continuous movement of friars, such attempted muzzling cannot have succeeded. At this very chapter (at which Munio himself was appointed vicar for the houses of León and Galicia) more than sixty friars were assigned to twenty-nine houses, including four (fr. Michael Danielis, fr. Fernandus Roberti [?], fr. P. Petri, fr. [. . .]-us Ordonii) to Zamora (Douais, 618–19 (Hernández, 'Pergaminos', 16)); AHN, Clero 3255/15.

8 *MHE*, ii. 59–63.

9 The assumption of Ballesteros (*Alfonso el Sabio*, 973) that the Dominicans were solidly pro-Sancho in their sympathies is mistaken. Fr. Aymar, the elect of Avila, was one of the last five bishops still with Alfonso X in January 1284 – 'que se connusco touieron en uerdat e en lealdat' (M.

González Jiménez, ed., *Diplomatario andaluz de Alfonso X*, Seville 1991, no. 520). Suero of Cádiz, another loyalist who was made to suffer for his loyalty after 1284, was also a Dominican and not a member of a military order, as suggested by J. Sánchez Herrero, *Cádiz. La ciudad medieval y cristiana*, Córdoba 1981, 228; G. Daumet, *Mémoire sur les relations de la France et de la Castille de 1255 à 1320*, Paris 1913, 189–90. See above, p. 82.

10 Causing Mortier to enquire indignantly (171 n. 4), 'Est-ce que saint Raymond de Pennafort n'était point Espagnol?'

11 W. A. Hinnebusch, *The History of the Dominican Order. Origins and growth to 1500*, i, New York 1965, 225.

12 In January 1284 Alfonso X's chancery recorded seven sees as vacant while sixteen were not mentioned at all, presumably because their bishops were attached to Sancho. In March 1286 the church of Salamanca was provided for, having been 'destituta pastoris propter diutinas et longas vacationes' (*Reg. Hon. IV* 320) and mulcted by the king while it remained so (see above, p. 81). In May 1286 the abbey of Oña had been without an abbot for more than fifteen years (*ibid.*, 509).

13 Rymer, *Foedera*, I. ii. 649; H. Wieruszowski, *Politics and Culture in Medieval Spain and Italy*, Rome 1971, 104–5.

14 H. Finke, *Acta Aragonensia*, iii, Berlin 1922, 1.

15 The payment was noted by Gaibrois, 'Fray Munio de Zamora', 141–2. Cf. her *Sancho IV*, i. 120, where Ordoño is described as one of the cardinals of Santiago, rather than cardinal bishop of Tusculum.

16 He was still alive on 25 September (Wadding, *Annales minorum*, v. 490–92). His successor, Giovanni Boccamazza, was created cardinal bishop of Tusculum on 22 December.

17 *Litt. encyc.*, 131–2.

18 *Dossier de l'Ordre de la Pénitence au XIII siècle*, ed. G. G. Meersseman, Fribourg 1961, 143–56, cc. 28, 33 ('Sorores vero sole non discurrent, maxime iuniores'), 47, 49–52.

19 'Sane cum quietis inclusio plus fragili feminarum sexui videatur competere quam viris, earumque discursus sit pro viribus restringendus . . .' (E. Martínez, *Colección diplomática del real convento de S. Domingo de Caleruega*, Vergara 1931, 350–54).

20 *Acta cap. gen.*, 241.

21 'Gratum Deo et ordini obsequium impendistis, quando magistro ordinis illatas nobis a religiosis quibusdam iniurias intimastis' (Finke, *Ungedruckte Dominikanerbriefe*, 140).

22 'Re vera ego non credidi tot mala aliquibus irrogata, nisi essent martirio coronandi' (*ibid.*).

23 See above, p. 78.

24 *Litt. encyc.*, 149.

25 *Litt. encyc.*, 148–50; Mortier, 252–6.

26 'contra iuris ordinem . . . ac contra ordinis privilegia et eciam instituta' (*Litt. encyc.*, 156).

27 *Litt. encyc.*, 151: '. . . nec vobis placeat novitate aliqua ordini nostro

admiracionem inducere, cum secundum Augustinum ipsa mutacio consuetudinis, eciam que utilitate militat, novitate conturbat, fratribus eciam multis dulcius esset mori, quam novitati huiusmodi subiacere'; *ibid.*, 152.

28 *Ibid.*, 151, 153.

29 'quo noster auditus tanta admiratione obstupuit, ut . . . animos in stuporem adduceret, oculos in lacrimas solveret, corda in merorem converteret, corpora cogeret in tremorem' (Douais, 340).

30 'quem . . . certitudinaliter novimus secundum carnis originem excellenter natum, excellenter dotatum, excellenter sensatum; secundum vero ordinem excellenter morigeratum et ab annis ineuntibus in hiis que sunt ordinis excellenter informatum; excellenter in hiis que ad Dominum, quantum novimus, timoratum, et in regimine ordinis multis clarorum virorum etiam apud Vestram Reverenciam testimoniis commendatum' (*ibid.*, 343).

31 'iuri non convenit, rationi obsistit, professionis nostre ordini contradicit' (*ibid.*, 340). Cf. Mortier, 264–7.

32 '. . . et sic status nostre religionis habere videbitur capita mostruosa, cum alterius conditionis sit corpus totum et alterius capita, sicut nostis' (Douais, 342). Mortier, 265, considers their conjecture 'not illusory'. For the larger discussion to which these anxieties refer, see J. A. Watt, 'Spiritual and temporal powers' in J. H. Burns (ed.), *The Cambridge History of Medieval Political Thought, c. 350–c. 1450*, Cambridge 1988, 382. In 1275 the prospect of the University of Paris having two rectors had been denounced as 'quasi monstrum' (O. Lewry, 'Corporate life in the University of Paris', 1249–1418, and the ending of the Schism', *Journal of Ecclesiastical History* 40 (1989) 513).

33 'si predicta concessio, quod advertat Dominus, stare debet, increscet subditorum irreverentia ad prelatos . . .' (Douais, 342).

34 *Ibid.*, 344.

35 'Quia vero multa frequenter falsa principi suggeruntur, non dubitamus, quin vobis de venerabili patre magistro ordinis multa falsa suggesta sint' (*Litt. encyc.*, 151).

36 '. . . Sentitis namque, quid turbacionis propter aliquorum vaniloquia [et] falsiloquia, ordo noster incipiat sustinere' (*ibid.*, 147).

37 According to Salimbene, while legate in Lombardy in 1278 Cardinal Latino had ordered the women there to wear their skirts shorter, though not daringly so (*Cronica*, 169).

38 'On ne craignait point de rappeler au Pape que son entourage pouvait ne pas lui dire toujours la vérité; et le Pape, – auquel les faiblesses humaines, loin d'être inconnues, apparaissent d'autant mieux qu'il est plus haut placé pour les voir, – ne trouvait pas mauvais qu'on les lui signalât. Des cardinaux, sortis de l'Ordre, lui avaient dit, sur la foi de délations injustes, que l'Ordre avait besoin d'être pacifié, corrigé, plus sagement administré, et lui avaient demandé tout pouvoir pour réaliser eux-mêmes ces améliorations' (268).

39 Cf. A. Dansette, *Histoire religieuse de la France contemporaine sous la*

Troisième République, ii, Paris 1952, 300–72; M. Larkin, *Church and State after the Dreyfus Affair. The separation issue in France*, London 1974, 134.

40 *Five Centuries of Religion*, iv, Cambridge 1950, 447.

41 'Aunque fueron sus prendas tantas, como testifican sus obras, y la benignidad con que se hazia amable a todos los Frayles; no debiò de caer muy en gracia a los Italianos, y Franceses, de quien la Nacion Española siempre ha sido aborrecida' (P. Fernández de Pulgar, *Teatro clerical apostolico y secular de las iglesias catedrales de España*, ii, Madrid 1680, 356). Cf. Peter Linehan, 'The accession of Alfonso X (1252) and the origins of the War of the Spanish Succession', in D. W. Lomax and D. Mackenzie, eds, *God and Man in Medieval Spain. Essays in honour of J. R. L. Highfield*, Warminster 1989, 59–79 (reprinted in *Past and Present in Medieval Spain* (Aldershot, 1992).

42 Mortier, 254.

43 *Ibid.*, 260–1.

44 *Ibid.*, 262.

45 *Ibid.*, 253. It might also be asked whether it was by pure coincidence that in August 1290, at about the time of his meeting with Munio, Nicholas IV instructed the Franciscan bishop of Burgos, fr. Fernando, to ensure that when visiting the nunneries of his diocese he was accompanied by two members of his order (*Reg. Nich. IV*, 3119).

46 Though the presence at the papal curia in the autumn of 1289 of Munio's confrère, Rodrigo González, former prior of the Spanish province and now archbishop of Compostela, deserves to be noted, as does that of Sancho IV's diplomatic envoys, for the former was an energetically zealous pastor and the latter were Franciscans (*Reg. Nich. IV*, 1511, 1817; García y García, *Synodicon Hispanum*, i (1981) 272–80). For the Franciscan envoys, see below, p. 117.

47 T. Ripoll, *Bullarium ordinis FF. Praedicatorum*, vii, Rome 1739, 48 no. 30; see above, p. 60. Cf. Herde, *Audientia litterarum contradictarum*, ii. 586–7.

48 Hinnebusch, 227, citing Gaibrois, 136–46. (To the point is the passage cited at p. 140 (=Castro, 194): 'Et con todesto [, senor,] que façie ffre Monio et los otros ffrades predicadores dexieron muchas veçes alas duennas que fussen contra lo que prometieron et iuraron al obispo don Suero.') Hinnebusch continues: 'Perhaps this memory was still fresh enough to be fitted together with the calumnies coming from France and the personal annoyances of Nicholas. That the pope so linked the facts to build a case against Munio is conjecture. We cannot say for certain that these are the things that lurk behind the phrase of Nicholas, "various causes that have recently emerged". We do know that he pursued the General relentlessly.'

49 *Acta. cap. gen.*, 260.

50 Better than anyone, perhaps, Sancho IV knew the identity of the culprits, Mortier observes (270). The king had been at Palencia in March 1291, but his presence there in the month in which the General Chapter met is not recorded (Gaibrois, *Sancho IV*, iii. nos. 347–61). For the Burgos incident see Linehan, 'A tale', 99–100.

꧁ ꧁ ꧁ ꧁ ꧁

51 AC Toledo, O.II.C.I.9; A.7.G.2.15a ('transiens per diocesim Palentinam'). The Italians had come to Castile to collect payments due to Master Andreas de Candulphis, archdeacon of Medina (Salamanca).

52 '. . . licet verisimiliter presumatur quod ad te pervenerit continentia seu notitia earundem' (Mortier, 271–2, n. 4). The General Chapter seems still to have been in session on 22 June, on which day the two friar-bishops, Suero of Cádiz and Blasius of Segovia, provided the Palencia and Valladolid houses with authorised copies of Nicholas IV's privilege *Dum sollicite* (Po. 22758) (AHN, Clero 185/1, 3501/3). Cf. Hinnebusch, 228: the General Chapter 'remained blithely ignorant of what had happened'.

53 Mortier, 278–93.

54 Though they had not affected his election, he had stated earlier: 'Ce motif de race n'influa en rien sur l'élection' (171 n. 4).

55 *Ibid.*, 280 n. 1.

56 *Ibid.*, 290, 292. Likewise, A. Linage Conde and A. Oliver in 1982, according to whom 'los historiadores serenos' attribute the clash to 'understandable animosity' on the pope's part (hostility to Sancho IV, Munio's nationality, the question of the 'third order') and regard the charge of 'debilidad en el gobierno' as a cover (*Historia de la Iglesia en España*, ii. 2, ed. J. Fernández Conde, Madrid 1982, 141). In fact no such charge was laid; that was both the point and the problem. These writers do not so much as mention the issue of Munio's personal reputation.

57 Mortier, 278, 293.

58 'On le mettait à la porte chargé d'honneurs, et lui, que l'on jugeait, extérieurement du moins, insuffisant pour gouverner l'Ordre des Prêcheurs, on l'élevait à une dignité supérieure. Il n'avait donc plus lieu de craindre une déchéance peu honorable. Sa personnalité était sauve' (*ibid.*, 263–4).

59 *Annales*, 208. The confusion dates back at least to Hernando de Castillo's History of the Order of 1612, and the story has lost nothing in the retelling. According to Fernández de Pulgar, in 1290 Sancho IV strongly urged Munio to accept the see (*Teatro clerical*, ii. 357). Cf. A. López Ferreiro, *Hist. de la santa iglesia de Santiago de Compostela*, v, Santiago 1902, 255–6.

60 Which would explain why, for example, the Dominicans of Salamanca acquired an exemplar of Martin IV's mandate concerning the tribulations of the Franciscans at Vienna (AHN, Clero 1895/4 (=Po. 21848), 9 Feb. 1282).

61 Finke, *Ungedruckte Dominikanerbriefe*, 138–9; *Litt. encyc.*, 139.

62 Cited in Mortier, 299 n. 1.

63 'Item, dixit quod non licet religiosis morari in curiis principum vel prelatorum. Respondeo: Hoc non dixi, sed dixi quod periculum est praedicatoribus religiosis morari in curiis principum saecularium propter periculum adulationis. Unde Mattheus . . .' (Faral, 'Les "Responsiones"', 340–41).

64 Mortier, 280. Regarding Olmedo's reliability see Quétif-Échard, *Scriptores*, ii. 168.

65 Cf. Kinkade, 'Alfonso X', 315, for Alfonso X's reference in his *Cantiga* 235 to the burning 'daqueles que non querian moller'. 'Mollire' can hardly have

been intended to mean masturbation (as it did a century later in the *De confessione mollitiei* ascribed to Gerson (T. N. Tentler, *Sin and Confession on the Eve of the Reformation*, Princeton 1977, 91–2)) or the 'crimen nefandissimum quod absurdissimum est etiam nominare' mentioned at the Barcelona provincial chapter of 1299 (Douais, 647 (Hernández, 'Pergaminos', 60)). Cf. J. Chiffoleau, 'Dire l'indicible. Remarques sur la catégorie du *nefandum* du XIIe au XVe siècle', *AÉSC* 45 (1990) 289–324.

66 *Acta cap. gen.* 266; *Litt. encyc.*, 159 ('Decus eciam castitatis iugiter reflorescat in nobis, quod foveant et ostendant victus sobrius, sermo castus, pudicus aspectus').

67 '... nullus vos voluptatis dulcor abducat' (*ibid.*, 160).

68 Though he did not fail to note Stephen of Besançon's election (*Annales*, 223).

CHAPTER FIVE

🌼🌼🌼🌼🌼🌼🌼🌼🌼🌼🌼🌼🌼🌼🌼🌼🌼🌼🌼🌼🌼🌼🌼🌼🌼

$\mathcal{M}$UNIO of Zamora was in disgrace. Even so, in 1291 the king of Castile continued to have need of as many friends in high places as he could muster. In the wider world Sancho IV had a multitude of problems to contend with, but the foremost of them, as well as the chief source of what little solace he enjoyed, was still his marriage. The king of Castile was related to Maria de Molina to a degree of proximity that was breathtaking even by late thirteenth-century standards. His grandfather, Fernando III, was also his wife's uncle; when they had married ten years earlier he was already betrothed to another; and for good measure, Maria was godmother to his bastard daughter. Successive popes shook their heads as much in sorrow as amazement. This was difficult, *very* difficult – difficult to the tune of 10,000 marks of silver, which was what it eventually cost to secure the legitimisation of Fernando IV, Sancho's heir. But that was not achieved until 1301, by which time Sancho had been dead for six years. As Nicholas IV observed in 1289 when declining Sancho's latest request for a dispensation, the Castilian marriage was flawed by a multitude of impediments.[1] It was a canonical conundrum. More than that, for a king whose nephews' claims to his throne enjoyed French as well as Aragonese support it was both a dynastic disaster and a diplomatic minefield. As it had done since the beginning of the reign, therefore, in and after 1291 the regularisation of his marriage occupied a central position in all the king of Castile's calculations.

So it was particularly unfortunate that at the papal curia Sancho IV was so completely outgunned by his French and Aragonese adversaries. Lacking diplomatic leverage there, the king of Castile was disproportionately dependent on those few forces that he could deploy. Hence his sending of Franciscan friars to plead his case with the Franciscan Pope Nicholas IV in November 1289.[2] Hence also the importance of the election of the Spaniard Munio as Master General of the Dominicans in 1285 and the significance of Munio's success in bringing the General Chapter of the Order to Palencia in 1291. On the international stage, however, Munio had now become a liability.

Even so, the king who had invested so heavily in the Dominican Order still had use for its friars, and for brother Munio in particular. At the Rome General Chapter in 1292 it was reported that one of the seven priors provincial who had been removed from office in the previous year, the Spanish provincial Brother Gil, had been unlawfully 're-elected'. For this act of defiance those responsible received a penance of three days' bread and water. It is difficult to resist the suspicion that Brother Gil was unsupported in his contumacy by the king at whose behest the Palencia General Chapter had authorised the establishment of three new houses of the Spanish province.[3] And it is certain that but for Sancho's active intervention the discredited Brother Munio would never have been hauled out of obscurity in February 1294 and 'elected' bishop of Palencia.

In the account of what ensued after the chapter vested their powers in two of their number, Simón, archdeacon of Carrión and Sancho González, abbot of Husillos, Munio's reluctance to accept preferment is repeatedly emphasised. Yet in less time than it took a candle to burn down the choice of the *compromisarii* fell on the ex-Master General. The king and queen both urged him to accept. So did the canons of Palencia. So too did Brother Nicolás, the prior provincial, together with the priors and brothers of the various convents who were in Palencia in such unusually large numbers on that February day. But Munio remained adamant in his refusal until, after consulting his brethren and the bishops of Coria and Túy, the provincial finally required him to accept election 'by virtue of holy obedience and for the remission of his sins'. All this, and Munio's eventual selfless capitulation, the record faithfully relates.[4]

What of course it does not relate, what was concealed at the time and has remained concealed ever since, are the handsome payments made by the king, accounted for in his chancery later that year, to the archdeacon of Carrión and the abbot of Husillos as well as to the prior and convent of the Palencia Dominicans. The going rate for conspiracy to simony in 1294 was 12,000 maravedís.[5]

As Sancho reminded the abbot and chapter of Valladolid in mid-March when he wrote instructing them to receive the new bishop in style on his return from his consecration by the archbishop of Toledo, Munio had done the royal couple some service.[6] But beyond the king of Castile's orbit those with a stake in the matter were less impressed, and soon the reverberations of the Palencia election were registering far afield. At the Montpellier General Chapter in late May, Brother Nicolás was deprived of office for his part in the affair (as well as for having permitted the election of Guillem de Moncada to the Catalan see of Urgel) and sentenced to a year of bread, water and the psalter.[7] The rebuke from Rome might have been more robust, had there been a pontiff to administer one. But not until July 1294 was the twenty-seven month vacancy created by Nicholas IV's death ended, and in the confusion of Celestine V's brief pontificate there was no opportunity for dealing with the likes of Sancho IV.[8] Meanwhile Bishop Munio was on the king's payroll and had been sent by him on a diplomatic mission to the court of the king of France.[9]

Then in December 1294 Boniface VIII became pope, and in April 1295 Sancho IV died. Deprived of his protector, *frey* Munio had now to brace himself for a renewal of the storm. It was not long in coming. In 1279 the Castilian bishops had complained about the threats and menaces which Alfonso X employed in order to impose creatures of his own upon vacant sees, and the Infante Sancho and his advisers had come up with the lame response that if such things did not occur then that was as well, and if they did then they ought not to in future.[10] But no one in 1279 had accused Alfonso X of going so far as to bribe the electors. Again, we do not know how well informed Boniface VIII was about the February 1294 election when in October 1295 he summoned the friar to give an account of his 'intrusion' into the see of Palencia. But on the strength of what he did know he had no hesitation in describing the affair as 'pernicious', 'odious' and 'abominable'.

Despite the vehemence of his language, however, it may still be wondered whether even at this date it was in fact the 'horrible abuse of secular power' and the prostitution of religious modesty to episco-pal ambition that was really at the root of the pontiff's fury.[11] After all, such considerations did not prevent him from confirming the elec-tion to the see of Urgel.[12] Nor were the episcopal prospects of either the abbot of Husillos or the archdeacon of Carrión materially affected by their involvement in the Palencia 'intrusion'.[13] But above all there is the fact that when at Rome in July 1296 Munio pleaded to be allowed to resign the see, in granting his request Boniface was able to refer to him as the 'former bishop of Palencia'.[14]

By July 1296 at latest, therefore, not only had the pope's earlier rancour evaporated, also the election of February 1294 was acknowledged (albeit inadvisably) to have been canonical. And a similar lack of moral outrage is observable in the pope's dealings at this stage with the archbishop of Toledo who had confirmed Munio's election and consecrated him. Like Munio, in October 1295 Archbishop Gonzalo Pérez had been summoned to Rome to explain his part in the friar's 'detestable intrusion' into the see, and to present himself there within three months of receipt of the summons.[15] But by the time the archbishop did eventually give an account of himself at Rome, a year to the very day after Munio had cleared his name, the pope was referring to the affair not as an intrusion but as an 'election', and was so completely reassured regarding the archbishop's conduct in the affair that in the following year he made him a cardinal.[16]

The contrast between the language of Boniface's letters in October 1295 and his demeanour in July 1297 could hardly be more marked: so marked indeed that in the seventeenth century it occurred to Pedro Fernández de Pulgar to wonder whether Toledo's historians had not conflated two distinct Gonzalos. Can the archbishop and the cardinal really have been one and the same man?, Fernández de Pulgar asked.[17] It was a fair question. In his attempt at an answer Fernández de Pulgar was certainly mistaken: Archbishop Gonzalo and Cardinal Gonzalo were unquestionably one and the same man.[18] But in his suspicion that there was an inconsistency in the story, he was wholly justified. The facts of the matter do not add up. There was a problem to be solved. Simply stated, as Fernández de Pulgar stated it himself, the problem is this. If the archbishop was innocent of complicity in what Boniface had previously described as Munio's 'intrusion' into the see of Palencia, then *a fortiori* so must Munio have been.[19] But in that case, if Munio was innocent, why was he prevailed upon to resign?

In normal circumstances, the explanation might have been what the outcome of the pope's meeting with Munio in July 1296 implied: that on investigating the matter the pope (wrongly as it happens) found no fault in Munio's election, and that Munio's early retirement was indeed entirely voluntary. But the circumstances were not normal. Regardless of what the pope may or may not have known about the irregularities committed in February 1294, in October 1295 he cannot have been unaware that Munio had a past – and a past which no responsible archbishop called upon to confirm his episcopal election could conceivably have discounted. In October 1295 Boniface might, therefore, have been expected roundly to have censured the archbishop. What in fact he did, and this ten months before he had heard Munio's account of the affair, was to send the archbishop assurances by letters close that, despite what was stated in the 'other letters' which he had been sent regarding 'the *frey* Munio affair' ('circa negotium fratris Munionis'), the archbishop need not bestir himself unduly. Although those 'other letters' had required his presence at Rome 'within a certain time', and despite the pontiff's keen desire to see him (a person 'most dear to us in Christ'), it would suffice if he came 'as soon as he could conveniently do so', he was now assured in this more confidential communication: 'quamcito comode poteris'.[20] At the end of 1295, Archbishop Gonzalo would have been justified in concluding that the pressure was off.

Then in July 1296 the wind changed. Within a fortnight of Munio's resignation of the see the archbishop was subjected to the full force of Bonifacian indignation. Since Munio's episcopal credentials were no longer in question, in accordance with the principle previously enunciated by Honorius IV no question remained regarding the archbishop's conduct in the matter: the cause having ceased, so ought the effect.[21] Yet now the cause was reactivated to the discomfiture of D. Gonzalo, who found himself not only suspected of collusion in the 'detestable and horrendous' events of February 1294 but also, despite the pope's recent emollient assurances, charged with 'persistent contumacy and continuous disobedience' for not having responded to the summons of October 1295. Suspended from the exercise of his jurisdiction, he was required to appear at Rome within the space of four months, failing which he would be deprived of office.[22]

In October 1295 the pope had told the archbishop to take his time, and this the archbishop had proceeded to do, for sufficient reasons which, with his usual prudence, he placed on record. If the death of Sancho IV had left the bishop of Palencia high and dry, the ensuing minority of Fernando IV left the archbishop of Toledo higher and drier still. In August 1295 he had been expelled from court. If the pontiff were aware of these 'great upsets in the kingdom', the archbishop reflected in February 1296, he would surely approve of his remaining in Castile and sending a proctor to Rome in his place.[23]

And of all this the pontiff unquestionably was aware. Earlier, when ostensibly the Palencia election had been an issue, Boniface VIII had assured the archbishop that there was . . . no hurry. It was only when the Palencia election was an issue no more that he charged the archbishop with having persisted in treating both him and the Roman Church with contempt.[24]

The conclusion must be that the pontiff's principal concern between 1295 and 1297 was not the Palencia election at all. There must have been a quite different reason for his sudden anxiety, so soon after his meeting with Munio in July 1296, to interview the archbishop without delay. But what may that reason and the source of this anxiety have been? In seeking to answer that question it is necessary to indulge in a measure of speculation regarding the overlapping private agenda of a number of Castilian personalities currently active in and around the papal curia.

Of course, if we possessed the record of Munio's interview with Boniface VIII, conjecture of this sort would not be required. In the absence of that information, however, it is not unreasonable to proceed from the assumption that the meeting at the end of which Munio emerged as 'olim episcopus Palentinus' had on the whole proved amicable. It may also have proved lengthy. With the kingdom of Castile beset by such 'great upsets', there was a whole range of subjects on which the pope would have wanted to interrogate the intimate of the late king – especially now that Munio's own ecclesiastical expectations were firmly buried in the past. For the same reason, and perhaps because he knew that he would not be returning to Castile in the near future – for who in his right mind would have chosen to do so in the summer of 1296? – Munio for his part may have been less guarded in his replies than he would otherwise have been.

Boniface may already have known a great deal about Munio's past. He would certainly have known much more about it than we do. Some of it he may have heard from Cardinal Latino Malabranca who, since assisting in the process of easing Munio out of the Master-Generalship, had been largely responsible for the election of Celestine V.[25] But for knowledge of Munio's more recent, Castilian, past, the pope must have been indebted to a Castilian informant. Someone therefore must have been talking at Rome just prior to the pope's summonses to Munio and the archbishop of Toledo in October 1295.

But who may this have been? With the papal curia swarming with

Castilians, then as it always was, the historian is in no position to lay charges, even less to seek a conviction. None the less, there was a particular Castilian ecclesiastic present there in those months, one who has figured earlier in this story and who in the autumn of 1295 had more reason than most for wishing to ingratiate himself with the pontiff. This was the new archbishop of Seville, D. Sancho González. He had been at the curia since July, and was currently under some pressure himself. Questions had been raised regarding his conduct while abbot of Lebanza, the secular abbacy in the church of Palencia which he had possessed during the course of his ascent of Castile's slippery ecclesiastical ladder, and in the month of November 1295 he was suspended from his see for a fortnight while inquiries into his alleged misdemeanours were instituted.

Now this Sancho González was the Sancho González who as abbot of Husillos had been immediately (and profitably) responsible for the election of Munio of Zamora as bishop of Palencia.[26] So he knew a great deal about that event, more than he chose to reveal, no doubt. But then so, of course, did others, and not least about the part that he had played on that occasion. Sancho González had a great deal to hide – and also the best of reasons for making a pre-emptive strike. By directing the pope's attention to the friar and the archbishop he might shift attention away from his own involvement in the affair. The stakes were high. He had much to lose. There was his reputation, for example, the reputation of the prelate who in July 1295 had been lauded by Boniface as one of those by whose merits the church's rights and liberties were preserved, the clerical estate rendered more peaceful and the people enabled to reap the advantages of joy and salvation.[27] There was also, of course, the consideration that the archbishopric of Seville was a prize not to be surrendered without a struggle.[28]

And some time since July 1295 someone had reported him to Rome, someone evidently with knowledge of the affairs of the church of Palencia. Investigation of his conduct as abbot of Lebanza might lead further, or so it may have seemed to Sancho González in the autumn of 1295. Less than two years had elapsed since the fatal election. Memories would still be fresh. The question of who it may have been who had delated him to Rome need not (indeed cannot) occupy us. Yet the question must surely have been in his own mind as he faced the inquiry which might cost him his archbishopric. Small wonder then if he was prepared to prevaricate regarding his role in the Palencia election, for which the reward he had received may now have seemed insignificant. But however he managed it, Sancho González emerged triumphant from the inquiry into his past, fully vindicated and with his morale so thoroughly restored that on returning to Castile he immediately justified the pope's panegyric of him by having his cross borne aloft in the city of Valladolid, thereby declaring primatial war on the archbishop of Toledo.[29]

Whatever he may have gleaned from the new archbishop of Seville, however, until his interview with *frey* Munio in the summer of 1296 Boniface VIII may still not have been fully informed about the Spanish phase of the former Master General's past. He may not have been aware, for example – for it was not a busy pope's job to read his predecessors' registers – that in September 1285 the Zamora Dominicans' complaints about Bishop Suero had been referred to . . . the archbishop of Toledo. Perhaps he never was aware. Perhaps he never reviewed the files. And, even if he did so in July 1296, perhaps he did not think it necessary to consider the question whether the archbishop had questioned Suero on the facts of the matter, and if not, why not,[30] or even to enquire what had become of that so-called convent. Dispersed, presumably, and the ground on which the brothers and sisters had disported themselves sown with salt, the author of *Periculoso* – the decree of 1298 which imposed strict rules of enclosure on 'certain nuns' who sound suspiciously like the Ladies of Zamora[31] – doubtless thought out loud while *frey* Munio murmured deferentially and peered distractedly at the countryside which lay beyond the window of the Anagni audience chamber.

It may have been so. Since we possess no account of what passed between that most torrential of pontiffs and the friar broken on the wheel, we have no means of knowing. In the circumstances in which *frey* Munio found himself as the papal gaze bore in upon him at that high-summer encounter, all that we can reasonably assume is that, whatever other issues may have been more or less skilfully skirted around, even casual conversation regarding Castilian affairs must sooner or later have touched on the question of the Castilian marriage and the letter of dispensation that Nicholas IV was rumoured to have granted the royal couple just twelve days before his death on 4 April 1292.

Rumoured to have. As Boniface declared in March 1297 when he pronounced the dispensation a gross forgery, the rumours had been circulating throughout the lengthy vacancy in the Roman Church that had followed Nicholas's death, the vacancy during which the Palencia election had taken place.[32] The existence of the fraud, and the extent of it, had come to light some three years previously[33] when one of the conspirators, 'Jacobus scriptor', a cleric from Constance, was apprehended and interrogated by the vice-chancellor of the Roman Church. It was a cloak-and-dagger story that Jakob told,[34] involving an international cast of three (or four): a story of an Englishman, a German and a Spaniard. But it was no joke.

Apart from Jakob the German, the improbable crew comprised Robert, the Englishman who, so the luckless Jakob claimed, had drawn him into the plot in the first place, and the shadowy Petrus on whose behalf the Englishman had first sought out the German, asking if he knew where in Rome there was a decent alchemist to be found. Oliverius, the fabricator of the dispensation, who was some sort of Frenchman[35] (and not to be trifled with on money matters; 'Vos truffans me', Jakob remembered him exclaiming), had been recruited later.

The brains of the team was Petrus, a Dominican friar who said he was the proctor of Sancho IV of Castile. It was he, *frey* Pedro, who had set the whole thing up and before they began had made them swear an oath of secrecy on the altar. If they could pull it off, he had promised them, they would all be rich, rich for ever ('imperpetuum divites'). He would have a bishopric, they could count on the richest pickings of Church and State that the kingdom of Castile had to offer, choice benefices and the highest offices in the king's household.[36] He spoke of a blank charter he had in his possession bearing the king of Castile's seal. Anything was possible. When the others hesitated and fretted about being excommunicated for forging papal letters, it was *frey* Pedro who stiffened their resolve. The next pope, when he was elected, would straighten matters out. The king of Castile was fighting Christendom's enemies on a daily basis ('cotidie'). All would be arranged. And, to their cost, the others believed him. They had only themselves to blame. *Frey* Pedro's limitations ought to have been apparent to them when, having engaged the alchemist Nicholas de Sancto Bricio (an absolutely *wonderful* little man) to make them a *bulla*, the Spaniard failed to provide the wherewithal. Then, as soon as he had the desired document in his possession, he disappeared, taking ship for Seville, courtesy of Sancho IV's Genoese admiral

125

Benedetto Zaccaria, and leaving Jakob the German in the lurch, significantly out of pocket, and with a considerable amount of explaining to do.[37]

Jakob the German's story is implausible on more than one count. But this is not surprising. Up before the vice-chancellor of the Roman Church, like the archbishop of Seville and the bishop of Palencia after him, no doubt Jakob was principally interested in saving his own skin. Even so, as in theirs, doubtless there were also elements of truth in his account. And it is these credible details that are of interest here, just as they will have been of interest to Boniface VIII when he studied the transcript of Jakob the German's story, as surely he did some time in the spring of the year 1297.

Amongst the particulars likely to have attracted the pope's attention was *frey* Pedro's reported claim that his reward from Sancho IV was to be a bishopric – a reward which he was prevented from claiming because he had left the Order. Another is the exclusively Dominican context within which the operation was conceived and executed. Jakob's first meeting with Brother Pedro had been in the friars' church of Santa Maria sopra Minerva. Their work done, the conspirators then made their escape from Rome in a galley moored beneath Santa Sabina, somewhere in the vicinity of the Order's other great church on the Aventine, where at that very time, May–June 1292, the General Chapter was in session and Brother Munio, the king of Castile's future bishop of Palencia, was in the process of undergoing public humiliation.[38]

The third is that blank royal charter – the 'blank charter with a great seal attached' – with the aid of which *frey* Pedro had enticed his partners into crime: an incriminatory object, if ever there was one, and, as Marcos Pous observes, an indication that the friar was acting with the knowledge either of the king himself or of 'a person of the first rank in the king's court'.[39] (The same thought may have occurred to Boniface VIII some time between 1296 and 1297.) Blank charters were almost common currency in late thirteenth-century Castile. Alfonso X had extorted them from his bishops, it had been reported in 1279.[40] Sancho IV found them useful too. At the beginning of the civil war of 1282–4 his father had denounced him for doing what he himself had done, in this case for providing his rebel brothers with 'chartas albas sigillatas sigillo' and using them to gain supporters. In 1287 Sancho had promised any number of 'cartas con nombres blancos' to Abrahen *el Barchilón*, farmer of the royal revenues.[41] But in the year 1292 nothing of the sort could conceivably have left the Castilian chancery without the knowledge of the king's chancellor and close confidant, that 'person of the first rank in the king's court' and speculator in blank cheques *par excellence*, Archbishop Gonzalo Pérez of Toledo.[42]

Then there is the further fact – of which of course Boniface could only have been aware if someone such as the new archbishop of Seville had drawn it to his attention – that since 1292 the Dominicans of Zamora had been in receipt of an annual pension from the king which they had not previously received, and which may or may not have represented a thank-offering to Brother Munio's old community in respect of shadowy services recently rendered.[43] But even without access to that privileged information, the probability is that some time between 11 and 23 July 1296 Boniface VIII concluded from what he had recently been told and what he had now re-read that he had uncovered an elaborate conspiracy involving a friar who had fled, a king who was dead, and (can it have been?) the archbishop who was so reluctant to come to Rome. Certainly all the signs were there.

In short, the terms in which Boniface VIII's modern biographer describes the Munio of Zamora affair ('one of the most mysterious . . . of his time') fail to carry conviction. 'A Castilian interlude hardly worth the solving' it was not.[44] For those with eyes to see in 1296, all the signs had been there at least since Jakob the German had confessed all (or all that he chose to confess) some time before April 1294.[45] But it was not until April 1297 that Boniface VIII thought it necessary to denounce the forgery and order his denunciation to be published from the pulpit throughout the Spanish peninsula – not, that is to say, until after his conversations of the previous summer with the *quondam* of Palencia, after his urgent summons to the archbishop, and after the archbishop's arrival in Rome in February or March 1297.[46]

When eventually he did appear, the archbishop evidently gave a thoroughly convincing account of himself and allayed whatever suspicions the pope may have been harbouring. This was to be expected. Archbishop Gonzalo Pérez was one of thirteenth-century Europe's great allayers of suspicions. Within no time he was making himself useful about the curia and advising the pope on the question of King Louis IX's claims to canonisation.[47] Indeed, so useful did he prove that at the end of 1298 Boniface raised him to the purple. So he stayed in Rome, in close proximity to Brother Munio. We do not know whether the two of them found time for a Roman reunion. Time was not on their side. In November 1299 the cardinal died, and in March 1300 *frey* Munio followed him to the grave.

Because the archbishop of Toledo never travelled light, the fact that he may have brought his Zamora dossier with him to Rome[48] does not necessarily mean that he was anticipating Zamora questions on his arrival there. Nor, for that matter, do the copies of the four letters from recent papal registers which he had made at this time (three of them relating to the recent clash between Pope Boniface and Philip IV of France, the other having to do with friars and bishoprics) necessarily indicate any continuing preoccupation either with recent events in the church of Palencia or with the question of friars in general.[49]

Notes

1 'impedimento multiplici quod in hac parte ingeritur obsistente' (*Reg. Nich. IV*. 1663 (published by A. Marcos Pous, 'Los dos matrimonios de Sancho IV de Castilla', Escuela Española de Arqueología e Historia en Roma, *Cuadernos de Trabajo* 8 (1956) 93–4)); Linehan, *History and the Historians*, 447, 540.

2 fr. Gundisalvus and fr. Nicholas (*Reg. Nich. IV*, 1663).

3 *Acta cap. gen.* 263, 266.

4 AC Toledo, X.2.A.2.1–1e published in Mortier, *Hist. des Maîtres Généraux*, i. 574–82. (It is to be noted that all AC Toledo documentation published by Mortier derives from Burriel's eighteenth-century transcriptions, and that these transcriptions are frequently unreliable.) The bishops of Coria and Túy, D. Alfonso and Juan Fernández de Sotomayor, dedicated curialists both, were successively the queen's chancellors (Gaibrois, *Sancho IV*, i. 44). For the use of candles, for this and other purposes, then and later and in Spain and elsewhere, see Linehan, *Spanish Church and the Papacy*, 256; M. Dykmans, *Le Cérémonial papal de la fin du Moyen Age à la Renaissance*, ii. *De Rome en Avignon ou Le Cérémonial de Jacques Stefaneschi*, Brussels and Rome 1981, 158–9; W. A. Christian, Jr., *Local Religion in Sixteenth-century Spain*, Princeton 1981, 47; A. Hobson, 'A sale by candle in 1608', *The Library*, 5th ser. 26 (1971) 215–33.

5 'A Sancho Gómez [*sic*], Abad de Fusiellos, XII mil. . . . Al Prior et al Convento de Palencia, CCCXXXII mrs. . . . Al Arcidiano Don Simón, XII mil mrs' (published in Gaibrois, *Sancho IV*, I. pp. lxxii, lxxiii). (The name of the abbot of Husillos was 'Sancius Gundisalvi' (González, not Gómez: Palencia, Archivo episcopal, Husillos no. 9).)

6 'Et bien sabedes de commo Frey Munio nos a fecho mucho seruiçio anos et ala Reyna' (M. Mañueco Villalobos and J. Zurita Nieto, *Documentos de la*

128

Iglesia Colegial de S. María la Mayor (hoy metropolitana) de Valladolid, ii, Valladolid 1920, 283–4). Munio had been consecrated at Toledo on 7 March (Mortier, 578).

7 *Acta. cap. gen.*, 275.

8 Despite the tradition (repeated by Hinnebusch, *History*, 229) that Celestine confirmed Munio's election.

9 Gaibrois, 'Fray Munio de Zamora', 134.

10 'que si non es assi es bien e si assi es non sea daqui adelant' (Linehan, 'Spanish Church revisited', 143).

11 *Reg. Bon. VIII*, 832; Mortier, 582.

12 *Reg. Bon. VIII*, 576 (December 1295); Quétif-Échard, *Scriptores*, i. 399. Guillem de Moncada was no less the king of Aragón's pensioner than Munio was Sancho IV's. Yet in December 1295 Boniface VIII sent him on a diplomatic mission to Sicily (Finke, *Acta Aragonensia*, i, Berlin 1908, 28; *Reg. Bon. VIII*, 851).

13 In 1295 and 1300 Boniface approved their appointments to the sees of Seville and Sigüenza respectively (*Reg. Bon. VIII*, 552, 3640).

14 *Reg. Bon. VIII*, 1636 (11 July 1296).

15 This was delivered to him on 2 January 1296 (AC Toledo, X.2.A.2.1f (published in Mortier, 582–3)).

16 *Reg. Bon. VIII*, 1898 (11 July 1297).

17 Fernández de Pulgar, *Teatro clerical*, ii. 360–1 (paginated 367).

18 Linehan, *Spanish Church and the Papacy*, 252.

19 'si auia probado su inocencia en la confirmacion, y consagracion de nuestro Obispo de Palencia Don Munio: como le quedò Don Munio sin el Obispado, pues estando sin culpa Don Gonçalo, tambien lo estava el Obispo Don Munio. Vna era la causa, y menor el delito en el Obispo, pues quando mucho se auia auido passivamente en la elecion' (*loc. cit.*).

20 AC Toledo, X.2.A.2.1a (ed. Mortier, ii. 583, misreading 'quamcito' as 'quanto'). The 'other letters' are those mentioned above in note 15.

21 See above, p. 83, note 37.

22 *Reg. Bon. VIII*, 1638 (23 July 1296): executor's letter, 18 October 1296 (AC Toledo, X.2.A.2.1g), Mortier, 584.

23 AC Toledo, X.2.A.2.1h: published (also from Burriel's copy) in Benavides, *Fernando IV*, ii. no. LXXVII, with the date, defective as it stands ('domingo doce dias andados . . .') corrected from 12 October to 11 November 1296. However, it evidently constitutes the archbishop's response to the summons presented to him on 2 January 1296 (see note 15 above), hence the date 12 February suggested here. For the Castilian situation in 1295, see Linehan, *History and the Historians*, 475–7, 526.

24 'qui nos et dictam sedem tandiu contempsit contemptibilem' (AC Toledo, X.2.A.2.1g).

25 P. Herde, *Cölestin V. (1294). (Peter vom Morrone). Der Engelpapst*, Stuttgart 1981, 67–8.

26 See above, p. 118.

27 'quarum industria et uirtute eedem ecclesie in suis iuribus et libertatibus

conseruentur, reddatur tranquillior cleri status et comodis salutis et gaudii plebs letetur' (Reg. Vat. 47, fo. 92ᵛ, no. 399 (*Reg. Bon. VIII*, 399)).

28 In the valuation recently undertaken by the papal chamber in order to estimate the level of *servitia communia* due to the Roman Church, the archbishop of Seville's annual income had been calculated at 7,800 florins (H. Hoberg, *Taxae pro servitiis communibus ex libris obligationum ab anno 1295 usque ad annum 1455 confectis*, Vatican City 1949, no. 121) (the figure for the year 1304. The figure given for 1295/6, 1,800 florins, is evidently an error).

29 His suspension had been imposed by 13 November and was lifted on 26 November 1295 (*Reg. Bon. VIII*, 552, 663). Cf. Mañueco Villalobos and Zurita Nieto, *Documentos de Valladolid*, iii (1920) 304–6.

30 It is in fact highly unlikely that the archbishop, newly returned to Castile in the autumn of 1285 after an absence of six or seven years, would have chosen to give priority to an investigation capable of complicating his relationship with Sancho IV. On 20 March 1286, 'multis et variis tam regis quam aliis negociis impediti', he sub-delegated the execution of another papal mandate which was already five months old (AHN, Clero 3022/10). Moreover, since the archbishop was at Segovia on this occasion, while the king was at San Sebastián, it cannot be assumed that he would have been with the court when it was at Zamora two months before (Gaibrois, *Sancho IV*, iii. nos. 102, 107).

31 'Wishing to provide for the dangerous and abominable situation of certain nuns, who, casting off the reins of respectability and impudently abandoning nunnish modesty and the natural bashfulness of their sex, sometimes rove about outside of their monasteries to the homes of secular persons and frequently admit suspect persons into these same monasteries, to the injury of those who by free choice vowed their chastity, to the disgrace and dishonor of the religious life, and the temptation of many . . .' Cf. J. A. Brundage and E. M. Makowski, 'Enclosure of nuns: the decretal *Periculoso* and its commentators', *Journal of Medieval History* 20 (1994) 143–55 (translation, 154).

32 *Reg. Bon. VIII*, 2335.

33 'adhuc eadem vacatione durante' (*ibid.*).

34 His testimony is published by Marcos Pous, 'Los dos matrimonios', 96–100.

35 'Credit' – it is Jakob speaking – 'quod esset Burgerundus vel Piccardus. Interrogatus qualiter sciret, dixit pro eo quod loquebatur in gallico' (*ibid.*, 98).

36 *Ibid.*, 97.

37 *Ibid.*, 99–100. The sequence of events related by Jakob seems to have occurred some time during 1292 when Sancho IV was indeed in Seville, engaged with the Genoese admiral in the siege of Tarifa. The terms in which the forged document justified dispensation of the royal marriage, as reward for the king's strenuous exertions against the enemies of the Faith ('intellecto inter cetera . . . quod ex jam percepta precordialissima devotione

expugnare cepistis Sarracenos vobis confines, crucis inimicos, et continue laboratis humiliare . . .' (*Reg. Bon. VIII*, 2335)) closely resembles the self-congratulatory language employed by Sancho's chancery that same year. Cf. A. López Dapena, *Cuentas y gastos (1292–1294) del rey D. Sancho IV el Bravo (1284–1295)*, Córdoba 1984, 343, 347; Gaibrois, *Sancho IV*, iii. p. cclxxxii. For Zaccarias's activities in 1292, *ibid.*, ii. 170 ff. (Was the servant 'Robinus' whom Brother Pedro sent from Genoa to visit the sick Jakob at Savona (Marcos Pous, 99) the admiral's man Micer Rofin, who is mentioned in Castilian sources? Cf. Gaibrois, ii. 180.)

38 Marcos Pous, 96 (the plot was hatched 'post mortem obitum eiusdem Nicholai [pape] circa mensem'), 99; Mortier, *Hist. des Maîtres Généraux*, 299. Nicholas IV died on 4 April 1292. Whitsun in that year, the day prescribed for the assembly of the General Chapter, fell on 25 May.

39 'membranam vacuam cui erat appensum unum magnum sigillum' (Marcos Pous, 97, 79).

40 'Facit etiam dominus Rex sigillari paginas vacuas per prelatos et perhibere testimonium de hiis que nec viderunt nec sciverunt' (Linehan, 'Spanish Church revisited', 143–4).

41 J. de Zurita, *Indices rervm ab Aragoniae regibvs gestarvm ab initiis Regni ad annvm MCDX . . .*, Zaragoza 1578, 172; Gaibrois, *Sancho IV*, i. p. clxxxviii.

42 Linehan, *Spanish Church and the Papacy*, 136–7; *idem*, *History and the Historians*, 475–8.

43 'A los freyres predicadores de Çamora dcclxiiii mr' (Hernández, *Las rentas del rey*, i. 188–9).

44 T. S. R. Boase, *Boniface VIII*, London 1933, 195, 198. Boase's summary account of the matter is otherwise exceptionally well informed.

45 In which month the then Cardinal Benedict Gaetani and two other cardinals had issued a warrant for the arrest of brother Petrus Hispanus OP 'de litterarum apostolicarum falcitate [*sic*] suspectum' (Finke, *Acta Aragonensia*, i. 14).

46 *Reg. Bon. VIII*, 2335 *ad fin.*

47 P. Linehan and F. J. Hernández, '"Animadverto": a recently discovered *consilium* concerning the sanctity of King Louis IX', *Revue Mabillon*, n. s. 5 (1994) 83–105.

48 There is no sign either at the Toledo archive or amongst the Toledo material in the Archivo Histórico Nacional of the instructions which he had had from Honorius IV in 1285 (see above, p. 2). Dr F. J. Hernández and the present writer have in preparation a full-length study of the career of Gonzalo Pérez.

49 Namely *Quorundam oculos*, prohibiting the election, postulation or provision of any mendicant 'ad aliquam extra administrationem sui ordinis praelaturam, in discordia de se facta' (VI 1.6.24) (AC Toledo, O.8.A.I.I). Earlier, presumably, the Dominicans of Toro had acquired an exemplar of *Petitio tua*, Nicholas IV's ruling regarding the procedures to be followed in the case of members of the Order elected to bishoprics (AHN, Clero 3572/12 (Po. 22816)).

CHAPTER SIX

'Ut eatis . . .'

$\mathcal{B}$RIEFLY reunited towards the end of their lives, in the year after
frey Munio's death the refulgent cardinal and the abject friar were
separated again. Both had been provided with splendid Roman
tombs, with the cardinal's in Santa Maria Maggiore one of the
wonders of the age, and the mosaic magnificence of the rehabilitated
Munio's in Santa Sabina to the south possibly designed to rival that
of Nicholas IV himself, the pope who had brought him down.[1] But
whereas the former Master General's remains stayed in Rome, the
cardinal's friends managed to persuade Boniface VIII to release his for
reinterment in Toledo. Their respective final resting-places in the
centres of Christendom and of the kingdom of Castile provide alternative vantage-points from which to survey some of the wider
implications of the succession of provincial incidents with which the
earlier chapters of this book have been concerned.

The sequence of events in and around the city of Zamora which were
to have such various consequences for some of those involved occurred
distressingly soon after the launching of one of the great pastoral ini-
tiatives of Christian history. The foundation of the Order of Preachers
can still be sensed as a new beginning. Loose-limbed friars roaming
Europe's roads, striding along beneath wide skies, are the 1220s person-
ified. From the beginning, itinerant preaching was central to the apostolic life to which Dominicans were committed. Christ's words to his
disciples on the eve of His Passion provided a favourite text: 'I have
chosen you, and ordained you, that ye should go ('ut eatis') and bring
forth fruit' (John 15.16). Although when Doña Caterina set off in the
1270s she went not to bring forth fruit but to sell it,[2] as recently as 1242
the emphasis had continued to be on keeping going and moving on.

As late as 1242 the Spanish friars still regarded themselves as, in a sense, the overnight guests of the Western Church. Though the proprietors of the ecclesiastical ghost town where they had bivouacked were nowhere to be seen, they felt they owed it to their hosts to leave the place as they had found it. The conclusion that the provincial chapter of that year expressed regarding the church which the Order had colonised at Pamplona reflected the Order's view of its relationship with the Church at large. The shell of the ruin on to which they had added their own habitation was to be kept intact. Friars intent on flying buttresses were to be restrained.[3]

Here was one view of the Dominicans, their own – friars as friends of the ecclesiastical environment, the preservers of old vaults and walls. Although to the eyes of others they more closely resembled immigrants than conservationists, if the Spanish evidence is typical neither characterisation is wholly appropriate. The signs suggest that in Spain after mid-century the Dominicans more closely corresponded to privileged squatters. From the record of *assignationes* (the details of the distribution of individual friars within and outside the province) it would appear that, although within the province their numbers continued to grow during these years, an increasing proportion of these new recruits were tending to stay put. Whereas 159 friars were assigned to 20 different houses in 1250, in 1275 (by which time at least another 10 houses had been established) only 62 of the brethren were directed to make a move.[4]

In Spain, as elsewhere, the friars were acquiring sedentary habits and accustoming themselves to sedentary status. By the mid-1270s the glad confident mornings and high-striding days were fast becoming a distant memory. Calculation had entered in. By 1319, when 'on account of the poverty of the see' fr. Juan Fernández OP was persuaded by his relations to decline the bishopric of Segorbe-Albarracín[5] – a place in need of first-generation mendicant ministrations, if ever there was one – those heroic days had gone for ever. In his study of the process of canonisation in the Christian West, André Vauchez has identified the 1260s as the decade during which the official Church drifted apart from the local churches and lost contact with those sources of devotion whose strength continued to be manifested in the confidence of the localities in their ability to recognise a saint for themselves.[6] At the same time the Order of Preachers, at least in parts of Spain, seems to have been experiencing its adolescence and exhibiting adolescent tendencies in claiming more and more house-room for itself. The events reported from Zamora in the 1270s suggest that they may even have been holding wild parties. The fact that it was the year 1264, the year of the ladies' establishment of themselves at Zamora, that Fr. Meersseman recorded as marking the moment of the progress of Dominican architecture from its infancy to its adolescence is presumably no more than a coincidence.[7] Also presumably, those events were untypical. Nevertheless, it remains necessary to relate the developments of which they were part to the new departures identified by Professor Vauchez.

If the number of *assignationes* were the only available index of this trend, it would have to be adjudged short-lived, since at the provincial chapter of Estella in 1281 more than 330 *assignationes* were decreed, and at Barcelona in 1299 as many as 550.[8] However, the 1290s also revealed other symptoms. For the Dominicans the 1290s was their most troubled decade to date. Historians sometimes ask why the Order of Preachers was spared the famous schism experienced by the Franciscans in these years. To many Dominicans at the time the question would have seemed unreal. By re-electing its prior provincial in defiance of the General Chapter's ordinance in 1291, the Spanish province declared open revolt, while at the Ferrara General Chapter in the previous year it had been thought necessary to legislate against an enemy within conspiring with forces without and dedicated to fomenting division and undermining the Order's good estate.[9]

Even so, even in 1290, the popes were still their friends. By a series of privileges – of which *Ad fructus uberes*, Martin IV's licence to them to exercise the parochial ministry without episcopal permission, was the most far-reaching – for almost half a century popes had regularly taken the friars' side against the ordinaries. And despite the view expressed at Pamiers in that year, that Nicholas IV's treatment of the Order was tantamount to an invitation to subjects everywhere to defy their 'prelates', the papacy's long-standing support of the mendicants still held. Rather than abrogate *Ad fructus uberes*, the Roman curia would see the University of Paris in ruins, the cardinal legate Benedetto Caetani informed the leaders of the French Church two months after the Pamiers meeting.[10] While the Parisian masters busied themselves with 'fabulous' and 'frivolous' issues to the detriment of 'useful' questions, the friars remained the Church's one sound member and the source of salvation for the many. The friars could rest assured that they would enjoy Martin IV's privilege for ever.[11]

But the high command of the Order was not so confident that its members were devoting themselves to 'useful' rather than 'curious' pursuits. Dabbling in urine was not regarded as a useful pursuit, for example, and the friars had been warned against doing so as early as 1249.[12] At Estella in 1281, while the rumours from Zamora must surely have been gathering pace, the provincial chapter had heard the Master General's thoughts on the subject,[13] and in February 1300 the supreme pontiff did what as cardinal legate he had promised that the Roman Church would never do.

Super cathedram, the decree which abrogated *Ad fructus uberes*, was promulgated midway between the deaths of Cardinal Gonzalo Pérez and Brother Munio. By means of an equitable settlement of the principal issues that had for so long been matters of contention, it sought to promote peace, charity and unity between the bishops and parish clergy on the one hand and the friars on the other. Two years later the pontiff was berating the mendicants in his public consistory for persisting in vexing the regulars. By March 1302 the Church's 'one sound member' had become 'those damned friars'.[14] Pope Boniface's revised estimate is a measure of what the 1290s had meant for the Order of Preachers.

According to *Super cathedram* the friars might continue to preach without licence both in their own churches and in public, though they were not to do so at the hour when the bishop was preaching in his cathedral: a long-standing injunction now given pontifical force.[15] But they were only to preach in other churches if invited. Nor, except with episcopal permission (which the pope was strangely confident the bishops would freely grant), were they to hear the confessions of the faithful. Further, they were required to surrender to the parish clergy a quarter of their income from funerals and 'from everything left to them, expressly or not, for whatever definite purpose, even from such bequests of which a fourth or canonical part is not claimed by custom or by law, and also a fourth part of bequests made at the death or at the point of death of the giver, whether directly or through a third party'.[16]

Every conceivable mendicant subterfuge had been anticipated; since 1290 Boniface VIII had come to know his friars. Even so, the attempt that *Super cathedram* represented to draw a line under the history of the previous eighty years depended for its efficacy on an unworkable fudge and sanctions beyond even Boniface VIII's control.[17] So its success was limited. In 1304, Boniface's successor, Benedict XI – a Dominican with views on the subject of 'novelty' and 'utility' which more closely resembled those expressed at Ferrara in 1290 than those voiced at Paris by Cardinal Benedetto in that year – rescinded the hydra-like measure which, he claimed, had succeeded in spawning seven new problems for every one it had settled – and though Benedict's successor, Clement V, restored it, controversy continued into the fourteenth century and beyond as to what *Super cathedram* actually meant.[18]

But at a time when no papal decree, however carefully drafted, was proof against the canonists' loophole-seeking sensors, it was not the eventual fate of *Super cathedram* that was significant. What was significant was that the decree enshrining the most serious setback to date in the history of the mendicant orders had been promulgated at all.

In considering the genesis of *Super cathedram*, with its castigation of the 'wicked acts' and 'evil living' to which 'dissensions and scandals' gave rise, it would of course not be right to give undue prominence to the events in Zamora with which the earlier chapters of this book have been concerned.[19] Yet, even if not directly responsible for *Super cathedram* – or for that matter for *Periculoso*[20] – recent lurid scandals within the Dominican Order can only have encouraged the shift in favour of diocesan and parochial integrity, respect for ancient landmarks and the prevention of trespass in other men's fields in accordance with which the decree of 1300 was promulgated.[21] As with the imminent settlement of the Burgos dispute in the cathedral chapter's favour,[22] ten years earlier such an outcome would have been unthinkable.

Amongst the previously exempt payments which *Super cathedram* made liable to parochial taxation were *carnalia*, those gifts to individual friars on account of friendship or family connexions which had contributed so much to the Order's material progress at Burgos, Zamora and elsewhere in the Spanish province. Together with the cardinal's corpse, let us, therefore, now return to the kingdom of Castile, or rather to the kingdom of León and to the convent of Poor Clares at Allariz in particular.

The Allariz convent was the establishment of Alfonso X's estranged queen, Violante of Aragón. Situated in the diocese of

Orense, as well as being one of the first places to declare openly for the Infante Sancho in March 1282, it was where the queen chose to be buried – symbolically perhaps, for in its Galician fastness Allariz was about as far as it was possible to venture from Seville, Murcia and Jerusalem, the locations specified by her husband to house his mortal remains. Violante's endowment of the convent was extremely lavish. By her will of April 1292 she bequeathed more than 200,000 maravedís 'de los de la guerra' to the place, with another 3,000 to its abbess, Sancha Eanes, and bequests too for her Franciscan executors, for the order's convent at Orense and for all Franciscan and Dominican foundations throughout Galicia. Individual friars attending her funeral were each to be provided with new habits to the value of 30 maravedís.[23] Earlier undertakings to be interred elsewhere, in Aragón with her mother Violante of Hungary and at Zamora – although it is not stated where 'en Çamora', the Clarissan convent is surely meant – the queen was at pains to revoke.[24]

The blessings of the Almighty and the Virgin, as well as her own and Alfonso X's, were invoked to ensure that her son King Sancho did not strive to frustrate Violante's intentions. Were he to do so, Sancho was to remain cursed through all eternity by God the Father and the Virgin – just as he had already incurred his earthly father's curse, the curse which haunted him for the remainder of his life.[25] The queen mother knew her son and his ways, no doubt. And the son was equally familiar with his mother's inveterate tendency to conspiracy. Indeed, for that reason he had already confiscated the extensive estates with which she had been endowed by Alfonso X forty years before, including the lordship of the towns of Valladolid, Plasencia, Ayllón, Estudillo, Coriel, San Estebán de Gormaz and Béjar,[26] and when he died in April 1295 he did so cursed by both his parents, which even in that age of family misunderstandings constituted a record of a sort.[27] Even so, as is apparent from the terms of the charters which the convent of Allariz received from him during his brief reign, however unfilial his relationship with his mother may have been, in his dealings with her favourite foundation Sancho IV was not unindulgent.

Nor, as those charters also demonstrate, was he oblivious to the realities of female mendicancy in his realms at the end of the century of Saints Dominic, Francis and Clare. In November 1290 Nicholas IV granted the Galician convent the rule that he had recently conceded to the Poor Clares of Blois.[28] The rule they received, these Poor Clares of Allariz, was the same rule as that which in 1263 the sister of Louis IX of France, the Blessed Isabel, had secured for her convent at Longchamp, a rule which, as well as to chastity and obedience, committed them to propertylessness.[29] But not to poverty, not to that poverty which Saint Clare herself had eventually been granted as a privilege. By the 1290s the requirements of the Clarissan communities of north-western Spain were less demanding. By then the houses of the Order rather resembled a species of dower house providing sheltered accommodation for ladies, many of them ladies *d'un certain âge*. And, as is usually the case with such arrangements, not all the ladies fitted in. One who failed to was Mayor Pérez. The other ladies at the Compostela convent said nasty things about her. She knew when she was not wanted. So off she went, taking her property in the parish of San Esteban de Trasmonte with her, very much in the spirit of the Dominican nuns of Metz whose bickerings and cries of 'I brought more to the cloister than you did' earned them a stiff rebuke shortly afterwards.[30]

It was in this same spirit, the spirit of limited-term investment rather than permanent commitment, that 'in order to enable them the better to serve God', Sancho IV's charter of July 1286, issued before their monastery was built, licensed the Ladies of Allariz to retain full control of their patrimonial possessions – 'as their order requires', the king stated, though in fact this was the very reverse of what their *rule* actually prescribed. According to that rule, they were to live 'sine proprio'. With Sancho's dispensation, however, they were to remain individually as free to purchase, inherit and otherwise acquire property as they had been before entering the convent.[31] In March 1291, by which time their buildings were up, Sancho intervened afresh, again at Violante's request, establishing one set of arrangements for the convent's ladies of rank ('del linage')[32] and another for 'las duennas delas villas e delos lugares', its 'town and country ladies' for whom a limit of 40,000 maravedís was set to the value of the lands of which they might dispose.[33]

Thus, although they were required by their rule only to receive communion through the convent's iron grille (that symbolic barrier against the outside world which María Reináldez had dared to approach at Zamora), the Ladies of Allariz were entirely at liberty to play the local property market.[34] The institution of a two-tier social system within their convent, of real ladies and 'other' ladies, is reminiscent of Zamora for other reasons, of course – and this is not surprising. For it was ladies from the Clarissan convent of Zamora, where Violante had previously chosen to be buried, who had provided the pioneering cadre of the Allariz community and in the summer of 1286 were to be found engaged in purchasing a site for themselves there. And it was the guardian of the Zamora Franciscans who four years later acted as the queen's agent in acquiring copies of papal privileges.[35]

Had life at Zamora in 1286 become as uncomfortable for these ladies as it had for those of the Dominican persuasion? Were they in flight from Bishop Suero too? If so, they were in for a shock. For in their new refuge they encountered even greater episcopal hostility than they had left behind. It was not the king who jeopardised the well-being of the new community of whose spiritual exertions he and other members of his family were now beneficiaries. As at Zamora, so at Allariz it was the local bishop who did so, refusing to consecrate their church and cemetery, threatening the Dominican bishop of Silves, D. Domingo, with suspension and excommunication when he came there to do so in April 1294, and remaining steadfast in his opposition for ten years or more after that.[36]

Amongst thirteenth-century Spain's episcopal friar-baiters, Don Pedro Yáñez de Noboa, bishop of Orense, easily outclassed D. Suero of Zamora. Deaf to all appeals for moderation whether from king or pope, in 1289 he had raised himself to that bad eminence by hijacking the corpse of a lady who had chosen to be buried with the Franciscans of his episcopal city, laying violent hands on the friars, and forbidding his canons to communicate with them. And, just as relations between the bishop and the Dominicans were being restored at Zamora,[37] at Orense worse followed: breach of sanctuary, murders committed by the bishop's men within the friars' precincts (including the cutting down of men crouching beneath the friars' altar and clinging to the crucifix, contempt of vestments, arson, and more besides). There was no end to the catalogue of episcopal enormities reported to Rome and after that to Avignon.[38]

Moreover, there appeared to be no prospect of an end to the bishop of Orense's recalcitrance. A prelate whose ancestry was as venerable as his qualifications for office were meagre, in 1308 he was reported to have remained excommunicate 'for six years or more'. In fact, he had been in rebellion for closer on twenty. And so he remained, the unrepentant embodiment of that threat to the institutional Church which Rome's promotion of the mendicants had caused to be voiced in Paris in the 1250s. There was no dealing with him. He was implacable. Here was a bishop wholly unamenable to the ordinary processes of canon law.[39]

Here was a bishop who had exposed the limitations of litigation. This in itself was nothing new. Forty years earlier Suero of Zamora had played fast and loose with Clement IV and had not been alone in doing so. But because he required its services for his own purposes, in the end Suero had been willing at least to temporise with the system. Bishop Pedro of Orense was made of sterner stuff, however. A different approach was called for, therefore, and the archbishop of Compostela and his colleagues were instructed to adopt it. Softly, softly, they were to bypass the ordinary processes, dispense with all the usual paraphernalia of justice, and report back.[40]

Clement V's directive was a landmark of a sort. It amounted to an admission that the system of delegate jurisdiction, the tentacles of which had reached into the remotest interstices of the Christian West for two centuries or more, had at last encountered an impenetrable obstruction. It also anticipated, to the letter, the measure designed to break the log-jam of litigation concerning beneficial and matrimonial cases *inter alia*, that 'simple, easy process . . . without the noise and rhetoric of a court of justice' which the General Council at Vienne was to enact in May 1312 and which, in his gloss on the decree, Johannes Andreae was to describe as 'entirely new law'.[41]

And so it was, 'entirely new law'. But the practice which it regularised was not new. The use of summary procedure in cases in which the ordinary operations of the Church's system had proved ineffective had its antecedents. In 1268, for example, it had been invoked to deal with a particularly complex beneficial wrangle.[42] Clement V's letter of March 1308 concerning the intractable bishop of Orense was, therefore, not its earliest formulation. However, in view of the extreme gravity of the charges against the bishop, it was highly significant, none the less. The rule of law as it had been administered against criminal prelates since the age of Gregory VII had been holed beneath the water-line.

What is more, it testifies to the ability of a bishop of the calibre of D. Pedro Yáñez de Noboa to defy with impunity both the rules of law to which he was subject. As the abbess of Allariz had complained in

March 1294, neither 'por carta de rroma' nor 'por cartas de nosso señor el Rey don Sancho' could the bishop be induced to consecrate her church and cemetery.[43] True, in March 1294 there was no pope either in Rome or anywhere else. Yet Sancho IV was then at the height of his powers. And the formidable Boniface VIII found D. Pedro no more biddable. Pope Boniface came and went, and when he went the bishop of Orense's reign of terror was still in place, principally because in 1295 Sancho IV had been succeeded by the 9-year-old Fernando IV, and in the ensuing anarchy the likes of D. Pedro Yáñez flourished.

The consequences of the royal minority in this case are recorded in a letter of April 1307 in which Fernando reprimanded his officials in Galicia for having sought to bring the bishop and chapter of Orense to book for demolishing the local Franciscan convent and carrying off the friars' stones and roof and wood. In doing so the officials had acted wrongly, the king informed them; this for two reasons. One, that the bishop, the chapter and the friars were churchmen and had therefore to 'seek justice' from the church's judge. The other, that when the bishop had raised the matter at the Cortes of Zamora, the king (such as he was in 1301) had ruled that the issue should be decided at Rome but that, as to the part they had played in the *britamiento* of the convent, he had pardoned them anyway.[44] Indeed, the king had pardoned them as long before as December 1296. He had done so at the behest of the bishop's nephews when he had been a child, had still been illegitimate, and was even more of a cipher than he was eleven years later.[45]

The circumstances in which the friars of Orense and their sisters at Allariz found themselves in the years after 1290 deserve to be related to the course of events at Zamora with which the earlier chapters of this book have been concerned. It would be possible to regard the development which had been witnessed at Zamora after 1285, from direct action to litigation, as an indicator of a sort, as confirmation of a process of progress. Some do. For some, the effectiveness of public authority is measurable in terms of the inclination of individuals to have recourse to a legal forum rather than to the hook on the wall by the door where their grandfathers had kept their rusty weapons. In this view of the past, the passage of the Middle Ages was marked by the murmur of quills penning writs in symphony with the gentle thud of swords being beaten into ploughshares.

The reports regarding the bishop of Orense seem to suggest other-

※ ※ ※ ※ ※

wise, however. Moreover, at least in Spanish terms, the bishop of Orense's case is far from unique. Rather than peaceful murmurings and gentle thuds, what is chiefly audible from the Spanish front is a series of clanks interspersed by curses and comminations. In Spain the shift from direct action to litigation seems to have been a matter of form rather than of substance. In Spain appellants packaged their petitions rather as the friars of Zamora were reported by Marina Rodríguez to have delivered their letters to the ladies, wrapped around lumps of stone.[46] 'I know that all Spaniards are impatient', the papal envoy Nicholas of Terracina observed in the report he submitted to Alexander IV in August 1257, after a series of particularly bruising encounters with Archbishop Benet de Rocaberti of Tarragona. 'That is their reputation, and experience confirms it.'[47] A pair of incidents separated by almost two centuries serves to confirm the envoy's experience that, in the fourteenth century as in the twelfth, when men went to law in Spain they did so with the same deadly purpose and with the same sense of total commitment with which elsewhere men went to war.

At Zamora one day early in the year 1158 a fisherman was on the point of selling a fine trout to a local shoemaker, when a member of a local noble household demanded the fish for his master. A crowd gathered. One thing led to another. The nobleman's man seized the shoemaker. The crowd seized the nobleman's man and, when the latter's friends arrived on the scene and they went into a nearby church to discuss their next move, the building was torched and all those within perished. The arsonists then packed up their belongings and left the city. From a place near the Portuguese border they then sent messengers to the king of León, Fernando II, begging his pardon but also requesting the removal of the governor, Ponce de Cabrera, whose son had died in the inferno. And the king acceded to their request, which it is difficult to imagine his contemporary Henry II of England doing in similar circumstances. This was the so-called 'Mutiny of the trout'. A good story, it lost nothing in the telling down the ages.[48]

The 'Tale of the pig' belongs to the 1330s, and is true. The pig lived at Covarrubias to the south of Burgos. But whose pig was it? That was the question. And where was it? That was another. The abbot of Salas, the dignitary of the chapter of Burgos who claimed it was his, was informed that two men of Covarrubias, the cleric Gil Pérez and the layman Gonzalvo González, had 'violently and injuriously' made off

143

with the animal. The charge, if true, was a charge of 'detinue of the said pig'. But *was* it true? Again, one thing led to another. A papal legate had recently issued a set of constitutions in defence of the ecclesiastical estate. In no time the legatine constitutions were invoked, the cleric and the layman, together with all those who may in any way have been implicated in 'the seizure ('raptus'), occupation and detention of the said pig', were excommunicated, Covarrubias was under interdict, and the living were being refused the sacraments and the dead denied ecclesiastical burial. In March 1335 the case of the Castilian quadruped reached Avignon, and the officials of a court upon which the affairs of the entire Church depended set about grappling with the case of the porcine subject of a king notorious for the robustness of his views on the matter of alien jurisdictions. By July 1336 the record of the preliminary pleadings alone ran to some 70 feet of paper and upwards of 20,000 words.[49] Had parchment still been in use the case of the Covarrubias pig must have had serious repercussions for the woollier inhabitants of Old Castile.

The particular circumstances of the fourteenth-century *casus belli* apart – and the role of pigs in the history of medieval Castile awaits its historian still[50] – the two stories have a single moral. Far from betokening a social sea change over two centuries, what in fact the recourse to advocacy rather than to arms signified was the unchanging nature of Spanish society. When growling and grimacing at them and sending them to Coventry failed to freeze the local Franciscans out of his city, the bishop of Orense had changed tack and set about smoking them out. D. Pedro Yáñez de Noboa had had even less to fear than usual when in April 1294 the bishop of Silves had appealed to the pope in Rome. In April 1294 there *was* no pope in Rome. Nor did Boniface VIII's installation deter D. Pedro from following the example of the men of Zamora a century and a half earlier and putting a match to the Franciscan convent.[51] At Orense, as in Spain at large, the old trusted remedies remained in place, obliging rulers to attempt to maintain order by adopting and adapting the example of Pope Clement V. Thus in 1329 Alfonso XI sought to put an end to the long-running dispute over the lordship of Illescas by overriding customary law and proceeding 'sin figura de juycio et non guardando orden de derecho'.[52] Historians have interpreted this measure as a manifestation of majesty. In fact, like the pope's on which it was modelled, it was as much an admission of impotence.

Nor in this respect was Spanish society so very different from other societies. Examples of the same adherence to old forms under new norms might be adduced from any area of the Christian West between 1158 and 1335. Yet in at least one respect, Spain *was* different. Whereas the history of Western Europe during these two centuries was a history of ever-rising population, Spain was different inasmuch as in Spain manpower continued at a premium.

As has been mentioned, when the Zamora arsonists asked the king to expel the governor whose son they had immolated, the king did as they asked. He did so after they had told him that unless he complied they would emigrate to Portugal.[53] Fifty kilometres to the west of Zamora, the Duero became the Douro and the course of the river marked the frontier between the kingdom of León and the kingdom of Portugal. At no time between the mid twelfth century and the mid fourteenth was any peninsular ruler able to view the prospect of mass emigration with any degree of equanimity. The poaching and protection of settlers represented an important part of D. Suero's episcopal activity.[54] The same was true of landlords elsewhere.[55] The manpower business was big business in medieval Spain. In the 1340s, when describing the state of collapse which Castile had reached in 1325, the chronicler of Alfonso XI concluded by reminding his readers that 'many of the inhabitants of the kingdom were abandoning the places where they lived and going off to settle in Aragon and Portugal'.[56]

Again, contemporary England provides a point of comparison. In England, not even in the worst years of the reign of Edward II, would the evacuation of the Marches and the Borders have been regarded as a synonym for anarchy. In 1325 England had men to spare. Christian Spain meanwhile, like the Latin kingdom of Jerusalem, was desperately short of them – as it had been for at least two centuries, and never more so than in the years after 1212, when just as the opportunities of Andalucía became available to the rulers of Castile, the human supply from north of the Pyrenees failed. Why this was so is yet another mystery. There were, to all appearances, richer pickings to be had in Spain after 1212 than ever before. There were also – also more than ever before – men and families north of the Pyrenees with no means of supporting themselves. Yet demand and supply failed to make contact. They did not come, not even from the Marches and the Borders.

Perhaps the experience of the last substantial contingent that had done so provides part of an explanation. The French warriors who had arrived in 1212 returned home before the battle of Las Navas de Tolosa was fought and won. The Castilian chroniclers attributed their defection to the fact that they were French. But perhaps the diarrhoea by which they were afflicted had as much to do with it, and the heat of the sun, which was too much for them, as the Castilians reported with unfeigned satisfaction.[57] Spain north of the Tagus was recognisably European, green to the eye and damp to the touch. Buttered toast in a stone house in the hills of moist Asturias was one thing. An adobe hacienda south of the Guadalquivir, endless olive oil and the prospect of stomach cramps in perpetuity may have seemed another. Be that as it may, for whatever reason, they did not come.

So the peninsular rulers, and the rulers of Castile in particular, were thrown back on their own human resources, and such was their anxiety to secure the Christian frontier that there was no expedient to which they would not have recourse. With the Church's local officers themselves so little committed to the cause, as the relatively trivial sums bequeathed by them to the *cruzada* would seem to indicate,[58] Alfonso X explored the possibility of exploiting Christian devotion, for example promoting shrines in the south in order to persuade the faithful to forsake Compostela in favour of the more powerful miracles available at Cartagena, and giving his blessing to Christian couples who, when the church bell rang to summon them to mass, opted instead to stay in bed for purposes of procreation.[59] And it was not only the laity who were the recipients of such encouragement. D. Suero granted rights of inheritance to settlers as an inducement to them to settle on his estates.[60] So too did the kings of Castile in their dealings with the Castilian clergy. In 1238 Alfonso's father, Fernando III (the Saint), had licensed the clergy of Guadalajara to bequeath their property to their children, and in 1271 Alfonso made similar provision for those of Almazán, Roa and Castrojériz in the dioceses of Osma and Burgos.[61]

Portugal, just down the road from Zamora, was different to the extent that Portugal was considerably smaller and the human shortfall proportionately less critical. So instead of condoning clerical concupiscence, the kings of Portugal taxed it and used it as a lever against the Portuguese episcopate. In 1224, and again in 1231, the bishop of Lisbon reported to Rome that, on the strength of a certain 'constitution' of King Afonso I, royal officials, with Jews and Moors in attendance, were in the habit of breaking in on priests by night and inspecting their beds.[62]

Meanwhile the kings of Castile were giving the clerical beds of their kingdom a wide berth, conniving at what went on in them, and hoping for the best. In doing so, however, they were encouraging a clerical tendency to venery for which, as both recent and more remote history amply demonstrated, the Castilian clergy needed no encouragement. Bishop Suero's investigation of the affairs of the Ladies of Zamora occurred exactly midway between the legation of Cardinal John of Abbeville and the decade during which the Archpriest of Hita, Juan Ruiz, was engaged in recording the sexual successes and disappointments of himself and his clerical brethren.[63]

In 1229 the French cardinal descended upon the peninsular kingdoms and confronted churchmen there with the legislation of the Universal Church promulgated at the Fourth Lateran Council fourteen years before. Amongst the many stern measures he decreed, the sternest by far concerned clerical concubinage. Clerics taken in fornication were to be excommunicated, suspended from their orders and deprived of their benefices. Their consorts were to be buried where the animals were buried. The legatine decrees caused universal dismay. Over the following century the bishops of Castile contrived by one means or another to have them modified, and little by little they persuaded popes to see the point and substitute fines.[64] Either there would be a Christian ministry, one feature of which would be the uncanonical items of washing on the line, or there would be no Christian ministry at all.

A century later and the washing on the line had become a feature of the local landscape. In the world of Juan Ruiz and Trotaconventos, the irresistibly repellent procuress of his *Libro de Buen Amor*, we are in the same world as that which had so shocked the cardinal in 1229, in the world of the 'prudent virgins' of Las Dueñas, as Honorius IV described them in 1286, and of the cathedral and diocesan clergy with whom D. Suero had to deal.

In August 1294 the archdeacon of Zamora, D. Pedro Anays, made a new will. He was a man of considerable substance, with property in more than seventeen localities and ready money to match. In addition to his lands, the combined value of the bequests he made and the sums owed him was well in excess of 50,000 maravedís. But he had brothers, nephews and nieces to provide for, and he provided for them generously. Amongst his beneficiaries, however, was a lady by name of Marina Gutierres, a lady with daughters, who was not a member of the family. Indeed it appears that the family was not on the best of terms with Marina Gutierres, for the archdeacon felt the need to stipulate that if any of his relatives attempted to deprive her of the land and houses which he had bequeathed to her, they were to forfeit their own bequests.[65] (It did not occur to him to curse them. Only kings and queens cursed their relatives.) The lady for whose eventual burial (not with the animals) the archdeacon now made provision had not figured in the will he had made five years earlier – but at that time the memory of his mother Doña Marina may still have been fresh in his mind.[66] Perhaps John of Abbeville ought to have done more to encourage mothers. It will be remembered that at the synod of Toro Bishop Suero Pérez had not concerned himself with clerical concubinage.[67]

'Although we are clerics, we are also men', another dean exclaims in the Archpriest of Hita's *Cántica de los clérigos de Talavera*, when yet again the clergy of Talavera had been required by the pope to manage without their ladies. They should therefore appeal to the king against this papal outrage:[68]

Demás que sabe el rey que todos somos carnales,
Creed se ha adolesçer de aquestos nuestros males.

The king must surely know how desperate our need is.
We look to him to save us from whatever new decreed is.

The dean's commitment to his clergy's carnal expectations had venerable antecedents all over Europe.

Out on the open road the friars continued to come and go, talking of . . . Talking of what? Deconstructing the latest *quaestio* perhaps? As the century advanced, and if the story that the old woman told is to be believed, perhaps not.

Having heard and appreciated his sermon earlier that day, the old woman met up with the preacher outside town and found him swapping blue jokes with a companion.
'Are you not the preacher who preached so well today?', she asked.
'Indeed I am', he replied. 'Why do you ask?'
'I ask, sir,' she said, 'for this reason. We have a young priest here who sings the mass most beautifully. But sometimes after mass he goes around the houses after the girls. And when he finds one he starts touching her

⁂ ⁂ ⁂ ⁂ ⁂

up. And when the girl says, "What you up to? Lay off. You just said mass", he answers: "Oh no, I'm not the one who said mass. The one who said mass was a priest. I'm a young man and I want it now."'

Though this story survives in a Spanish version, its original setting was not necessarily Spanish.[69] The exploits of the Ladies of Zamora, however, unquestionably were. They belonged to the same real world and to the same century as the clergy of Sepúlveda who, when threatened by their bishop with separation from their concubines, clubbed together and formally bound themselves 'to defend and assist one another and their churches against the bishop and to take the case to Rome'.[70] This was prudent on their part – and, to judge by the evidence of the *Libro de Buen Amor*, also more or less effective.

The virgins of Zamora were prudent too; indeed they were nothing if not prudent. They are also of interest to the historian of medieval morals and manners. The snapshot of them parading around their cloister, parodying a funeral procession in lamentation for the exclusion of their paramours; Doña Estefanía dining alone; Doña Caterina de Zamora *entertaining* alone, the dalliance believed to have ensued confirming all the former Master General's worst fears on the subject of *familiaritas* and of the eventual consequences of those 'wandering eyes' that so haunted him, of those nunnish glances which, once they had exercised themselves in the service of feminine vanity within the cloister, were capable of pinioning a man, even through holes in the wall.[71] Or through the grille, which Humbert's Rule called *rota* and insisted must be 'inseparably' secure, or through that barrier against contact with the outside world, their barred and double-barred window.[72] From the very beginning of the female Order, for the very reason that they were taboo, the grille and window separating them from that world exercised a special fascination for the women looking out.[73]

Assignations in the choir, clinches at the gate, and nuns in the oven fending off tumescent friars: the whole added up to a sad betrayal of high hopes recently entertained. Spirited though they may have been, however, it is the ministrations of the social anthropologist that the Ladies of Zamora require, not those of the student of psychosomatics. For all the anxiety to view the host reported of those of them who were excommunicated, their averagely respectable appetite for the sacraments betrays none of the unbridled enthusiasm of the Ursulines of Loudun in the 1630s.[74] Even less does it smack of heretical tendencies.[75] Though the refusal of some of these restless dowagers to give evidence on oath in 1279 might be suspected of indicating something of the sort, religious heterodoxy is hardly to be imputed to them. Rather than to any susceptibility on their part to advanced theological opinions, the Ladies' concerted refusal to co-operate with don Suero's enquiry is attributable to a combination of their collective disdain for a jumped-up bishop and their commitment to the obligation they were under never to reveal the particulars of their Rule either to him or to anyone else.[76]

That apart, however, who would ever have thought that this 'tragicomédie monacale', as Américo Castro described it from his limited knowledge of the affair,[77] this tragi-comedy of the cloister could conceivably have had such far-reaching consequences? Who, in July 1280 when the prioress of Las Dueñas wrote to the cardinal in Rome, would ever have imagined that within ten years her reports (whether true or not) of claustral escapades in one of thirteenth-century Europe's least visited corners, her descriptions (whether real or imagined) of friars 'entering the enclosure with the young nuns and behaving with them disgracefully, embracing them and making free with them and saying such things to them as men of their cloth ought not to say; and even stripping themselves of their garments, and parading around the place naked as the day they were born, and dressing up in the sisters' clothes and dressing the sisters up in theirs, and also doing other wicked things which we cannot bring ourselves to describe',[78] would have brought low the Master General of the Dominican Order himself? But, equally, what may have been in the mind of that other prioress three centuries later, Soeur Jeanne des Anges, prioress of the Ursulines of Loudun, when, feeling herself spurned by the dashing local priest of rakish reputation, she set in train that course of events which was to deliver the object of her fantasies to the most gruesome of fates and reduce her community to the basest depths of human degradation?[79] And which of us, when he surveys the newspaper press a further 300 years on, will fail to recognise human nature's capacity for encouraging history to repeat itself yet again? For

> . . . great things spring from little:- Would you think,
>   That in our youth, as dangerous a passion
> As e'er brought man and woman to the brink
>   Of ruin, rose from such a slight occasion,
> As few would ever dream could form the link

Of such a sentimental situation? ...
[...]
'Tis strange, – but true; for truth is always strange,
Stranger than fiction: if it could be told,
How much would novels gain by the exchange![80]

Notes

1 J. Garms, R. Juffinger, B. Ward-Perkins, *Die Mittelalterlichen Grabmäler in Rom und Latium vom 13. bis zum 15. Jahrhundert*, i, Rome and Vienna 1981, 277–8; Julian Gardner, *The Tomb and the Tiara. Curial tomb sculpture in Rome and Avignon in the later Middle Ages*, Oxford 1992, 51–2, 83, 88–9; J. Fernández Alonso, 'El sepulcro del Cardenal Gonzalo (García Gudiel) en Santa María la Mayor', *Anthologica Annua* 35 (1988) 483–516.

2 D. L. d'Avray, *The Preaching of the Friars. Sermons diffused from Paris before 1300*, Oxford 1985, 45–6, 53–4; see above, p. 49.

3 'Item volumus et mandamus quod opus ecclesie Pampilone inceptum coaptetur corpori antiquae ecclesiae, ita quod neque arcus, neque parietes antiquae ecclesiae destruantur' (Douais, 608 (Hernández, 'Primeras actas', 20)). Cf. G. Meersseman, 'L'architecture dominicaine au XIIIe siècle. Législation et pratique', *AFP* 16 (1946) 166.

4 Douais, 611–12, 618–19 (Hernández, 'Primeras actas', 27–32; 'Pergaminos', 14–19).

5 P. L. Llorens Raga, *Episcopologio de la diócesis de Segorbe-Castellón*, Madrid i, 1973, 142.

6 A. Vauchez, *La Sainteté en Occident aux derniers siècles du Moyen Age d'après les procès de canonisation et les documents hagiographiques*, Rome 1981, 117–18.

7 'L'architecture', 173.

8 Douais, 625–30, 637–46, 650 (Hernández, 'Pergaminos', 28–37, 44–59, 65–6).

9 *Acta cap. gen.*, 266 (above, p. 118); 257: 'ne aliquis verbo vel facto ad divisionem nostri ordinis audeat laborare, vel absolucionem cuiuscumque prelati, vel immutacionem generalis status nostri ordinis ... cum personis constitutis extra obedienciam nostri ordinis studeat procurare.'

10 See above, p. 103; 'Vero dico vobis, antequam curia Romana a dictis fratribus hoc privilegium ammoveret, pocius studium Parysiense confunderet' (H. Finke, *Aus den Tagen Bonifaz VIII*, Münster-in-W., 1902, p. vii).

11 *Ibid.*, pp. v ('Hoc enim membrum solum sanum reperimus'), vi–vii.

12 Douais, 610 (Hernández, 'Primeras actas', 25); Linehan, *Spanish Church and the Papacy*, 315.

13 '... orationi devote crebra et utilis lectio non curiosa succedat' (Douais, 631–2). 'Curiosity' was not invariably intellectual curiosity, however. Amongst the nuns of Metz, for example, it found expression in the latest

fashions, especially silkware (R. Creytens, 'Les "admonitiones" de Jean de Luto aux moniales dominicaines de Metz (*c.* 1300)', (*AFP* 21 (1951) 227)). Cf. 'Rule', 346: 'Edificia sororum sint humilia, curiositate uel superfluitate non notanda.'

14 'Et papa dixit: . . . quamvis multum in ea [*Super cathedram*] clericos gravaverimus, maledicti fratres ultra decretalem non cessant eos contra et ultra eam indecenter agravare' (Finke, p. xlviii).

15 See above, p. 10.

16 Conc. Vienne 1311–12, c. 10 (Extrav. commun. 3.7.2 (Friedberg, ii. 1161–4)); translated in Tanner, *Decrees*, i. 365–9.

17 If the bishops were to refuse to grant licences to hear confessions, then friars were to be enabled to do so 'de plenitudine apostolice potestatis'. If the friars were to seek to circumvent the rules regarding their receipts from funeral payments etc. ('quod absit') then, the pope reminded them, they would be faced with a strict totting-up ('districta ratio') at the last judgement. Cf. R. C. Trexler, 'The bishop's portion: generic pious legacies in the late Middle Ages in Italy', *Traditio* 28 (1972) 409–10.

18 Decree *Inter cunctas*, February 1304 ('. . . sicque, dum ansam solvisse se credidit, nodum ligasse videtur, et septem, uno Hydrae amputato capite, suscitasse. Nec mirum, quia plerumque pariunt novitates discordiam; praesertim, dum ab eo, quod diu aequum visum est, per novam constitutionem receditur, nec, quare recedatur, utilitas evidens vel alia causa subest') (Extrav. commun. 5.7.1 (Freidberg, ii. 1296–1300)); T. M. Izbicki, 'The problem of canonical portion in the later Middle Ages: the application of "Super cathedram"', *Proceedings of the Seventh International Congress of Medieval Canon Law*, ed. P. Linehan, Vatican City 1988, 459–73.

19 '. . . nec ignoramus quod dissensiones et scandala pravis actibus aditum praeparant, rancores et odia suscitant, et illicitis moribus ausum praebent' (*loc. cit.*).

20 See above, p. 124.

21 'Quia vero transgredi non debemus terminos a patribus constitutus, aut falcem in messem mittere alienam' (X 3.29.5 (Friedberg, ii. 555; Celestine III, 1199)). The maxim was quoted both by William of Saint-Amour (Faral, 341) and by the friar in his discourse on the sacrament of penance in *Libro de Buen Amor*, 1146c: 'Non deve poner omne su foz en miese ajena.'

22 Linehan, 'A tale', 102–5.

23 M. Martínez Sueiro, 'Fueros municipales de Orense', *Boletín de la Comisión Provincial de Monumentos Históricos y Artísticos de Orense* 4 (1910) 127; A. López, 'Convento de S. Clara de Allariz', *Estudios Franciscanos* 8 (1912) 380–84. For the early history of the house see P. García Barriuso, 'Documentación sobre la fundación, privilegios y derechos históricos del monasterio de Santa Clara de Allariz', *Liceo Franciscano* 42 (1990) (*Santa Clara de Allariz. Historia y vida de un monasterio*) 11–45.

24 There had been a Clarissan house at Zamora since 1237 (ACZ, 11/1; I.

Omaechevarría, 'Origenes del monasterio de Santa Clara de Zamora', *AIA*, 2ª época 44 (1984) 483–92).

25 'E ruego e coniuro al rey por dios e por santa Maria et por la bendiçion de dios e de santa Maria primeramiente e de si por la de su padre et de su madre, e porque depare dios que en [MS 'quien'] lo a el ffaga quandol mester ffuere, ca todos por esto an de passar, que non embarge nin desapodere a los mios manssessores de ninguno daquelos lugares que yo tengo ffasta que todas mis debdas sean pagadas e mis mandas cunplidas. E si lo non ffiziere demandegolo dios e santa Maria su madre enel cuerpo et enel alma e en todas las cossas que del fueren, et lo que la mi alma lazrare por ello demandegelo dios enla suya e nunca gelo perdone . . . E si por abentura quisiere alguno enbargar esto que yo fago en alguna manera aya la maldiçion de Dios e de santa Maria ssu madre' (López, 'Convento de S. Clara', 383, corrected against the original (AHN, Clero 1429/5)).

26 Probably in 1288 (R. Kinkade, 'Violante of Aragón (1236?–1300?): an historical overview', *Exemplaria Hispanica* 2 (1992–3) 14). In September 1290 Nicholas IV denounced those responsible for appropriating 'bona quamplurima que ad dotalicium suum spectant . . . et adhuc illa detineant taliter occupata' (Reg. Vat. 45, fo. 77ᵛ (*Reg. Nich. IV*, 3216)).

27 Linehan, *History and the Historians*, 487.

28 By means of a registral cross-reference ('ut in regesto primi anni eiusdem domini Nicolai capitulo cxxviiii (RV. 44, fos. 32ʳ-34ᵛ); RV. 45, fo. 107ᵛ, 9 November 1290 (*Reg. Nich. IV*, 244, 3804)).

29 'Quaelibet . . . semper vivat in obedientia et castitate, sine proprio' (Wadding, *Annales Minorum*, iv. 507–15, 507). Cf. L. Oliger, 'De origine regularum ordinis S. Clarae', *Archivum Franciscanum Historicum* 5 (1912) 436–7.

30 'me multociens pravis oprobiis incuperando (*leg.* opprobriis vituperando) sine mei merito atque iure et extra monasterium me contra meam voluntatem indebite deiecerunt' (M. de Castro, 'El real monasterio de Santa Clara, de Santiago de Compostela', *AIA*, 2ª época 43 (1983) 47; Creytens, 'Les "Admonitiones" de Jean de Luto', 226.

31 'Et por les ffazer bien et merçed et por que puedan seruir meior a Dios, tenemos por bien e mandamos que aya, segund su orden manda, libremiente todos los sus heredamientos que ovieren de su patrymonio o de compras, de gananças o de donaçiones. Et que puedan heredar, seyendo en la orden, todos los bienes de sus herederos, asi como los erederian non seyendo enella. Et que los puedan vender a quien quissieren, saluo a ordenes o a caualleros o a otro ome, por que nos perdiessemos el nuestro derecho' (Gaibrois, *Sancho IV*, iii. no. 123 (29 July 1286)). Cf. Graña Cid, 'Primeras clarisas', 690, 699–700.

32 '. . . que puedan auer todos sus heredamientos libres e quitos entrando enla orden e seyendo y, assi como ssi ffuessen al mundo, pora darlos ala orden o fazer dellos aquello que mas pro ffuere al lugar' (*ibid.*, no. 349).

33 Though none was set on sales to members of their own families completed within a year of entry (*ibid.* (=AHN, Clero 1429/4, a damaged document. I

have emended some of Gaibrois's conjectural readings)). Cf. García Barriuso, 'Documentación', 18–25.

34 Wadding, iv. 510 ('per cratem autem ferream per quam communionem accipiunt'). Cf. Appendix 11: 'Maria Reinaldi [. . .] contra mandatum [priorisse] uenit ad cratem' (see above, p. 49).

35 M. de Castro, *La provincia franciscana de Santiago. Ocho siglos de historia*, Santiago de Compostela 1984, 202–7; García Barriuso, 'Documentación', 17, 23.

36 Gaibrois, *Sancho IV*, iii. no. 486 (July 1293); López, 'Convento de S. Clara', 132–4; García Barriuso, 'Documentación', 45.

37 On 28 January 1293 the full complement of eleven bishops of the province of Compostela, Pedro of Zamora included, published a 40-day indulgence in favour of the Dominicans of Benavente (AHN, Clero 3524/16).

38 *Reg. Nich. IV*, 1281; Martínez Sueiro, 'Fueros' 4 (1910) 121–6; Gaibrois, *Sancho IV*, ii. 111–12.

39 Wadding, vii (1733) 457–8; M. del M. Graña Cid, 'La Iglesia Orensana durante la crisis de la segunda mitad del siglo XIII', *Hispania Sacra* 42 (1990) 701–2.

40 '. . . summarie, de plano, sine strepitu et figura iudicii ac indagine non solemni diligentius ueritatem . . . ad nostram presenciam quamcitius transmissuri ut informari possumus exinde quid per nos in huius negotio sit agendum' (Wadding, *loc. cit.* (Reg. Vat. 55, fo. 52^r: *Reg. Clem. V*, 2593)).

41 Clem. 2.1.2, *Dispendiosam* (Tanner, *Decrees*, 363); *Glossa ordinaria* ad v. *Dispendiosam* (*Liber Sextus decretalium D. Bonifacii papae VIII. Clementis pape V constitutiones. Extravagantes, tum viginti D. Johannis papae XXII tum communes*, Turin 1620, col. 86). For the date of the decree, see S. Kuttner, 'The date of the constitution "Saepe", the Vatican manuscripts and the Roman edition of the Clementines', *Mélanges Eugène Tisserant* IV, Studi e Testi 234, Vatican City 1964 (reprinted in Kuttner, *Medieval Councils, Decretals, and Collections of Canon Law*, London 1980), 428, and references cited there.

42 *Reg. Clem. IV*, 622; E. Cerchiari, *Capellani papae et apostolicae sedis Auditores Causarum Sacri Palatii seu Sacra Romana Rota . . . relatio historica–iuridica*, iii, Rome 1919, 49. See also C. Lefebvre, 'Les origines romaines de la procédure sommaire aux XII et XIII s.', *Ephemerides Iuris Canonici* 12 (1956) 149–97.

43 López, 'Convento de S. Clara', 133.

44 'Et esto quelo façedes sin rraçon e sin derecho siendo ellos e los frades sobredichas [*sic*] perssonas de sancta iglesia e deuan conprir derecho por el iuiz dela iglesia. Demas que ya me esta querella fue dada del obispo en las cortes de çamora et yo mande por sentençia que pues el pleito era en la corte de Roma que por y ouiessen su derecho, e sobre esto que uos mostraren una mi carta de perdon por que yo perdonara el britamiento del dicho monesterio al obispo e aaquellos que y fueron' (AC Orense, *Privilegios*, IV. 5). Cf. the wildly inaccurate transcript of the whole letter in *Documentos del Archivo Catedral de Orense*, i, Orense 1914–22, 235–6.

❀ ❀ ❀ ❀ ❀

45 E. Duro Peña, 'Catálogo de documentos reales del Archivo de la Catedral de Orense (844–1520) (*Miscelánea de textos medievales* i, Barcelona 1972, no. 137) (cf. nos. 151, 153).

46 Appendix II [5].

47 'Scio omnes hispanos impatientes esse, ut fama predicat et facta demonstrant' (J. Blanch, *Arxiepiscopologi de la Santa Església Metropolitana i Primada de Tarragona*, i, Tarragona 1951, 165–6). As he reports, in the course of his tour of duty Nicholas had visited the court of Alfonso X. He would, therefore, have had the opportunity of testing his hypothesis on Bishop Suero of Zamora.

48 J. González, *Regesta de Fernando II*, Madrid 1943, 26–7, tells it straight. Cf. E. Fernández-Xesta y Vázquez, '"El Motín de la trucha" y sus consecuencias sobre don Ponce Giraldo de Cabrera', *Primer Congreso de la Historia de Zamora*, iii, Zamora 1991, 261–83.

49 L. Serrano, *Cartulario del Infantado de Covarrubias*, Silos 1907, 179–81. The document is preserved at the Archivo Colegial de Covarrubias. I owe my knowledge of its dimensions and extent to Francisco Hernández, in whose forthcoming study of the culture of Castilian litigation in this period 'el pleito del cerdo' will loom large.

50 Cf. Peter Linehan, 'Segovia: a "frontier" diocese in the thirteenth century', *English Historical Review* 96 (1981) (reprinted in *Spanish Church and Society*) 496. E. P. Evans, *The Criminal Prosecution and Capital Punishment of Animals*, London 1906, 140–1, reports cases of swine arraigned on capital charges elsewhere in Europe in this period.

51 *Reg. Bon. VIII*, 1108.

52 H. Grassotti, 'En torno al señorío de Illescas' in *Estudios medievales españoles*, Madrid 1981, 303–28; F. J. Hernández, *Los cartularios de Toledo. Catálogo documental*, Madrid 1985, no. 518; Linehan, *History and the Historians*, 633.

53 R. Pastor de Togneri, *Resistencias y luchas campesinas en la época del crecimiento y consolidación de la formación feudal. Castilla y León, siglos X–XIII*, Madrid 1980, 143–4.

54 Sánchez Rodríguez, 'La diócesis', 163.

55 For the activity of *habitatores* in the diocese of Cuenca in the 1260s, luring settlers southwards to Seville, see Linehan, 'The *gravamina*', 749.

56 *Crónica de Alfonso XI*, ed. C. Rosell, Biblioteca de Autores Españoles 66, Madrid 1875, 197.

57 Linehan, *History and the Historians*, 295–6.

58 This judgement is based on the evidence of wills of this period from Toledo and León as well as Zamora. At Zamora the dean Pedro Anays in 1289 and Bishop Pedro II in 1302 left 100 and 50 maravedís respectively for the recovery of captives, a provision which indicates that they had the Spanish crusade in mind (ACZ, 18/10, 12/15) (see above, pp. 147–8). Such, evidently, was the extent of his disenchantment with the regime that in 1285 Bishop Suero stipulated that his bequest of 1,000 maravedís was 'pro seruicio et liberacione terre sancte Iherosolomitane'. There is something as

pathetic as it is wholly characteristic about Suero's commitment to the
Holy Land just as the Christian presence there was about to be expunged
altogether. (The sum of 1,000 maravedís was not as princely a bequest as it
may appear, for it was 'monete de la guerra', the devalued currency issued
by Alfonso X after 1265. Cf. Hernández, *Las Rentas del rey*, i.
pp. clxv–clxxii. Throughout his will D. Suero distinguished carefully
between bequests expressed in terms of 'money of the war' and those 'in
good money'.)

59 *Ibid.*, 510–14.
60 Martín Rodríguez, 'Campesinos vasallos', 12–13.
61 *Ibid.*, 510; González, *Reinado de Fernando III*, iii (1986) no. 623.
62 A. D. de Sousa Costa, *Mestre Silvestre e Mestre Vicente, juristas da contienda entre D. Afonso II e suas irmãs*, Braga 1963, 115, 183–4.
63 For the historical 'Johannes Roderici archipresbiter de Fita' in the year 1330, see F. J. Hernández, 'The Venerable Juan Ruiz, archpriest of Hita', *La Corónica* 13 (1984) 10–22. Cf. H. A. Kelly, *Canon Law and the Archpriest of Hita*, Binghamton 1984, dating the *Libro de Buen Amor* to the later years of the fourteenth century.
64 Linehan, *Spanish Church and the Papacy*, 29–30, 35–53.
65 ACZ, 18/20, edited (but incompletely and misdated to 1284) by Coria Colino, 'Clerigos prestamistas', 354, 356–7.
66 He may even still have had her on his hands. The references to her in the will of 31 August 1289 are inconclusive (ACZ, 18/10).
67 See pp. 24–5 above.
68 *Libro de Buen Amor* 1697cd.
69 R. Foulché-Delbosc, ed., 'Une règle des Dominicains, texte castillan du xive siècle', *Revue Hispanique* 8 (1901) 504, 508.
70 Linehan, 'Segovia: a "frontier" diocese', 484.
71 'Si qua [. . .] oculos uagos habens per claustrum uel domum ad uanitates sepe direxerit' (this was counted a slight fault); 'Si qua in aliquem oculum fixerit' (this was grave) ('Rule', 344). Cf. the constitutions of Montargis, 1250, which called a spade a man: 'Si qua in *virum* aliquem oculum fixerit . . . ' (ed. Creytens, 'Les constitutions primitives', 77).
72 'Rule', 347: 'in ipso muro inseparabiliter adherens'; 'Porro omnes supradicte fenestre uel fenestrelle ferrate sic disponi debent, uel per duplicacionem ferrature uel per acutos clauos, quod inter exteriores et interiores nullus possit interuenire contactus.'
73 See above, p. 139. The Rule was clear. No sister was to go 'ad fenestram locutorii secularium' except under escort ('Rule', 342). Cf. Creytens, 'Les constitutions primitives', 73.
74 See below, p. 163; A. Huxley, *The Devils of Loudun*, London 1952.
75 The documentation contains no trace whatsoever of the presence of such influences at Zamora, nor, despite its title – 'Santa María de las Dueñas de. Zamora. ¿Beguinas o monjas? El proceso de 1279' – does the article by M. L. Bueno Domínguez contain so much as a reference to Beguines there.

76 'Rule', 348.
77 'Une charte léonaise', 195.
78 See above, p. 57.
79 Huxley, chapters 1–4, especially pp. 100–1.
80 Byron, *Don Juan*, Canto XIV. c–ci.

APPENDICES[1]

❀ ❀

I.a

Zamora, 26 March 1264

Noverint universi presentes literas inspecturi quod nos S. dei gratia Çamorensis
episcopus et nos capitulum eiusdem ecclesie, premisso habito diligenti
tractatu super uenditione domorum, ortorum et tocius loci que olim fuerunt
fratrum minorum que nos habemus ultra flumen facienda dompne Exemene
et dompne Eluire filiabus Roderici Pelagii olim militis Çamorensis,
considerantes quod ipse uolebant ibi monasterium construere et habitum et
ordinem fratrum predicatorum assummere, intelligentes pium desiderium
earundem, perpendentes etiam quod prefatus locus honori pocius quam
utilitati nobis existat, attendentes etiam debita quibus nos dictus episcopus
propter procuratam utilitatem nostre ecclesie tenebamur in hoc, noster
tractatus et deliberatio comunis resedit quod nos dictis dominabus et aliis
cum ipsis dictam ordinem ingressuris ibidem dictum locum cum suis
pertinenciis uenderemus. Unde sciant cuncti presens scriptum cernentes
quod nos prefatus episcopus et capitulum Çamorense domos et ortos et
totum predictum locum que olim fuerunt predictorum fratrum minorum
uendimus cum omnibus iuribus et pertinenciis suis, sicut dicti fratres
minores habebant, dictis dominabus scilicet dompne Exemene et dompne
Eluire pro tribus millibus et CCC morabitinis legionensibus. Et confitemur
quod statim satisfecerunt nobis in pecunia numerata de mille morabitinis.
Et ad cultum divini nominis ampliandum concedimus eis sub conditionibus
que in alia cedula continentur quod ibi construant monasterium et habitum
ordinem [*sic*] fratrum predicatorum assumant ipse et omnes alie que,
inspirante Domino, cum eis ibi uoluerint assummere ordinem supradictam.
Et nos prefatus episcopus promittimus dictis dominabus scilicet dompne
Exemene et dompne Eluire dictum habitum et ordinem nos daturos.
Volumus autem quod residuum precii taliter soluant nobis: placet nobis et
concedimus quod postquam in predicto loco duodecim domine in predicto
habitu et ordine fuerint constitute donec de precio [*sic*] residuo nobis plene
fuerit satisfactum, exceptis uestibus, suppelectilibus, culcitris et stramentis
suis et lectis, medietatem aliorum bonorum vel precii eorundem que extunc
ingredientes monasterium earum tempore ingressus secum attulerint dicte

domine soluant nobis. Et nos prefati episcopus et capitulum Çamorenses sub obligatione bonorum nostrorum et ecclesie Çamorensis promittimus predictum locum prefatis dominabus et earum successoribus, si quis eas super predicti loci proprietate aut possessione in iure impetierit, quantum de iure fuerit defensuros et eas seruare indempnes. Et ut hec omnia in dubium uenire non possint nos episcopus et capitulum Çamorenses presentem cartam sigillis nostris fecimus communiri. Et nos Eluira Roderici et Exemena Roderici quia sigillum proprium non habemus rogamus abbatem de Morerola et abbatem Vallisparadisi et abbatem Sancti Michaelis de Monte ut huic carte sigilla sua ducerent appendenda. Et nos supradicti abbates ad preces supradictarum dominarum presenti carte sigilla nostra duximus apponenda. Actum est hoc Zamore .vii kal. Aprilis, era M.CCC.secunda, anno domini M.CC.LX.quarto.

[Zamora, Archivo de las Dueñas; ACZ, 13/57]

I.b

Zamora, 26 March 1264

In dei nomine. Que prouida et utili dispositione geruntur ne tractu temporis cum labilis sit hominum memoria obliuione tollantur suadet ratio ut in scriptis cuncta ordinabiliter reddigantur. Scriptura enim nutrit memoriam et labentiam [*sic*] cuncta perpetuat et confirmat. Idcirco presentis scripti serie notum sit omnibus presentibus et futuris quod nos S. diuina permissione episcopus et capitulum Çamorense, uolentes cultum diuini nominis ampliare in ciuitate et diocesi Çamorense prout debitum officii nostri requirit, damus uobis domine Eluire Roderici et domine Exemene Roderici licentiam construendi monasterium sub regula beati Agustini et institutionibus ordinis fratrum predicatorum in loco Sancte Marie in quo fratres minores iusta [*sic*] Sanctum Frontonem antiquitus habitabant sub scriptis pactis, conditionibus et promissionibus in perpetuum inuiolabiliter obseruandis. Et nos Eluira Roderici et Exemena Roderici, uolentes sub regula sanctimonialium beati Agustini et fratrum predicatorum constitutionibus in supradicto loco domino famulari, promittimus bona fide pro nobis et successoribus nostris canonicam obedientiam subiectionem et reuerenciam venerabili patri domino S. episcopo Zemorensi [*sic*] et eius successoribus canonice intraturis. Promittimus inquam saluis supradicti ordinis institutis ita quod in monasterio nostro uisitatio et institutio et destitutio fiat secundum instituta ordinis fratrum predicatorum, sicut alie domine eiusdem ordinis uisitantur, et priorisse in eodem ordine instituuntur et destituuntur. Nichilominus tamen concedimus quod episcopus Zamorensis qui pro tempore fuerit habeat uisitationem et correctionem in monasterio nostro, habeat etiam ibidem procurationem cum monasterium nostrum ad statum uenerit pinguiorem et censuram ecclesiasticam in monasterio nostro exercere ualeat, saluis supradicti ordinis institutis. Promittimus insuper quod decimas de possessionibus nostris in ciuitate et diocesi Çamorense habitis et habendis et de nostrorum animalium nutrimentis integre exsoluemus ecclesie cathedrali et aliis ecclesiis ciuitatis et diocesis Çamorensis iuxta ordinationem episcopi et capituli Zamorensis. Promittimus etiam quod nec parrochiam nec parrochianos habebimus absque licentia et auctoritate domini episcopi et capituli Zamorensis nec contra uoluntatem eorum quempiam parrochianum ciuitatis uel diocesis Zamorensis ad sepulturam ecclesiasticam admittemus. Spondemus etiam bona fide sub iuramento pro nobis et successoribus nostris quod nullam impetrabimus indulgentiam, nullum priuilegium quin etiam supradicta integre et fideliter in perpetuum prout superius expressimus obseruemus. Et si forsitan contigat per aliquem impetrari nullo utemur tempore impetratis absque consensu et beneplacito episcopi et capituli Çamorensis. Insuper promittimus quod supplicabimus domino pape cum instantia ut omnia supradicta per sedem apostolicam confirmentur. Et ut hoc in dubium uenire non possit nos episcopus et capitulum Zamorense presentem cartam sigillis nostris fecimus comuniri. Et nos Eluira Roderici et Exemena Roderici quia sigillum proprium non habemus rogamus abbatem de Morerola et abbatem Vallisparadisi et abbatem Sancti Michelis de Monte ut huic carte sigilla sua ducerent apponenda. Et nos supradicti abbates ad preces supradictarum dominarum presenti carte sigilla nostra duximus apponenda. Actum est hoc Zamore .vii. kal. Aprilis, era M.CCC.secunda, anno domini M.CC.LX.quarto.

[ACZ, 13/57b (remains of five seals]

II

Zamora, July 1279

Cum nos S. dei gratia Zamorensis episcopus, Deum habentes pre oculis et desiderantes reformationem et bonum statum monasterii monialium Sancte Marie ordinis Sancti Augustini que portant habitum fratrum predicatorum, quod monasterium est iuxta Sanctum Frontonem prope Zamoram, clamore et fama tam quarumdam dictarum monialium quam populi nobis referentibus multas rixas et discordias habitas i..ter moniales predictas, iuxta officii nostri debitum descenderimus ad uisitandum monasterium supradictum, Viris religiosis uidelicet domino M. abbate de Moreruella, Dominico Petri quondam abbate Vallis Paradisi ordinis Cisterciensis nobis adiunctis,

Inasmuch as we Suero, by the grace of God bishop of Zamora, having God before our eyes and being desirous of the reform and good estate of the convent of nuns of Santa María of the Order of Saint Augustine who wear the habit of the friars preacher, which monastery is situated near San Frontis close by Zamora, uproar and rumour of certain of the said nuns as well as of the local people having drawn to our attention the many quarrels and discord dividing the said nuns, in accordance with the duty of our office came to visit the said convent, with the assistance of the venerable the lord M. abbot of Moreruela and Domingo Pérez sometime abbot of Valparaíso, of the Order of Cîteaux, and with M. Vicéncez treasurer and

ac cum M. Vincentii thesaurario et P. Benedicti magistroscolarum senioribus ecclesie nostre et Saluatore Petri canonico Zamorensi, ad dictum monasterium personaliter accedentes quamlibet monialem eiusdem monasterii, singillatim supradictis personis presentibus et monialibus apparentibus in claustro ipsius monasterii requisiuimus diligenter ut quelibet monialis per obedienciam qua tenebatur nobis et ordini tam in spiritualibus quam in temporalibus super reformatione et bono statu ipsius monasterii nobis exponeret ueritatem, et quelibet monialis exposuit prout sequitur in hunc modum.

P. Benítez *magisterscolarum*, seniors of the church of Zamora and Salvador Pérez canon of the said church in attendance, arriving there in person, in the presence of the aforementioned persons and of the nuns convened in the cloister of the said convent, addressing each nun of the aforesaid convent in turn we diligently required of them that, by virtue of the obedience by which they are obliged to us and their order in matters both spiritual and temporal, each should declare to us the truth concerning the reform and good estate of their convent. And each nun declared to us as follows, in this manner.

1] Domina Maria subpriorissa iurata et interrogata dixit quod[2] Marina Dominici et domina Catherina Zamorensis uenerunt de nocte cum baronibus scilicet cum Petro Petri clerico qui erant extra et uocabant alias moniales que erant in monasterio scilicet dominam Sthephaniam[3] et portabant litteram et dabant dicte Sthephanie. Interrogata si fuerunt obedientes priorisse sue dixit quod aliqui sic, aliqui non, et maior pars fuerunt inobedientes. Alique confesse fuerunt de inobedientia, alique non. Interrogata qui extraxerunt Mariam de Xiuilia et Mariam Vallisoletani, dixit quod plures. Interrogata que, non respondit set dixit quod ille propria auctoritate recesserunt a monasterio. Interrogata que esset apta ad prioratum respondit quod Marina Roderici soror domine Orobone uel Mariam [*sic*] Alffonsi Legionensis. Interrogata si Petrus Petri habet familiaritatem cum aliqua moniali respondit quod sic. Cum qua? Cum domina Catherina.

On oath and under interrogation, Doña María sub-prioress stated that Marina Domínguez and Doña Caterina de Zamora came by night with some men, in particular the cleric Pedro Pérez, from outside the convent and called to some of the nuns within, in particular to Doña Stefanía, and brought with them a letter which they passed to Doña Stefanía. Asked whether the nuns were obedient to their prioress, she said that some were and some were not; most were not. Some had made confession of their disobedience, others not. Asked who had released María de Sevilla and María de Valladolid, she said many had. Asked who, she did not reply but said that they had left the convent of their own volition. Asked who was fit for the office of prioress, she said Marina Rodríguez, the sister of Doña Orobona, or María Alfónsez de León. Asked whether Pedro Pérez had intercourse with any of the nuns, she said yes. With whom? With Doña Caterina.

2] Domina Xemena iurata et interrogata dixit quod silencium non seruatur. Item dixit quod omnes confessate fuerunt sed plures non acceperunt corpus Christi. Item dixit quod excommunicate uolebant intrare ecclesiam ad uidendum corpus Christi. Priorissa claudebat portam ecclesie, percutiebant moniales portas ecclesie. Interrogata de creatione priorisse, respondit quod sub priorissam [*sic*].

On oath and under interrogation, Doña Jimena stated that silence is not observed. She said that they had all made their confessions but that most did not receive communion. She said that those who were excommunicated wanted to enter the church to view the host. The prioress shut the church door but the nuns hammered at them. Asked about the appointment of a prioress, she said the sub-prioress [would be fit].

3] Domina Perona iurata et interrogata si constitutiones et regule sunt seruate dixit quod non, quod silencium non seruatur nec ore non bene recitantur. Moniales non sunt confessate. Ille que recesserunt a monasterio sine licencia recesserunt. Causa scandali est quod Maria Martini fouet partem ecclesie Zamorensis. Et dixit ipsa Perona quod displicet ei quod episcopus Zamorensis habet uisitare monasterium. Item dixit quod domina Maria subpriorissa esset apta ad monasterium in priorissam.

On oath and under interrogation as to whether the constitutions and rules had been observed, Doña Perona said no; also that silence is not observed and that the hours are not recited properly. The nuns had not made their confessions. Those who had left the convent had left without permission. The cause of the scandal is that María Martínez is on the side of the church of Zamora. She said that it gave her no pleasure to have the bishop of Zamora visiting the convent. She also said that the sub-prioress Doña María is fit to be prioress of the convent.

4] Domina Katherina Zamorensis dixit quod domina Xemena et subpriorissa erant apte in priorissam ad monasterium. Item dixit quod uendidit tres caperas panis de Montamarta et plus non uendidit.

Doña Caterina de Zamora said that Doña Jimena and the sub-prioress were fit to be prioress at the convent. She said that she had sold three measures[4] of wheat from Montamarta but not more.

5] Marina Roderici iurata et interrogata dixit quod non seruatur silencium. Item dixit quod domina Stephania portabat litteram eiectam per parietem. Postquam dominus episcopus recessit a monasterio remansit monasterium in discordia. Turpia uerba fuerunt prolata contra priorissam dicendo caraça o merina

On oath and under interrogation, Marina Rodríguez stated that silence is not observed. She said that it was Doña Stefanía who had brought in the letter thrown over the wall. After the lord bishop left the convent the place had remained in turmoil. The prioress had been called shocking names, such as

quod non habuerat bene prioratum. Item quando iecerunt lapides in coro cantauerunt Te Deum Laudamus, et ipsa priorissa tunc clausit se ad portam. Subpriorissa esset apta ad monasterium in priorissam. Eluira Petri et plures alie extraxerunt Mariam de Xiuilia et Mariam de Valladolit de compedibus.

caraça and 'sheep', because she had done a poor job as prioress. When the nuns threw stones in the choir they sang a *Te Deum* and the prioress locked herself behind [?] a door. The sub-prioress was fit to be prioress of the convent. Elvira Pérez and many others released María de Sevilla and María de Valladolid from the stocks.

6] Domina Columba iurata et interrogata dixit quod scandalum ortum est quia mandauit dominus episcopus quod non uenirent predicatores ad monasterium. Dixit eciam quod non erant obedientes Marie Martini priorisse et insurrexerunt contra eam. Interrogata que sunt, respondit quod omnes moniales que fecerant altare quando erant excommunicate et turpia uerba dicebant ei, et incluserunt priorissam ad portam et dicebant quod priorissa erat aleuiosa. Dixit eciam quod domina Orobona o Katerina de Benauento essent apte in priorissam.

On oath and under interrogation, Doña Columba stated that the trouble had started because the lord bishop had banned the friars from the convent. She said that they were not obedient to María Martínez and rose up against her. Asked who they were, she said all those who set up the altar when they were excommunicated and said shocking things to the prioress and shut her behind a door and called her traitor. She also said that Doña Orobona or Caterina de Benavente were both fit for the office of prioress.

7] Maria Reinaldi iurata et interrogata dixit quod silencium non seruatur. Alique confessate fuerunt, alique non. Alique receperunt corpus Christi, alique non. Item quando proiecerunt litteras cantauerunt Te Deum Laudamus quia dicebant quod moniales incorpore erant ordini fratrum predicatorum. Audiuit dici quod Eluira Petri dehonestauerat male priorissam. Ista Eluira Petri, Ines Dominici et domina Stephania et alie quamplures extraxerunt Mariam de Valleoleti de compedibus. Scandalum est ortum ratione fratrum predicatorum. Subpriorissa esset apta in priorissam.

On oath and under interrogation, María Reináldez stated that silence is not observed. Some nuns made their confessions, others not. Some received communion, others not. When they threw the letters in they sang the *Te Deum* because (they said) the nuns were now incorporated into the Order of Preachers. She had heard it said that Elvira Pérez had slandered the prioress badly. The same Elvira Pérez, together with Ines Domínguez, Doña Stefanía and many others, had freed María de Valladolid from the stocks. The trouble had started because of the friars preacher. The sub-prioress was fit to be prioress.

8] Maria Vincencii iurata et interrogata dixit quod silencium non seruatur. Aliquando fuerunt obedientes priorisse, aliquando non. Ista monialis et Eluira Petri et alie quamplures extraxerunt Mariam de Xiuilia et Mariam Vallisoletanam de compedibus de consilio maioris partis monialium quia dictum fuit quod moniales erant incorporate ordini fratrum predicatorum. Te Deum Laudamus cantauerunt, turpia uerba dixerunt priorisse Marie Martini. Subpriorissa esset apta in priorissam. Scandalum ortum est ratione fratrum predicatorum.

On oath and under interrogation, María Vicéncez stated that silence is not observed. Sometimes the nuns obeyed the prioress, sometimes not. Together with Elvira Pérez and various other nuns, she had freed María de Sevilla and María de Valladolid from the stocks at the behest of the majority of the community, because it had been said that they were now incorporated into the Order of Preachers. They sang the *Te Deum* and used bad language to the prioress María Martínez. The sub-prioress was fit to be prioress. The reason for the trouble was the friars.

9] Arnalda Eimenerez iurata et interrogata dixit quod regula nec constituciones non seruantur. Scandalum ortum est quia ille que sunt exparte predicatorum non diligerunt illas que sunt obedientes ecclesie Zamorensi nec uolunt eis loqui. Ille que sunt exparte predicatorum non fuerunt obedientes priorisse Marie Martini et turpia uerba dixerunt ei dicendo[5] ei caraça et mastina, et impulerunt priorissam graui modo. Principaliores fuerunt Marina Romani et domina Johanna et domina Catherina Zamorensis. Expulerunt priorissam de claustro et dehonestauerunt eam turpibus uituperiis et ista turpia dixerunt priorisse ad maiorem dehonestationem in presencia illarum que obediebant ei, et tenebant et habebant proprium scilicet denarios. Interrogata que, respondit quod ille que fouent partem predicatorum. Subpriorissa et Maria Martini sunt apte in priorissas [*sic*]. Ille littere que fuerunt proiecte in coro

On oath and under interrogation, Arnalda Eiménerez stated that neither the rule nor the constitutions were observed. The trouble had arisen because those nuns who favoured the friars had no time for those who sided with the church of Zamora, and were not on speaking terms with them. The nuns who favoured the friars defied the prioress María Martínez. They called her bad names, *caraça* and 'bitch', and battered her very badly. The chief offenders were Marina Románez, Doña Juana and Doña Caterina de Zamora. They drove the prioress from the cloister and slandered her with shameful language, and these horrid things they said to the prioress in order to discredit her in the presence of those of the nuns who were obedient to her. They had and retained private possessions, namely money. Asked who, she said the nuns who favoured the friars. The sub-prioress and María Martínez are both fit to be prioress. The letters thrown into the choir were

emanauerunt exparte predicatorum ut credit, et tunc cantauerunt Te Deum Laudamus quia dicebant quod erant incorporate ordini fratrum predicatorum. Item dixit quod Catherina recepit litteram a Petro Petri clerico per foramina. De auditu dixit quod Catherina recepit tabulas cereas a quodam juuene scriptas per foramina. Item interfuit P. Petri clericus et quidam alii quando exiuit de monasterio Catherina. Item Theresa Arnaldi uituperauit Mariam Martini pessimis uituperiis et insurrexerunt contra eam. Que sunt exparte predicatorum.[6] M. Dominici turpes cantilenas dixit priorisse.

sent in by the party of the friars (she believed). And the *Te Deum* was then sung because they said that they were now incorporated into the Order of Preachers. She said that Caterina had received a letter through a hole in the wall from the cleric Pedro Pérez. She had heard it said that Caterina also received wax tablets written by a young man, also through the wall. Pedro Pérez was there and so were various others when Caterina went out of the convent. Teresa Arnáldez vilified María Martínez with the most horrible insults and they rose up against her. [. . .] M. Domínguez sang nasty songs against the prioress.

10] Domina Perona Zamorensis iurata et interrogata dixit quod fuerunt obedientes priorisse Marie Martini nisi pro paucis oleribus [*sic*][7] et pro clauibus quod ei non fuerunt obedientes. De litteris proiectis in coro respondit ut cetere. Subpriorissa est apta in priorissam.

On oath and under interrogation, Doña Perona de Zamora stated that the nuns were obedient to the prioress María Martínez except [. . .] and in respect of the keys. As to the letters thrown into the choir she answered as the rest. The sub-prioress is fit for the office of prioress.

11] Maria Alfonsi Legionensis iurata et interrogata dixit quod regula et constitutiones non seruantur. Silencium non seruatur. Maria Martini et ista pars seruant. Alia pars que fouet predicatorum [*sic*] non seruant. Scandalum ortum est ratione fratrum predicatorum. Maria Martini et subpriorissa domina Maria et pars eius, scilicet Marie Martini, obediunt ecclesie Zamorensi, et alia pars que sunt plures que fouent partem predicatorum sunt inobedientes ecclesie Zamorensi. Monasterium erit in pace si Marie [*sic*] de Xiuilia, Maria Vallisoletana, Katherina,

On oath and under interrogation, María Alfónsez de León stated that the rule and the constitutions are not observed. Silence is not kept. María Martínez and her group keep it, the pro-mendicant group do not. The trouble had arisen because of the friars preacher. María Martínez and the sub-prioress Doña María and their group (that is, María Martínez's group) are obedient to the church of Zamora. The rest, who are in the majority and favour the friars, are not obedient to the church. The convent would be at peace if María de Sevilla, María de Valladolid, Caterina, Miorovida and

Miorouida et earum secaces non fuerint in monasterio. Plures non fuerunt obedientes Marie Martini et subpriorisse et errauerunt priorisse grauiter et turpia uerba dehonestando priorissam dixerunt ei. Interrogata que fuerunt, respondit quod pars que fouet partem predicatorum, et cominabantur ei scilicet priorisse. Conspirauerunt contra eam scilicet priorissam ut facerent sibi [*sic*] malum, et de litteris eiectis in coro et de Te Deum Laudamus, reddendo rationem ut supradicte, respondit sicut cetere. Cantilenas malas et turpes fecerunt priorisse Marie Martini dum erat priorissa. Subpriorissa est apta ad officium priorisse.

their hangers-on were not in the convent. There were many who disobeyed María Martínez and the sub-prioress and abused the prioress shamefully and dishonoured her with disgraceful language. Asked who these were, she said those of them who favour the friars and threatened her (namely, the prioress). They conspired against her (namely, the prioress) in order to harm her. As to the letters thrown into the choir and the *Te Deum* she answered as the rest, giving the same account as theirs. They composed bad and shameful songs against the prioress María Martínez when she was prioress. The sub-prioress is fit for the office of prioress.

12] Domina Margarita de Benauento iurata et interrogata respondit quod regula et constitutiones seruantur aliquando sic, aliquando non. Silencium [*sic*]. Item dixit quod quodam tempore non obedierunt Marie Martini priorisse. Interrogata que fuerunt, respondit quod Eluira Petri, Ines Dominici, Perona Franca et alie que fouent partem predicatorum. Catherina recipiebat litteras per foramina. Habet famam cum P. Petri clerico. Turpia uerba dixerunt priorisse. Dicebant quod non erat priorissa earum sed priorissa beati Augustini. Nec uolebant ei obedire, et habuerunt comunem tractatum super hoc quod non obedirent ei. Turpes cantilenas fecerunt priorisse. Perona fecit cantilenam cum qua priorissa irascebatur. De priora [*sic*] creanda respondit quod subpriorissa. De litteris proiectis in coro et de Te Deum Laudamus reddendo rationem respondit ut cetere.

On oath and under interrogation, Doña Margarita de Benavente stated that the rule and constitutions are sometimes observed, sometimes not. Silence (likewise?). She said that there was a time when the nuns had not been obedient to the prioress María Martínez. Asked who, she named Elvira Pérez, Ines Domínguez, Perona Franca and others who favour the party of the preachers. Caterina received letters through holes in the wall. She is said to be having an affair with the cleric Pedro Pérez. They said shocking things about the prioress. They used to say that she was not their prioress but Saint Augustine's. They did not wish to obey her. They made common cause not to obey her. They made up dirty songs; Perona composed one that enraged the prioress. As to the election of a prioress, she opted for the sub-prioress. As to the letters thrown

13] Domina Stephania iurata et interrogata respondit quod non seruatur silencium quia quelibet ad opus sui iret. Discordia est in monasterio. Item dicit quod appellationes facte fuerunt de consilio et mandato fratrum predicatorum. Item multa sunt amissa per priorissam Maria [*sic*] Martini. Subpriorissa est apta ad officium priorisse. Domina Stephania mandauit cantare Te Deum Laudamus.

into the choir and the *Te Deum*, she answered with the same account as the rest.

On oath and under interrogation, Doña Stefanía stated that silence is not observed because each nun went about her own business. There is discord in the convent. She says that the appeals were sent on the advice and instructions of the friars preacher. Many things were let slip by the prioress María Martínez. The sub-prioress is fit for the office of prioress. It was Doña Stefanía who was responsible for the chanting of the *Te Deum*.

14] Maria Martini[8] iurata et interrogata respondit quod regula nec constitutiones non seruantur. Silencium non seruatur. Aliquando moniales receperunt litteras et dona a fratribus predicatoribus per mulieres et per foramina, quas cedulas habebant mulieres scriptas in digitis. Item moniales uiuunt in discordia pro eo quod fratres predicatores frequentabant monasterium et dissolucionem faciebant cum monialibus in eodem. Et ista monialis dixit fratri Didaco ut inhiberet fratribus nec[9] ad monasterium hoc uenirent. Diuise sunt moniales, quedam sunt exparte fratrum predicatorum, quedam seruiunt ecclesie Zamorensi. Dissolutio erat quia fratres predicatores denudabant se coram monialibus et quidam frater nudus induit tunicam Domine Xemene que erat ad opus sui coram monialibus. Diuina officia non celebrantur nec in oris ad hoc deputatis. Et ille frater qui induit tunicam fecit rimas Ines Dominici. Item insurrexerunt contra priorissam Mariam Martini dicendo quod non erat priorissa et quicumque eam diceret priorissam peccabat mortaliter quia non erat priorissa nisi trium. Turpia uerba dixerunt ei et cominabantur ei et spoliauerunt priorissam officio priorisse, et specialiter Domina Xemena et subpriora et Domina Sthephania, Marina Roderici et omnes alie que erant exparte predicatorum et iuuabant istas moniales in hac spoliatione. Domina Perona et Maria de Xiuilia occuparunt linteamina que erant super altaribus et postmodum restituerunt priorisse. Domina Xemena habuit reliquias et nunquam habeunt[10] eas. Claues quibus priorissa fuerat spoliata nunquam recuperauit priorissa. Item Domina Xemena nunquam fuit obediens priorisse licet priorissa iniungebat ei in uirtute obediencie. Et alie erant inobedientes ei et licet dabat penitentiam eis non seruabant, et nullam obedientiam seruabant ei. Petrus Petri clericus uenit ad monasterium, dixit quod moniales erant incorporate ordini fratrum predicatorum et quod ducerent priorissam captam. Et hoc asserebat ut recederet priorissa, alioquin caperetur priorissa et duceretur per tibias et daretur ei mortem. Catherina exiuit ab hordine et homines fratrum predicatorum receperunt eam qui erant prope monasterium. Et Petrus Petri erat ad Sanctum Frontonem et iuit cum ea per aldeolas. Et Petrus Petri, presente Catherina, uendidit triticum en Montamarta. Postmodum misit[11] litteram priorisse ut recederet a monasterio que erant exparte predicatorum et Catherine. Interrogata quis esset apta ad officium priorisse respondit quod Domina Orobona. Arnalda et Marina Garsie et eius filia et alie plures fecerunt cantilenas Marie Martini dum esset priorissa. Perona Franca percussit priorissam et inclusit eam cum aliis monialibus. Item Maria Reinaldi inpulit priorissam et contra mandatum suum uenit ad cratem. Miorouida cum haberet contencionem cum quadam moniali post completorium, et[12] diuisisset eas strinxit priorissam inter duo janua taliter quod habuit emittere sanguinem. De litteris proiectis in coro et Te Deum Laudamus respondit ut[13] cetere. Item Domina Sthephania dehonestauit matrem et auiam priorisse et genus suum, uituperando eam, et nolebat comedere cum aliis ad mensam in refectorio sed in quadam camera separata quam abstulit ei Maria Martini dum esset priorissa. Item recepit litteram Domina Sthephania, propter quam litteram priorissa Maria Martini grauiter fuit percussa in dormitorio. Eluira Petri quia priorissa[14] dedit ei penitenciam fecit insultum contra eam cum digitis ad oculos nec erat ei obediens quando uocabatur ad capitulum.

15] Xemena Petri iurata et interrogata respondit quod regula et constitutiones et silencium [sic]. Discordia est in monasterio occasione fratrum predicatorum quia frater Munio dixit quod auferret habitus Domine Orobone. Maria Reinaldi cum fratre Bernabe, Ines Dominici cum fratre Nicholao, Marina Dominici Taurensis cum fratre Iohanne Dauiancos, qui se denudauit in monasterio coram monialibus, Theresa Arnaldi cum fratre Petro Guterii, qui intrauit monasterium et iuit ad coquinam, clausus fuit ibi et exiuit, et moniales cum metu suo incluserunt se in furno et habuerant suffocari.[15] Et Deus uelit quod nunquam fratres predicatores uenirent monasterio. Isti erant amasii eorum. Item priorisse Marie Martini erant inobedientes omnes que erant exparte predicatorum. Vituperabant priorissam et uocabant priorissam Marie [sic] Martini filiam heretici. Item quedam conuerse ibant per uillam et in ponte inuenerunt duos fratres predicatores, et alter eorum dedit pelizco in tibia, et illa conuersa dixit ei. Item Ines Dominici habebat duos fratres amasios, scilicet fratrem Johannem Dauiancos et fratrem Nicholaum. Et frater Johannes Dauiancos sedit cum ista in infirmaria in uno lecto, et dixit frater Johannes Dauiancos: 'Mia mengengelina, non diligatis puerum sed diligatis me senem quia magis ualet bonus senex quam malus puer.' Et quando predicabat ueniebat per coros et dicebat 'ibi mia mongelina'. Domina Sthephania denudauit fratrem Egidium et postmodum uestiuit eum. Ines Dominici et Maria Reinaldi fecerunt hoc idem fratri Dominico Iohanni. Haec supradicta fuerunt causa scandali. Ines Dominici, Eluira Petri, Domina Johanna, Maria Reinaldi dimittebant completorium et ibant sine licencia ad bibendum, et dicebant: 'Recitet priorissa Maria Martini completorium con las clerigales.' Et nisi essent predicatores longe melius esset monasterium quam sit. Moniales que fouent partem fratrum

predicatorum procurarunt se eximi si possent a iurisdictione domini
episcopi. Perona ueya, Maria de Xiuilia et Miorouida dixerunt quod
uerberarent episcopum, de auditu deponit. De litteris proiectis in coro et de
Te Deum Laudamus respondit ut cetere. Marina Romani, M. Giraldez,
Eluira Petri, Domina Iohanna, Ines Dominici, M. Reinaldez extraxerunt
Mariam de Xiuilia et Mariam de Valladolit de compedibus et iuerunt cum
candalis incensis ad ecclesiam. Subpriorissa est apta in priorissam.

16] Sol Martinez iurata et interrogata. Regula et constitutiones non seruantur.
Silencium non seruatur. Discordia uenit occasione fratrum predicatorum
quia nolebant[16] auferre iurisdictionem episcopi et dare sibi. Et ista et
quedam alie non consenserunt. Fratres predicatores ueniebat [*sic*] ad
monasterium frequenter et loquebantur cum puellis separate. Et frater
Munio cominatus est istis que fouebant partem ecclesie Zamorensis quod
caperet eas et poneret eas perpetuo in catenis. Fratres predicatores aliqui
dabant zonas sutas cum serico puellis amasiis suis et moniales dabant
sudarios et superzonas fratribus amasiis suis. Frater Johannes Dauiancos
denudauit se coram monialibus. Frater Martinus Picamillo et alius frater
loquebantur cum singulis puellis, scilicet Perona Franca et M. Reinaldi in
dormitorio. Frater Dominicus Johannis, frater Egidius erant[17] infirmaria et
denudauerunt se et puelle induebant eos. Domina Sthephania, M. Reinaldi
et plures alias [*sic*] et cingebant eos, et domina Sthephania dicebat quod
habebat saraberas fratris Egidii de nocte et tenebat eas pro amore eiusdem
fratris. Item contra mandatum episcopi domina Xemena et domina
Sthephania, domina Perona et quedam alie aperuerunt portam maiorem
fratribus predicatoribus et locute sunt cum eis ad portam. Frater Johannes
Johannis dixit in monasterio: 'Aqui casamiento de bon lugar pora frei
Nicholas.' Dixit sic et incontinenti habuit amorem de Ines Dominici. Frater
Petrus Guterrii discurrebat per monasterium et metu eiusdem puelle
absconderunt se in furno. Et frater Johannes de Auiancos currebat in
monasterio contra moniales. Haec fuerunt causa scandali. Et dixit quod
omnes que fouebant partem predicatorum erant inobedientes Marie Martini
priorisse et dicebant uituperalia mala ei. Et M. Reinaldi et Perona Franca
impulerunt priorissam dicendo ei: 'Aleuiosa, dedisti litteras falsas', et alia
multa dicebant uituperia priorisse que non sunt dicenda. Pars que fouebat
partem predicatorum procurabant se eximi a iurisdictione episcopali, sed
domina Xemena et domina Sthephania erant principaliores. Miorouida et
Maria de Xiuilia, fustes tenentes in manu, et Perona uoluerunt uerberare
dominum episcopum. Fere omnes moniales habent proprium. Catherina
recepit litteras per foramina a Petro Petri clerico et fuit et est infamata cum
eodem clerico. Et de litteris proiectis in coro et de Te Deum Laudamus
respondit ut cetere. Item Maria de Xiuilia et M. Vallisoletana uoluerunt
ponere Mariam Martini dum erat priorissa in cathenis. Excommunicate
celebrabant diuina alta uoce.

17] Domina Catherina de Benauento iurata et interrogata respondit quod
regula et constitutiones non seruantur. Scandalum est ortum ratione fratrum

predicatorum. Alique fouent partem predicatorum, alique seruiunt ecclesie Zamorensi. Ines Dominici, domina Johanna, M. Rainaldez, Perona Franca habebant fratres predicatores amasios, et iste abluebant pannos fratrum, et postmodum remotis uiris incedebant processionaliter per claustrum ponendo sibi adinuicem nomina fratrum cantando cantum ac si mortuum tenerent presentem. Pars que fouet partem predicatorum cominata est parti seruienti ecclesie Zamorensi dicendo quod ista que fouebat partem ecclesie Zamorensis incarceraretur perpetuo propter litteram missam ab episcopo que lecta fuit in capitulo in qua continebat quod fratres predicatores non uenirent ad monasterium. Item dum ista incenderet lampades moniales clamabant contra eam malo modo quia M. Martini dum esset priorissa dedit penitentiam Eluira [*sic*] Petri. Hae Eluira Petri et Sancia Garsie insurrexerunt contra priorissam eundo cum digitis ad oculos dicendo[18] priorisse: 'Falsa et demoniada quia fecisti fratres predicatores expelli a monasterio propter clericos.' Perona Franca dixit contra priorissam: 'Merina, bacallar, caraça, asnal', dicendo quod Gundisaluus Petri erat falsus qui portauerat litteras episcopi et littere episcopi erant false. Pars que fouebat partem predicatorum erant inobedientes priorisse. Maria Reinaldi impulit priorissam Mariam Martini. M. de Xiuilia impulit priorissam Mariam Martini. Iterum Eluira Petri dixit illud idem prout superius dictum est. Item ille qui erant excommunicate proiciebant contra portam ecclesie lapides et clauserunt portam. 'Prodest uobis domina quod domina Xemena est uobiscum. Alioquin non exiretis extra et ibi moriemini fame.' Pars que fouet partem predicatorum procurarunt se eximi a iurisdictione domini episcopi et subici fratribus predicatoribus. De litteris proiectis in coro et de Te Deum Laudamus respondit ut cetere. Subpriorissa est apta ad officium priorisse.

18] Marina Dominici Taurensis dixit quod regula nec constitutiones non seruantur. Silencium non seruatur. Subpriora est apta ad officium priorisse.

Marina Domínguez de Toro said that neither the rule nor the constitutions are observed. Nor is silence observed. The sub-prioress is fit for the office of prioress.

19] Eluira Dominici Zamorensis iurata et interrogata. Silencium non seruatur. Ore non recitantur. Subpriorissa est apta in priorissam.

On oath and under interrogation, Elvira Domínguez: silence not observed, hours not recited. Sub-prioress fit for office of prioress.

20] Mariam [*sic*] Sugerii iurata et interrogata. Silencium non seruatur. Ore non recitantur. Subpriorissa est apta ad officium priorisse.

On oath and under interrogation, María Suaréz: silence not observed, hours not recited. Sub-prioress fit for office of prioress.

21] Ines Dominici iurata et interrogata. Silencium non seruatur. Ore non recitantur. Domina M. de Xiuilia uel domina Xemena in priorissam.

On oath and under interrogation, Ines Domínguez: silence not observed, hours not recited. Doña María de Sevilla or Doña Jimena for prioress.

22] Maria Dominici Zamorensis. Silencium non seruatur. Ore non recitantur. Domina Xemena est apta ad officium priorisse.

María Domínguez de Zamora: silence not observed. Doña Jimena is fit for the office of prioress.

23] Miorouida de Tauro. Silencium non seruatur. Ore non semper recitantur. Marina Dominici Taurensis in priorissam.

Miorovida de Toro: silence not observed, hours not always recited. Marina Rodríguez for prioress.

24] Eluira Petri Zamorensis. Ore non semper recitantur. Silencium non seruatur. Marina Roderici uel Maria de Xiuilia in priorissam.

Elvira Pérez de Zamora: hours not always recited, silence not observed. Marina Rodríguez or María de Sevilla for prioress.

25] M. de Xiuilia. Silencium non seruatur. Non ueniunt ad oras. Subpriora est apta ad officium priorisse.

María de Sevilla: silence not observed, they do not attend hours. Sub-prioress is fit for office of prioress.

26] Theresa Arnaldi. Ore non recitantur. Subpriora est apta ad officium priorisse.

Teresa Arnáldez: hours not recited. Sub-prioress is fit for office of prioress.

27, 28, 29] Marina Roderici Taurensis, Domina Xemena, Domina Stephania. Subpriorissa est bona sed est debilis et hae sunt[19] ad officium priorisse.

Marina Rodríguez de Toro, Doña Jimena, Doña Stefanía: sub-prioress good but weak. Suggest themselves for office of prioress.

30] Sancia Garsie dixit silencium non seruatur. Domina Xemena uel subpriora est apta ad officium priorisse.

Sancha Garcés said that silence is not observed. Doña Jimena or the sub-prioress is fit for the office of prioress.

31] Domenga Iohannis. Silencium non seruatur. Domina Xemena, M. de Xiuilia, Marina Dominici Taurensis sunt apte ad officium priorisse.

Domenga Yuáñez: silence not observed. Doña Jimena, María de Sevilla and Marina Domínguez de Toro all fit for office of prioress.

32] Velasquida Zamorensis. Silencium aliquando non seruatur. Subpriora est apta ad officium priorisse.

Velasquida de Zamora: silence sometimes not observed. Sub-prioress fit for office of prioress.

33] Domina Iohanna. Silencium non seruatur. Domina Xemena, M. de Xiuilia, Marina Domingues de Tauro sunt apte ad officium priorisse.

Doña Juana: silence not observed. Doña Jimena, María de Sevilla and Marina Domínguez de Toro fit for office of prioress.

34] Domina Sancia Taurensis. Silencium non seruatur. Dum sedent ad mensam indifferenter

Doña Sancha de Toro: silence not observed. While sitting at table they chatter idly. In church they do not

loquuntur et in ecclesia non ueniunt ad horas. Domina Xemena o domina Esteuania Fernandez sunt apte ad officium priorisse. Ista Sancia monuit eas ut obedirent episcopo et ipse ei noluerunt credere. Et taliter faciat dominus episcopus quod moniales corripiantur et corrigantur. Et non uidit quod fratres loquerentur cum monialibus nec moniales cum fratribus nam ipsi cauebant se ab ea.

Et ne hoc possit in dubium euenire, Nos S. dei gratia Zamorensis episcopus presentem cartam sigillo nostro fecimus comuniri. Et nos supradicti M. abbas de Moreruella et Dominicus Petri monacus Vallis Paradisi Cisterciensis ordinis, et P. Benedicti magisterscolarum et M. Vincencii thesaurarius Zamorensis a domino S. episcopo conuocati huic visitationi prescripte interfuimus et sigilla nostra apposuimus in testimonium ueritatis[20]. Actum est hoc Zamore in claustro prefati monasterii mense Iulii anno Domini Millesimo.CC.septuagesimo nono.

attend hours. Doña Jimena or Doña Stefanía Fernández are fit for the office of prioress. The said Sancha warned the nuns that they should obey the bishop, but they would have nothing of it. Let the bishop do what is necessary to discipline the nuns and bring them into line. She had not observed the friars talking with the nuns, nor the nuns with the friars, because the friars steered well clear of her.

And for the avoidance of doubt, we Suero, by the grace of God bishop of Zamora, cause this present record to be confirmed with our seal. And we, the aforesaid M. abbot of Moreruela and Domingo Pérez monk of Valparaíso of the Order of Cîteaux, and P. Benítez *magisterscolarum* and M. Vicéncez treasurer of Zamora, being summoned by the lord bishop don Suero to attend the visitation here recorded, were present thereat and have attached our seals in testimony of the truth. Dated in the cloister of the aforesaid convent in the month of July in the year of the Lord 1279.

ACZ, 13/61

III

Zamora, 15 February 1288

Noscant omnes presentes litteras inspecturi quod Nos Petrus divina miseratione Zamorensis episcopus et nos Alfonsus eiusdem Zamorensis ecclesie decanus una cum toto ipsius ecclesie capitulo, propositas nobis pias illustrissimi domini Sancii dei gratia regis Castelle et Legionis preces intelligentes ac videntes ad divinum sacre religionis esse cultum in regnis sibi creditis ampliandum, suum etiam mandatum suscipientes [. . .] gratiam apostolicam ut sorores monasterii Sancte Marie de ultra pontem Zamorensis civitatis sint libere sub cura magistri ordinis predicatorum et prioris provincialis Hyspanie qui pro tempore fuerint ac aliorum fratrum eiusdem ordinis, sicut sorores de Maiorito et de Calaroga et cetere que sunt ordini dictorum fratrum incorporate sorores, ut autem earundem sororum honus et cura de quibus extitimus hactenus solliti super dictorum fratrum humeros quos dei

⁂ ⁂ ⁂ ⁂ ⁂

credimus domesticos et servos absque cuiuslibet in posterum contradictionis
obice mera possint libertate manere, non obstantibus conditione seu
conditionibus, composicione seu composicionibus inter reverende memorie
dominum Suggerium [. . .] quondam Zamorensis ecclesie episcopum[21] et
Nos ac dictas sorores initis seu quacumque actoritate vallatis, gratis ac libere
renunciamus omni iuri siquid in [. . . . . .] sororum monasterio et in istis
sororibus habebimus vel eramus in posterum habituri quo ad omnia
supradicta, salvis decimis spiritualibus omnium possessionum et annalium
quas predicte sorores habent vel habiture sunt in civitate et diocesi
Zamorensi, quas quidem decimas integre et sine aliqua diminutione solvere
teneantur ecclesie nostre et aliis parrochialibus ecclesiis Zamorensis diocesis,
et quod teneantur respondere eciam episcopo et ordinariis ecclesie
Zamorensis prout continetur in decretali novella de privilegiis que incipit
Volentes. Ne vero dicte nostre libere voluntatis concessum possint in dubium
nostris successoribus devenire presentem litteram nostris appensis sigillis
fecimus roborari. Actum est hoc Zamore XV kal. marcii anno domini
M.CC.LXXXVii.

[Zamora, Archivo de las Dueñas]

Notes

1 In the texts which follow the orthography of the originals has been
retained. Punctuation has been provided in order to assist what appears to
be the sense. [. . .] and [. . . . . .] represent, respectively, an illegible word
and what appear to be two illegible words.
2 'dixit quod' above line, indicating perhaps an insertion in the scribe's draft
unnecessarily transposed into this, his fair copy.
3 One or more names evidently omitted.
4 'caperas': word not identified.
5 MS. 'clicendo'.
6 Words missing here.
7 'Pro paucis oleribus', literally: 'for a few vegetables', meaning 'for some
trivialities'. Cf. E. L. Llorens, *La negación en español antiguo con referencias
a otros idiomas, Revista de Filologia Española,* Anejo XI, Madrid 1929,
185–92.
8 For translations of the next four testimonies see pp. 48–9, 50–2 above.
9 *sic,* for 'ne'.
10 *sic,* for 'restituit'.
11 *sic,* for 'miserunt'.
12 *suppl.* 'quando priorissa'.
13 'ut' repeated, marked for deletion.
14 MS. 'priorissam', the 'm' marked for deletion.
15 Although the sentence has no main verb, its sense is clear enough.
16 *sic,* for 'volebant'.
17 *suppl.* 'in'.

18 'quia ista fouebat' marked for deletion.
19 *suppl.* 'apte'.
20 The fold of the document is pierced for the attachment of *six* seals.
21 MS. has full stop here.

BIBLIOGRAPHY

Aguade Nieto, S., 'En los orígenes de una coyuntura depresiva. La crisis agraria de 1255 a 1262 en la Corona de Castilla', in *De la sociedad arcaica a la sociedad campesina en la Asturias medieval. Estudios de historia agraria*, Alcalá de Henares 1988, 335–70.

Almeida, F. de, *História da Igreja em Portugal*, ed. D. Peres, i, Porto 1967.

Ballesteros y Beretta, A., *Alfonso X el Sabio*, Barcelona 1963.

Barbiche, B., *Les Actes pontificaux originaux des Archives Nationales de Paris*, ii, Vatican City 1978.

Barraclough, Geoffrey, 'The chancery ordinance of Nicholas III, a study of the sources', *Quellen und Forschungen aus italienischen Archiven und Bibliotheken* 25 (1933/4) 192–250.

Bartlett, Robert, *The Making of Europe. Conquest, colonization and cultural change 950–1350*, Harmondsworth 1994.

Beltrán de Heredía, V., 'Examen crítico de la historiografía dominicana en las provincias de España y particularmente en Castilla', *AFP* 35 (1965) 195–248.

Benavides, A., *Memorias de D. Fernando IV de Castilla*, 2 vols, Madrid 1860.

Benito Ruano, E., 'La Iglesia española ante la caída del Imperio latino de Constantinopla', *HS* 11 (1958) 5–20.

Bennett, R. F., *The Early Dominicans*, Cambridge 1937.

Blanch, J., *Arxiepiscopologi de la Santa Església Metropolitana i Primada de Tarragona . . . Transcripció i prologació de Joaquim Icart*, i, Tarragona 1951.

Boase, T. S. R., *Boniface VIII*, London 1933.

S. R. E. Cardinalis S. Bonaventurae, *Opera omnia*, ed. A. C. Peltier, xii, Paris 1868.

Brett, E. T., *Humbert of Romans. His life and views of thirteenth-century society*, Toronto 1984.

Brundage, J. A., *Law, Sex and Christian Society in Medieval Europe*, Chicago and London 1987.

——and E. M. Makowski, 'Enclosure of nuns: the decretal *Periculoso* and its commentators', *Journal of Medieval History* 20 (1994) 143–55.

Bueno Domínguez, M. L., 'Las mujeres de Santa María de las Dueñas de Zamora: la realidad humana', in *Las mujeres en el Cristianismo medieval. Imágenes teóricas y cauces de actuación religiosa*, ed. A. Muñoz Fernández, Madrid 1989, 237–45.

——'Las tensiones del episcopado de Palencia y él de Zamora. Siglos XIII y XIV', *Actas del II Congreso de Historia de Palencia. 27, 28 y 29 de abril de 1989*, Palencia 1990, ii. 401–11.

——'Santa María de las Dueñas de Zamora. ¿Beguinas o monjas? El proceso de 1279', *HID* 20 (1993) 85–105.

Bullarium Ordinis Fratrum Praedicatorum, i, Rome 1729.

Canellas López, A. (ed.), *Colección diplomática del Concejo de Zaragoza*, Zaragoza 1972.

Cartulario de la Universidad de Salamanca (1218–1600), ed. V. Beltrán de Heredia, i, Salamanca 1970.

Castro, Américo, 'Une charte léonaise intéressante pour l'histoire des moeurs', *Bulletin Hispanique* 25 (1923) 193–7.

Castro, M. de, *La provincia franciscana de Santiago. Ocho siglos de historia*, Santiago de Compostela 1984.

——'El real monasterio de Santa Clara, de Santiago de Compostela', *Archivo Ibero-Américano* 43 (1983) 3–61.

Cerchiari, E., *Capellani papae et apostolicae sedis Auditores Causarum Sacri Palatii seu Sacra Romana Rota . . . relatio historica-iuridica*, iii, Rome 1919.

Chartularium Studii Bononiensis. Documenti per la storia dell'Università di Bologna dalle origini fino al secolo XV, pubblicati per opera dell'Istituto per la Storia dell'Università di Bologna, vols viii, x, xi, Bologna 1927, 1936, 1937.

Chiffoleau, J., 'Dire l'indicible. Remarques sur la catégorie du *nefandum* du XIIe au XVe siècle', *AÉSC* 45 (1990) 289–324.

Christian, W. A., Jr., *Local Religion in Sixteenth-century Spain*, Princeton 1981.

Clasen, S., 'Tractatus Gerardi de Abbatisvilla "Contra adversarium perfectionis Christianae"', *AFH* 31 (1938) 276–329; 32 (1939) 89–200.

Congar, Y. M.-J., 'Aspects ecclésiologiques de la querelle entre mendiants et séculiers dans la seconde moitié du XIIIe siècle et le début du XIVe', *Archives d'hist. doctr. du M. A.* 36 (1961–2) 35–161.

Coria Colino, J., 'Clerigos prestamistas. El mundo de los negocios en una ciudad medieval: Zamora (siglo XIII–XIV)', *El pasado histórico de Castilla y León*: Actas del I Congreso de Historia de Castilla y León, i, Burgos 1983, 343–58.

——'El pleito entre cabildo y concejo zamoranos de 1278: análisis de la conflictividad jurisdiccional. Concejo, cabildo y rey', *Primer Congreso de Historia de Zamora*, iii. *Medieval y moderna*, Zamora 1991, 285–303.

Corominas, J., *Diccionario crítico etimológico de la lengua castellana*, Madrid and Berne 1954.

Coulton, G. G., *Five Centuries of Religion*, iv, Cambridge 1950.

Creytens, R., 'Les "Admonitiones" de Jean de Luto aux moniales dominicaines de Metz (*c.* 1300)', *AFP* 21 (1951) 215–27.

——'Les constitutions primitives des soeurs dominicaines de Montargis (1250)', *AFP* 17 (1947) 41–84.

Crónica de Alfonso X, ed. C. Rosell, Biblioteca de Autores Españoles 66, Madrid 1875, 3–66.

Crónica de Alfonso XI, ed. C. Rosell, Biblioteca de Autores Españoles 66, Madrid 1875, 173–392.

Dansette, A., *Histoire religieuse de la France contemporaine sous la Troisième République*, ii, Paris 1952.

Daumet, G., *Mémoire sur les relations de la France et de la Castille de 1255 à 1320*, Paris 1913.

d'Avray, D. L., *The Preaching of the Friars. Sermons diffused from Paris before 1300*, Oxford 1985.

Decrees of the Ecumenical Councils, trans. N. P. Tanner, London and Washington, DC 1990.

Dillard, Heath, *Daughters of the Reconquest. Women in Castilian town society, 1100–1300*, Cambridge 1984.

Documentos del Archivo Catedral de Orense, i, Orense 1914–22.

Douie, D. L., *The Conflict between the Seculars and the Mendicants at the University of Paris in the Thirteenth Century*, Aquinas Paper no. 23, London 1954.

Duro Peña, E., 'Catálogo de documentos reales del Archivo de la Catedral de Orense (844–1520) (*Miscelánea de textos medievales* 1), Barcelona 1972, 9–145.

Duvivier, C., *La Querelle des d'Avesnes et des Dampierre jusqu'à la mort de Jean d'Avesnes, 1257. Les Influences françaises et germaniques en Belgique au XIIIᵉ siècle*, ii, Brussels 1894.

Dykmans, M., *Le Cérémonial papal de la fin du Moyen Age à la Renaissance*, ii. *De Rome en Avignon, ou Le Cérémonial de Jacques Stefaneschi*, Brussels and Rome 1981.

Echániz Sans, M., *Las mujeres de la Orden Militar de Santiago en la Edad Media*, Salamanca 1992.

Emery, R. W. 'The Second Council of Lyons and the mendicant orders', *Catholic Historical Review* 39 (1953) 257–71.

——*The Friars in Medieval France. A catalogue of French mendicant convents, 1200–1550*, New York and London 1962.

Evans, E. P., *The Criminal Prosecution and Capital Punishment of Animals*, London 1906.

Faral, E., 'Les "Responsiones" de Guillaume de Saint-Amour', *Archives d'hist. doctr. du M.A.* 18 (1950–1) 337–94.

Férotin, M., *Recueil des chartes de l'abbaye de Silos*, Paris 1897.

Fernández Alonso, J., 'El sepulcro del Cardenal Gonzalo (García Gudiel) en Santa María la Mayor', *Anthologica Annua* 35 (1988) 483–516.

Fernández Conde. J., ed., *Historia de la Iglesia en España*, ii. 2, Madrid 1982.

Fernández de Pulgar, P., *Teatro clerical apostolico y secular de las iglesias catedrales de España*, ii, Madrid 1680.

Fernández Duro, C., *Memorias históricas de la ciudad de Zamora, su provincia y obispado*, i, Madrid 1882.

Fernández-Xesta y Vázquez, E., '"El Motín de la trucha" y sus consecuencias sobre don Ponce Giraldo de Cabrera', *Primer Congreso de la Historia de Zamora*, iii, Zamora 1991, 261–83.

Ferrer-Vidal, M., 'Los monasterios femeninos de la Orden de Santiago durante la Edad Media', in *Las Ordenes Militares en el Mediterráneo occidental (s. XII–XVIII)*. Coloquio celebrado los días 4, 5 y 6 de mayo de 1983, Madrid 1989, 201–14.

Finke, H., *Acta Aragonensia*, 3 vols, Berlin 1908–22.

——*Aus den Tagen Bonifaz VIII*, Münster-in-W. 1902.

——*Ungedruckte Dominikanerbriefe des 13. Jahrhunderts*, Paderborn 1891.

Fletcher, R. A., *The Episcopate in the Kingdom of León in the Twelfth Century*, Oxford 1978.

Foulché-Delbosc, R., 'Une règle des Dominicains, texte castillan du XIVe siècle', *Revue Hispanique* 8 (1901) 504–10.

Freed, John B., *The Friars and German Society in the Thirteenth Century*, Cambridge, Mass. 1977.

Fueros leoneses de Zamora, Salamanca, Ledesma y Alba de Tormes, ed. A. Castro and F. de Onis, i, Madrid 1916.

Fugedi, E., 'La formation des villes et les ordres mendiants en Hongrie', *AESC* 25 (1970) 966–87.

Gaibrois de Ballesteros, M., *Historia del reinado de Sancho IV de Castilla*, 3 vols, Madrid 1922–8.

——'Fray Munio de Zamora', *Eine Festgabe zum siebzigsten Geburtstag . . . Heinrich Finke* (Vorreformationsgeschichtliche Forschungen. Supplementband), Münster-i.-W. 1925, 127–46.

García Barriuso, P., 'Documentación sobre la fundación, privilegios y derechos históricos del monasterio de Santa Clata de Allariz', *Liceo Franciscano* 42 (1990) (*Santa Clara de Allariz. Historia y vida de un monasterio*) 11–107.

García de Cortázar, J. A., *La sociedad rural en la España medieval*, 2nd edn, Madrid 1990.

García y García, A. (ed.), *Synodicon Hispanum*, 6 vols to date, Madrid 1981– .

Gardner, Julian, *The Tomb and the Tiara. Curial tomb sculpture in Rome and Avignon in the later Middle Ages*, Oxford 1992.

Garms, J., Juffinger R. and Ward-Perkins, B., *Die Mittelalterlichen Grabmäler in Rom und Latium vom 13. bis zum 15. Jahrhundert*, i, Rome and Vienna 1981.

Glorieux, P., 'Les polémiques "contra Geraldinos". Les pièces du dossier', *Archives d'hist. doctr. du M. A.* 6 (1934) 5–41.

——'"Contra Geraldinos". L'enchaînement des polémiques', *Archives d'hist. doctr. du M. A.* 7 (1935) 129–55.

Gómez Pérez, J., 'Elaboración de la Primera Crónica General de España y su trasmisión manuscrita', *Scriptorium* 17 (1963) 233–76.

Goñi Gaztambide, J., *Historia de los obispos de Pamplona*, i, Pamplona 1979.

González, Julio, *Regesta de Fernando II*, Madrid 1943.

——*Reinado y diplomas de Fernando III*, 3 vols, Córdoba 1980–6.

González Jiménez, M. (ed.), *Diplomatario andaluz de Alfonso X*, Seville 1991.

——'Alfonso X y las oligarquias urbanas de caballeros', *Glossae* 5–6 (1993–4) 195–214.

Graña Cid, M. del M., 'La Iglesia Orensana durante la crisis de la segunda mitad del siglo XIII', *Hispania Sacra* 42 (1990) 689–720.

——'Las primeras clarisas andaluzas. Franciscanismo femenino y reconquista en el siglo XIII', *Archivo Ibero-Américano* 54 (1994) 661–704.

Grassotti, H., 'En torno al señorío de Illescas' in *Estudios medievales españoles*, Madrid 1981, 297–328.

Grundmann, H., *Religiöse Bewegungen im Mittelalter. Untersuchungen über die geschichtlichen Zusammenhänge zwischen der Ketzerei, den Bettelorden und der religiösen Frauenbewegung im 12. und 13. Jahrhundert und über die geschichtlichen Grundlagen der deutschen Mystik*, 2nd edn, Hildesheim 1961.

Guadalupe, M. L., 'El tesoro del cabildo zamorano: aproximación a una biblioteca del siglo XIII', *Studia Historica, Historia medieval,* 1 (1983) 167–80.

Herde, Peter, *Beiträge zum päpstlichen Kanzlei- und Urkundenwesen im dreizehnten Jahrhundert*, 2nd edn, Kallmünz 1967.

——*Audientia litterarum contradictarum. Untersuchungen über die päpstlichen Justizbriefe und die päpstliche Delegationsgerichtsbarkeit vom 13. bis zum Beginn des 16. Jahrhunderts*, 2 vols, Tübingen 1970.

——*Cölestin V (1294). (Peter vom Morrone). Der Engelpapst*, Stuttgart 1981.

Hernández, F. J. 'Alfonso X in Andalucia', *HID* 22 (1995) 293–306.

——(ed.), *Los cartularios de Toledo. Catálogo documental*, Madrid 1985.

——(ed.), *Las rentas del rey. Sociedad y fisco en el reino castellano del siglo XIII*, 2 vols, Madrid 1993.

——'The Venerable Juan Ruiz, archpriest of Hita', *La Corónica* 13 (1984) 10–22.

Hernández, R., 'Pergaminos de actas de los capítulos provinciales del siglo XIII de la Provincia Dominicana de España', *Archivo Domenicano* 4 (1983) 5–73.

——'Las primeras actas de los capítulos provinciales de la Provincia de España', *Archivo Domenicano* 5 (1984) 5–41.

Hilger, W., *Verzeichnis der Originale spätmittelalterliche Papsturkunden in Osterreich 1198–1304*, Vienna 1991.

Hinnebusch, W. A., *The History of the Dominican Order. Origins and growth to 1500*, i, New York 1965.

Hoberg, H., *Taxae pro servitiis communibus ex libris obligationum ab anno 1295 usque ad annum 1455 confectis* (Studi e Testi 144), Vatican City 1949.

Hobson, A., 'A sale by candle in 1608', *The Library*, 5th ser. 26 (1971) 215–33.

Humbert de Romanis, *Opusculum tripartitum*, ed. Edward Brown, *Appendix ad Fasciculum rerum expetendarum & fugiendarum . . . sive tomus secundus*, London 1690.

——*Sermones . . . Acc. epistola de tribus votis substantialibus, et aliis quibusdam exercitiis*, Venice 1603.

Huxley, Aldous, *The Devils of Loudun* [1952], London 1994.

Izbicki, T. M., 'The problem of canonical portion in the later Middle Ages: the application of "Super cathedram"', *Proceedings of the Seventh International Congress of Medieval Canon Law*, ed. P. Linehan, Vatican City 1988, 459–73.

Jiménez Soler, A., 'La política española de Jaime II', in *Eine Festgabe zum siebzigsten Geburtstag . . . Heinrich Finke* (Vorreformationsgeschichtliche Forschungen. Supplementband), Münster-i.-W. 1925, 169–84.

Johannes Andreae, *Liber Sextus decretalium D. Bonifacii papae VIII. Clementis*

☙ ☙ ☙ ☙ ☙

papae V constitutiones. Extravagantes, tum viginti D. Johannis papae XXII tum communes, Turin 1620.

Jordan of Saxony, *Libellus de principiis Ordinis Praedicatorum Iordani de Saxonia*, ed. H. C. Scheeben, MOPH 16, Rome 1935.

Juan Gil de Zamora, *De preconiis Hispanie*, ed. M. de Castro y Castro, Madrid 1955.

Kelly, H. A., *Canon Law and the Archpriest of Hita*, Binghamton 1984.

Kinkade, R. P., 'Alfonso X, *Cantiga* 235, and the events of 1269–1278', *Speculum* 67 (1992), 284–323.

——'Violante of Aragón (1236?–1300?): an historical overview', *Exemplaria Hispanica* 2 (1992–3) 1–37.

Kłoczowski, J., 'Dominicans of the Polish province in the Middle Ages', The Christian Community of Medieval Poland. Polish Historical Library, 2; Wrocław 1981, 73–118 (reprinted in Kłoczowski, *La Pologne dans l'Église médiévale*, Aldershot 1993).

Kuttner, S., 'The date of the constitution "Saepe", the Vatican manuscripts and the Roman edition of the Clementines', *Mélanges Eugène Tisserant* IV, Studi e Testi 234, Vatican City 1964, 427–52 (reprinted in Kuttner, *Medieval Councils, Decretals, and Collections of Canon Law*, London 1980).

——'Die Konstitutionen des ersten allgemeinen Konzils von Lyon', *Studia et documenta historiae et iuris* 6 (1940) 70–131 (reprinted in Kuttner, *Medieval Councils*).

Ladero Quesada, M. A., *Fiscalidad y poder real en Castilla (1252–1369)*, Madrid 1993.

Lalou, E., 'Les tablettes de cire médiévales', *BÉC* 147 (1989) 123–40.

——'Inventaire des tablettes médiévales et présentation générale', in *Les Tablettes à écrire de l'Antiquité à l'époque moderne*, ed. E. Lalou, *Bibliologia* 12, Turnhout 1992, 233–88.

Langbein, J. H., '*Albion's* fatal flaws', *Past & Present* 98 (1983) 96–120.

Larkin, M. *Church and State after the Dreyfus Affair. The separation issue in France*, London 1974.

Lefebvre, C., 'Les origines romaines de la procédure sommaire aux XII et XIII s.', *Ephemerides Iuris Canonici* 12 (1956) 149–97.

Le Goff, J., 'Apostolat mendiant et fait urbain dans la France médiévale: l'implantation des ordres mendiants. Programme-questionnaire pour une enquête', *AÉSC* 23 (1968) 335–52.

——'Ordres mendiants et urbanisation dans la France médiévale', *AÉSC* 25 (1970) 924–46.

Lewry, O., 'Corporate life in the University of Paris', 1249–1418, and the ending of the Schism', *Journal of Ecclesiastical History* 40 (1989) 511–23.

Libro de Buen Amor, ed. J. Corominas, Madrid 1967.

Linehan, Peter, 'The *gravamina* of the Castilian Church in 1262–3', *EHR* 85 (1970), 730–54 (reprinted in Linehan, *Spanish Church and Society 1150–1300*, London 1983).

——*The Spanish Church and the Papacy in the Thirteenth Century*, Cambridge 1971.

🙰 🙰 🙰 🙰 🙰

——'The Spanish Church revisited: the episcopal *gravamina* of 1279', in B. Tierney and P. Linehan, eds, *Authority and Power. Studies on medieval law and government presented to Walter Ullmann on his seventieth birthday* (Cambridge 1980), 127–47 (reprinted in *Spanish Church and Society*).

——'Spanish litigants and their agents at the thirteenth-century papal curia', in S. Kuttner and K. Pennington, eds, *Proceedings of the Fifth Congress of Medieval Canon Law . . . 1976*, Vatican City 1980, 487–501 (reprinted in Linehan, *Past and Present in Medieval Spain*, Aldershot 1992).

——'Segovia: a "frontier" diocese in the thirteenth century', *EHR* 96 (1981), 481–508 (reprinted in *Spanish Church and Society*).

——'The accession of Alfonso X (1252) and the origins of the War of the Spanish Succession', in D. W. Lomax and D. Mackenzie, eds, *God and Man in Medieval Spain. Essays in honour of J. R. L. Highfield*, Warminster 1989, 59–79 (reprinted in *Past and Present in Medieval Spain*, Aldershot, 1992).

——'A tale of two cities: capitular Burgos and mendicant Burgos in the thirteenth century', in *Church and City 1000–1500. Essays in honour of Christopher Brooke*, ed. D. Abulafia *et al.*, Cambridge 1992, 81–110.

——*History and the Historians of Medieval Spain*, Oxford 1993.

——'The Church and feudalism in the Spanish kingdoms in the eleventh and twelfth centuries', *Atti della dodecisima Settimana internazionale di studio, Mendola, 24–28 agosto 1992*, Milan 1995, 303–31.

——and F. J. Hernández, '"Animadverto": a recently discovered *consilium* concerning the sanctity of King Louis IX', *Revue Mabillon*, n. s. 5 (1994) 83–105.

Livros velhos de linhagens, ed. J. M. Piel and J. Mattoso, *Portugalliae Monumenta Historica*, n. s. 1, Lisbon 1980.

Llorens, E. L., *La negación en español con referencias a otros idiomas*, *Revista de Filologia Española*, Anejo XI, Madrid 1929.

Llorens Raga, P. L., *Episcopologio de la diócesis de Segorbe-Castellón*, Madrid 1973.

Loperráez Corvalán, J., *Descripción histórica del obispado de Osma*, 3 vols, Madrid 1788.

López, A., 'Convento de S. Clara de Allariz', *Estudios Franciscanos* 8 (1912) 281–4, 380–7; 9 (1912) 132–41.

López, J., *Tercera parte de la Historia General de Sancto Domingo y de su Orden de Predicadores*, Valladolid 1613.

López Dapena, A., *Cuentas y gastos (1292–1294) del rey D. Sancho IV el Bravo (1284–1295)*, Córdoba 1984.

López Ferreiro, A., *Historia de la santa iglesia de Santiago de Compostela*, v, Santiago de Compostela 1902.

MacDonald, R. A., 'Law and politics: Alfonso's program of political reform', in R. I. Burns, ed., *The Worlds of Alfonso the Learned and James the Conqueror. Intellect and force in the Middle Ages*, Princeton 1985, 150–202.

MacKay, Angus, 'A typical example of late medieval Castilian anarchy? The affray of 1458 in Alcaraz', in *Medieval and Renaissance Studies in Honour of R. B. Tate*, ed. R. Cardwell and I. Michael, Oxford 1986, 81–93.

——'Courtly love and lust in Loja', in *The Age of the Catholic Monarchs*,

1474–1516. Literary Studies in Memory of Keith Whinnom, ed. A. Deyermond and I. Macpherson, *BHS* Special Issue, Liverpool 1989, 83–94.

Madoz, P., *Diccionario geográfico-estadístico-histórico de España y sus provincias de Ultramar*, 16 vols, Madrid 1846–50.

Mañueco Villalobos, M. and J. Zurita Nieto, *Documentos de la Iglesia Colegial de S. María la Mayor (hoy metropolitana) de Valladolid*, vols ii, iii, *El siglo XIII*, Valladolid 1920.

Marcos Pous, A., 'Los dos matrimonios de Sancho IV de Castilla', Escuela Española de Arqueología e Historia en Roma, *Cuadernos de Trabajo* 8 (1956) 7–108.

Martín, J.-L., 'Fuentes y estudios zamoranos', *Primer Congreso de Historia de Zamora*, iii. *Medieval y moderna*, Zamora 1991, 11–25.

Martín Rodríguez, J.-L., *Campesinos vasallos del obispo Suero de Zamora (1254–86)*, Salamanca 1981.

Martínez, E., *Colección diplómatica del real convento de S. Domingo de Caleruega*, Vergara 1931.

Martínez Sueiro, M., 'Fueros municipales de Orense', *Boletín de la Comisión Provincial de Monumentos Históricos y Artísticos de Orense* 4 (1910) 1–7, 25–34, 49–54, 73–84, 121–30; 5 (1911) 1–10, 33–45, 57–61, 81–94, 105–12, 129–35, 153–62.

Meersseman, G. G., 'L'architecture dominicaine au XIIIᵉ siècle. Législation et pratique', *AFP* 6 (1946) 139–90.

——*Dossier de l'Ordre de la Pénitence au XIII siècle*, Fribourg 1961.

Monumenta diplomatica S. Dominici, ed. V. J. Koudelka, MOPH 25, Rome 1966.

Mortier, D. A., *Histoire des Maîtres Généraux de l'Ordre des Frères Prêcheurs*, ii, Paris 1905.

Moxó, S. de, 'De la nobleza vieja a la nobleza nueva. La transformación nobiliaria castellana en la baja Edad Media', *Cuadernos de Historia* 3 (1969) 1–270.

Mundy, J. H., *Men and Women at Toulouse in the Age of the Cathars*, Toronto 1990.

Nüske, G. F., 'Untersuchungen über das Personal der päpstlichen Kanzlei 1254-1304', *Archiv für Diplomatik* 20 (1974) 39–240; 21 (1975) 249–431.

Oliger, L., 'De origine regularum ordinis S. Clarae', *Archivum Franciscanum Historicum* 5 (1912) 181–209, 413–47.

Omaechevarría, I., 'Orígenes del monasterio de Santa Clara de Zamora', *Archivo Ibero-Américano* 44 (1984) 483–92.

Ostolaza, M. I., *Colección diplómatica de S. María de Roncesvalles (1127–1300)*, Pamplona n. d.

Pardo, M., 'Le roi Rodrigue ou Rodrigue roi', *Imprévue* 6 (1983) 61–105.

Pastor de Togneri, R., *Resistencias y luchas campesinas en la época del crecimiento y consolidación de la formación feudal. Castilla y León, siglos X–XIII*, Madrid 1980.

Pásztor, E., 'Contributo alla storia dei Registri Pontifici del secolo XIII', *Bullettino dell'Archivio Paleografico Italiano*, 3rd ser. 1 (1962) 37–83.

Pérez Martín, A., 'Estudiantes zamoranos en Bolonia', *Studia Zamorensia* 2 (1981) 23–66.

———'El Ordo iudicarius "Ad summariam notitiam" y sus derivados', *Historia. Instituciones. Documentos* 8 (1981) 195–266; 9 (1982) 327–423.

Presilla, M. E., 'The image of death and political ideology in the *Cantigas de Santa Maria*' in *Studies on the 'Cantigas de Santa Maria': Art, Music, and Poetry. Proceedings of the International Symposium on the 'Cantigas de Santa Maria' of Alfonso X, el Sabio (1221–1284) in commemoration of its seven hundredth anniversary year – 1981 (New York, November 19–21)*, ed. I. J. Katz and J. E. Keller, 403–57.

Procter, E. S., *Curia and Cortes in León and Castile 1072–1295*, Cambridge 1980.

Ptolemy of Lucca, *Die Annalen des Tholomeus von Lucca in doppelter Fassung nebst Teilen der Gesta Florentinorum und Gesta Lucanorum*, ed. B. Schmeidler, *MGH, SS* rer. Germ. N. S., VIII, Berlin 1930.

———*Historia ecclesiastica*, ed. L. A. Muratori, *Rerum Italicarum Scriptores*, xi, Milan 1727.

Quétif, J. and Échard, J., *Scriptores Ordinis Praedicatorum recensiti*, i, Paris 1719.

Quintana Prieto, A. (ed.), *La documentación pontificia de Inocencio IV (1243–1254)*, 2 vols, Rome 1987.

Represa, A., 'Genésis y evolución urbana de la Zamora medieval, *Hispania* 32 (1972) 525–45.

Ripoll, T., *Bullarium ordinis FF. Praedicatorum*, vii, Rome 1739.

Willielmi Rishanger, quondam monachi S. Albani, et quorundam anonymorum, Chronica et annales, ed. H. T. Riley, Rolls Series, London 1865.

Rodrigo Jiménez de Rada, *Historia de rebus Hispanie sive Historia Gothica*, ed. J. Fernández Valverde, Corpus Christianorum Continuatio Mediaevalis 72, Turnhout 1987.

Rodríguez Fernández, J., *Los fueros locales de la provincia de Zamora*, Salamanca 1990.

Rodríguez Pazos, M., 'Privilegios de Sancho IV a los franciscanos de la provincia de Santiago (1284) y de Castilla (1285)', *Archivo Ibero-Américano*, 2ª época 36 (1976) 529–52.

Rosa Pereira, I. da, 'Livros de direito na Idade Media', *Lusitania Sacra* 7 (1964–6), 7–60.

Rouse, R. H. and M. A. Rouse, 'The vocabulary of wax tablets', in *Vocabulaire du livre et de l'écriture au Moyen Age*, ed. O. Weijers, Turnhout 1989, 220–30.

Ruiz, T. F., 'The transformation of the Castilian municipalities: the case of Burgos 1248–1350', *Past & Present* 77 (1977) 3–32.

———, 'Expansion et changement: la conquête de Séville et la société castillane 1248–1350', *AÉSC* 34 (1979) 548–65.

———'Two patrician families in late medieval Burgos: the Sarracín and the Bonifaz' in *The City and the Realm. Burgos and Castile 1080–1492*, Aldershot 1992, no. VI, 1–26.

———*Crisis and Continuity. Land and town in late medieval Castile*, Philadelphia 1994.

Ruiz Asencio, J. M., *Colección documental del Archivo de la Catedral de León*, viii, (1230–1269), León 1993.

Rymer, T., *Foedera*, I. ii, London 1816.

Salimbene de Adam, *Cronica*, ed O. Holder-Egger: *MGH, SS.* XXXII, Hanover and Leipzig 1905–13.

Sánchez Herrero, J., *Cádiz. La ciudad medieval y cristiana*, Córdoba 1981.

Sánchez Rodríguez, M. A., 'La diócesis de Zamora en la segunda mitad del siglo XIII', *Primer Congreso de Historia de Zamora*, iii. *Medieval y moderna*, Zamora 1991, 147–71.

Scheffer-Boichorst, P., 'Zur Geschichte Alfons X von Castilien', *MIöG*, 9 (1888) 226–48.

Schmidt, T., *Die Originale der Papsturkunden in Baden-Württemberg 1198–1417*, Città del Vaticano 1993.

Schmitt, J.-C., *La Raison des gestes dans l'Occident médiéval*, Paris 1990.

Serrano, L., *Cartulario del Infantado de Covarrubias*, Silos 1907.

Sousa Costa, A. D. de, *Mestre Silvestre e Mestre Vicente, juristas da contenda entre D. Afonso II e suas irmãs*, Braga 1963.

Tentler, T. N., *Sin and Confession on the Eve of the Reformation*, Princeton 1977.

Thomson, W. R., *Friars in the Cathedral. The first Franciscan bishops 1226–1261*, Toronto 1975.

Tierney, B., *Religion, Law, and the Growth of Constitutional Thought 1150–1650*, Cambridge 1982.

Trenchs Odena, J. and M. J. Carbonell, 'Tablettes de cire aragonaises (XIIᵉ-XVᵉ siècle)', *BÉC* 151 (1993) 155–60.

Trexler, R. C., 'The bishop's portion: generic pious legacies in the late Middle Ages in Italy', *Traditio* 28 (1972) 397–450.

——'Le célibat à la fin du Moyen Age: Les religieuses de Florence', *AESC* 27 (1972) 1329–50.

Vauchez, A., *La Sainteté en Occident aux derniers siècles du Moyen Age d'après les procès de canonisation et les documents hagiographiques*, Rome 1981.

——'Les stigmates de S. François et leurs détracteurs dans les derniers siècles du Moyen Age', École Française de Rome, *Mélanges d'Archéologie et d'Histoire* 80 (1968) 595–625.

Veríssimo Serrão, J., *Portugueses no Estudo de Salamanca*, i, *(1250–1550)*, Lisbon 1962.

Vilaplana, M. A., 'El Tumbo Negro de Zamora', in *Homenaje a D. Agustín Millares Carlo*, i, Las Palmas 1975, 69–87.

Wadding, L., *Annales Minorum*, iv, v, vi, Rome 1732, 1733, 1733.

Watt, J. A., 'Spiritual and temporal powers': J. H. Burns (ed.), *The Cambridge History of Medieval Political Thought, c. 350–c. 1450*, Cambridge 1988, 367–423.

Wieruszowski, H., *Politics and Culture in Medieval Spain and Italy*, Rome 1971.

Wirth, J., 'Sainte Anne est une sorcière', *Bibliothèque d'Humanisme et de Renaissance* 40 (1978) 449–80.

Zurita, J. de, *Indices rervm ab Aragoniae regibvs gestarvm ab initiis Regni ad annvm MCDX . . .*, Zaragoza 1578.

INDEX

Abbreviations used: abb.: abbot; (a)bp: (arch)bishop; card.: cardinal; ch.: church; kg: king; Ord.: Order; q.: queen

Abrahen *el Barchilón*, 126–7
Afonso I, kg of Portugal, 146
Afonso III, kg of Portugal, 10, 79
Alcocer (Guadalajara), Clarissan house, 10
Alexander IV, pope, 5, 10, 11, 12
Alfonso X, kg of Castile, 11, 17, 19, 20, 78, 84, 126, 146
Alfonso XI, kg of Castile, 88, 144
Alfonso Eanes, proctor, 90n27
Alfonso Garcés de Carvajal, knight, 61
Alfonso de Molina, infante of Castile, 84, 90n31
Alfonso Tellez, nobleman, 90n31
Allariz (Orense), Clarissan house, 137–42
  rule of, 138–9
Astorga
  bp Martín González, 85
Aviancos, Juan de, OP, 1, 50, 51
Avila
  bp-elect Aymar OP, 38n124, 110n9
  ch. of S. Mateo (Ord. Santiago), 5
  'T', cantor of, 54

Badajoz, 23
Bartlett, Robert, 17

Beatriz, q. of Portugal, 10
Benavente, 56, 80
Benedict XI, pope, 137
Berengarius de Azanuy, proctor, 83
Blanca, cousin and sister-in-law of Sancho IV, 88
Blois
  Clarissan house, 138
Boniface VIII, pope, 119–27
  decretal *Periculoso*, 124, 137
  Super cathedram, 136–7
Braga
  Geraldus Laurentii, archd. of Neiva, 89n21
Bueno Domínguez, M., 41–2, 46–7
Burgos, 19
  bp Fernando OFM, 113n45
  Cortes of (1274), 26
  Dominicans at, 3, 12

Cádiz
  bp Juan Martínez OFM, 138n124
  bp Suero OP, 111n9, 114n52
Caetani, Benedetto, card. deacon of St. Nicholas in Carcere Tulliano, 135
  see also Boniface VIII, pope
Caleruega
  Dominican nuns of, 27–8, 100
Cartagena, 146